Object Relations
Theory
and Religion

Object Relations Theory and Religion

CLINICAL APPLICATIONS

Edited by
Mark Finn & John Gartner

PRAEGER

Westport, Connecticut
London

Library of Congress Cataloging-in-Publication Data

Object relations theory and religion : clinical applications / edited
    by Mark Finn and John Gartner.
            p.   cm.
    Includes bibliographical references and index.
    ISBN 0–275–93518–3 (alk. paper)
    1. Object relations (Psychoanalysis)—Religious aspects.
    2. Psychoanalysis and religion.   3. Psychology, Religious.
    I. Finn, Mark.   II. Gartner, John, 1958–
    RC489.025025   1992
    616.89′17—dc20   91–42787

British Library Cataloguing in Publication Data is available.

Library of Congress Catalog Card Number: 91–42787
ISBN: 0–275–93518–3

First published in 1992

Praeger Publishers, 88 Post Road West, Westport, CT 06881
An imprint of Greenwood Publishing Group, Inc.

Printed in the United States of America

The paper used in this book complies with the
Permanent Paper Standard issued by the National
Information Standards Organization (Z39.48–1984).

10 9 8 7 6 5 4 3 2 1

Contents

Introduction   vii

1   **The Deep Structure of Religious Representations**
    John McDargh   1

2   **The Capacity to Forgive: An Object Relations Perspective**
    John Gartner   21

3   **The Functions of Faith: Religious Psychodynamics in
    Multiple Personality Disorder**
    David G. Benner   35

4   **God-Representation as the Transformational Object**
    Edward P. Shafranske   57

5   **God-Representations in Adolescence**
    Mark R. Banschick   73

6   **Psychoanalytic Treatment with a Buddhist Meditator**
    Jeffrey Rubin   87

7   **Transitional Space and Tibetan Buddhism: The Object
    Relations of Meditation**
    Mark Finn   109

 8 **Between Religious Psychology and the Psychology of Religion**
    Benjamin Beit-Hallahmi   119

 9 **Images of God: A Study of Psychoanalyzed Adults**
    Marilyn S. Saur and William G. Saur   129

10 **Religious Behavior in the Psychiatric Institute 500**
    Michael H. Stone   141

    Afterword by Ana-Maria Rizzuto   155

    Bibliography   177

    Index   189

    About the Editors and Contributors   197

Introduction

The relationship between psychoanalysis and religious experience is one of the major recurring questions at the heart of the psychoanalytic enterprise. Like any perennial question, it can be set aside for a while, but inevitably, it returns. Any apparently new formulation of psychoanalysis creates new opportunities for the reconsideration of its most fundamental issues. Both religion and psychoanalysis are deeply concerned with the nature of loving, and of course, hating in human life. It seemed for a while that so-called drive theory had rendered religious experience an epiphenomenal antique embarrassing to a clear-thinking psychoanalyst. However, the emergence of the importance of early relationships articulated by the family of object relations theories opened a door through which religious life can again center psychoanalytic discussion perhaps under friendlier intellectual circumstances. As Mitchell (1984) points out,

The designation 'object relations theory' has been used with reference to a wide range of very different kinds of formulations: from Klein's rich and complex depiction of unconscious fantasy, to Fairbairn's highly abstract schematic structural model, to Bowlby's ethologically-based theory of attachment, to Winnicott's epigrammatic paradoxes and pithy observations about children, to Mahler's powerfully evocative portrayal of the longing for symbiotic fusion, to Jacobson's casuistic emendations of Freud's drive theory. (p. 473)

He goes on to say: "Most broadly, object relations concepts serve as a new model for viewing all of development, offering an alternative metapsychology, supplying a hermeneutics fundamentally different from drive theory'' (p. 497). It is to this broad sense of object relations theory, which Greenberg and Mitchell (1983) term ''relational,'' that the present volume is committed.

Rizzuto's (1979) *The Birth of the Living God* took the bold step of employing object relations theory to the clinical study of an individual's religious representations and arguing that religious representations are an inherent aspect of psychological organization that are profoundly revealing of a person's relational world. The present volume is a collection of applications of this more open sensitivity established by Rizzuto to a range of cases. It grew out of a 1987 symposium at the American Psychological Association in New York.

Rizzuto begins her book by stating that it is not about religion, and while a similar claim can be made for the present volume, it would be disingenuous not to say that there is an underlying apologetic for at least the potentially adaptive role of religion. In the spirit of a symposium, we asked Ana-Maria Rizzuto for a critical appraisal of these chapters. This appears as the afterword. To include commentary on commentaries partakes, we hope, in the wisdom of the Talmud, where text and commentary exist on the same page. For this reason, we also have included Beit-Hallahmi's critique of the recruitment of object relations theory in the service of religious apologetics. With the notable exception of Beit-Hallahmi, most of the authors have some sort of active religious commitment. At the same time, all of the authors also have an investment in maintaining an analytic attitude. The religious commitments of the authors vary from Christian to Jewish to Buddhist. The neutrality toward psychic contents in psychoanalysis brings with it an implicit ecumenism. Perhaps this investment or desire is reflected by Gregory Bateson in describing his book, *Angel's Fear*.

As I write this book, I find myself still between the Scylla of established materialism with its quantitative thinking, applied science, and controlled experiments on one side, and the Charybdis of romantic supernaturalism on the other. My task is to explore whether there is a sane and valid place for religion somewhere between these two nightmares of nonsense. Whether, if neither muddle headedness nor hypocrisy is necessary to religion, these might be found in knowledge and in art the basis to support an affirmation of the sacred that would celebrate natural unity. (p. 64)

Such an agenda is not needed to appreciate the value of object relations theory in studying religious phenomena, but honesty requires making it clear to the reader. Knowing it helps make sense of the collection.

Vergote (1988) offers a point of view that perhaps creates a possibility of avoiding either reductionism or reactionary apologetics. He states:

To open new possibilities does not mean, however, that religion is simply a dim reflection of a positive mystical faculty latent in the psyche. My refusal to entangle the bonds between religion and the psychic system is as firm as my refusal to sever them. These two orders of activity, although distinct, become so closely related that one can say of this type of psychology what St. Augustine said about philosophy: true religion is true psychology, and true psychology, in turn, is true religion. . . . It is my contention that religion is so intimately enmeshed in the walls of psychological circumstances that religious pathology is always an effect of psychic causality. (pp. 29–31)

Vergote's position can be understood as establishing a basis for genuine technical neutrality. Both reductionism and apologetics partake of potential countertransference distortions. It is our hope that this volume can make a small contribution toward an approach to religious material in the lives of patients freer of bias of any sort.

Chapter 1

The Deep Structure of Religious Representations

John McDargh

For some considerable time now, I have been wrestling with understanding the peculiarity of religious imagery and how it is that in the lives of some persons, the received symbols of a religious tradition have the uncanny power to mobilize powerful energies for personal growth and transformation. For other persons, those images remain inert, lifeless and irrelevant, or worse, must be positively rejected if vital living is to proceed. The clue to this problem I have concluded is to imagine that theological symbols are rather like water lotus. Although, like these flowers, theological images may be observed, compared, and classified in terms of their surface presentation and formal characteristics, their genuine vitality and life—for better or worse—is drawn from their hidden roots sunk in the depth of personal interiority and fed by the individual's unique and distinctive developmental history. Thus while religious images have communal or public meanings about which theologians may dispute, the meanings that matter, at least for the psychotherapist or pastoral counselor, are the peculiar, idiosyncratic uses that the individual makes of these symbolic forms for his or her most private purposes.[1]

The preceding statement may strike some readers as painfully obvious. Yet it is surprising how often the otherwise careful clinician, who begins with the assumption that she has no a priori knowledge of all that a client means when he refers to his father or mother, will nevertheless presume that she knows exactly what is intended when the client refers to "God." The beginning of all wisdom, as Socrates tried to teach us, is to acknowledge our essential ignorance.

Nowhere is this healthy agnosis more needed then when dealing with religious material in a clinical situation. We are on the road to genuine understanding when we recognize that indeed we do not know what our clients mean the first time they refer to their God. How then shall we find out? "I need a way of seeing in the dark," as the psychiatrist in Peter Shaffer's play "Equus" put it. In less poetic terms, we need both a theory and a research methodology that is adequate to the complexity, mysteriousness, and existential significance of the religious material that we may be privileged to come upon in the course of our therapeutic practices.

An important basis for just such a theory with which to "see in the dark" has been the formulations of psychoanalyst Ana-Maria Rizzuto based on her extensive surveys and interviews of an inpatient population and the observations drawn from her clinical practice.[2]

The significant advances of this work beyond the classical psychoanalytic discussion of religion are twofold. First, this research challenges both Freud's linkage of the God representation exclusively to the figure of the oedipal father and Freud's assumption that the God representation, once formed, remains forever tied to its infantile origins, frozen as it were under the conditions of its psychic constitution. In contrast, Rizzuto presents evidence demonstrating that our early childhood experience, both of father and mother but also of grandparents and other significant adults, may be psychically elaborated into conscious, preconscious and unconscious representations linked to the word-symbol "God." These, like the memorialized representations of the actual historical parents, are shown to undergo defensive and adaptive distortions, changes, and corrections. Over the course of a life, they have an enduring role to play within the inner world of the human person.

The second paradigm-shifting advance beyond Freud then is the way in which Rizzuto, appropriating Winnicott's notion of transitional object phenomena, describes this role of the God representation in a manner that recognizes its potentially positive and healthy function.[3] As Rizzuto puts it, "People's dealings with their God are no more, and no less, complex than their dealings with other people—either in early childhood or in any other age; that is, they are imperfect, ambiguous, dynamic and, by their very nature, have potential for both integrating and fragmenting their overall psychic experience."[4]

This capacity to integrate total psychic functioning, or to maintain "psychic equilibration," is the way in which Rizzuto most generally describes the value for health and maturity of religious representations. The essential accuracy of both of these theoretical advances will be assumed in this chapter. Where we hope to build upon Rizzuto's contribution is in suggesting a more nuanced account of what we might term the "deep structure" of a religious representation, specifically, its roots in aspects of self-experience that are prelinguistic—what Eugene Gendlin was pointing to with his language of feeling or "felt sense" and what Christopher Bollas implies with his phrase, "the unthought known."[5] First, the context in Rizzuto.

In her work, Rizzuto makes a suggestive distinction between concepts and "images" or "representations." She writes:

When dealing with the concrete fact of belief, it is important to clarify the conceptual and emotional differences between the concept of God and the images of God which, combined in multiple forms, produce the prevailing God representation in a given individual at a given time. The concept of God is fabricated mostly at the level of secondary-process thinking. This is the God of the theologians, the God whose existence or non-existence is debated by metaphysical reasoning. But this God leaves us cold. The philosophers and mystics know this better than anybody else. This God is only the result of rigorous thinking about casuality. Even someone who believes intellectually that there must be a God may feel no inclination to accept him unless images of previous interpersonal experience have fleshed out the concept with multiple images that can now coalesce in a representation that he can accept emotionally.[6]

It is not difficult to picture the kind of phenomena that would seem to support this distinction. A sophisticated theologian who had thought his notions of God had been properly and critically demythologized is amazed to discover in a moment of personal crisis that he was spontaneously evoking the God of his childhood bedtime prayer. Another individual who had found most "God is love" language inexplicable and distasteful is similarly surprised to find that it made emotional sense to her only when an experience in therapy put her in vital touch, for the first time as an adult, with a long repressed memory of the solacing presence of her maternal grandmother.

One could multiply such examples, but one suspects the more examples one supplied, the less clear the distinction between "concept" and "image" would begin to appear. The theoretical separation between the two is ultimately unsatisfying for two reasons. The first is that, as Paul Pruyser argued, abstract ideals and beliefs can themselves function as love objects. In other words, they can be related to in ways that serve to support the individual's sense of being a coherent, cohesive, and "beloved" self.[7] The second reason is that a model that locates conscious and unconscious representations of the divine as somehow "beneath" conceptual formulations still leaves unanswered the question of what lies "below" these representations. Rizzuto's reply, suggested above, would be: "images of previous interpersonal experience." This is helpful, but only as a beginning, for we might well inquire further what kinds of interpersonal experience are most crucial for the formation of representations of God or the divine. Are there some kinds of experience that arguably must be privileged over others? To use the metaphor introduced earlier, asking these questions will lead us further down the roots of religious representation into its dark and watery source in human psychic life.

At this point our investigation of the deep structure of religious representations may be advanced by picking up on William James' analysis of the relationship between idea/concept and feeling. As James investigated the difference between living and dead religious ideas or religious symbols, he distinguished between those that are purely notional and those that are in some measure tethered to or expressive of an underlying primary experience or feeling. In the dimension of feeling, James held, we find "the deeper source of religion" so that "philosophical and theological formulas are secondary products, like translations of a text into another tongue." According to this model, a religious claim becomes credible to us only insofar as it connects with an underlying process of religious experiencing.[8]

"Articulate reasons," he wrote, "are cogent for us only when our inarticulate feelings of reality have already been impressed in favor of the same conclusions."[9] James thus shifts our focus from the distinction between concept and representation and invites us to examine instead whether and how a religious statement, at whatever level of abstraction or concreteness, represents the passage into language of our "inarticulate feelings of reality." To press further and ask what those "feelings of reality" may be that are constitutive of religious experiencing is to find oneself out on the boundary between psychological and theological reflection. Although all intellectual structures erected on this disputed turf have a provisional character, we will propose one that is suggested by the convergence of a contemporary theological discussion regarding the nature of faith with the emergent insights of psychoanalytic object relations theory.

FAITH AND THE MAKING OF MEANING

Wilfred Cantwell Smith, distinguished scholar of comparative religions, has demonstrated over his life's work that the modern, popular understanding of religious faith as involving assent to or affiliation with a set of beliefs and doctrines (as in the question, "To what faith do you ascribe?") is a distortion of the traditional Jewish, Christian, Muslim, and even Hindu use of the term. Smith showed that originally and properly, "faith" was intended to be descriptive of an individual's total way of being in relationship to what was experienced as ultimately real and trustworthy in the universe.[10] Faith, to put it simply, is less of a noun and more of a verb. Protestant theologian James Fowler, wedding this insight to constructive developmentalist psychology, proposed that we can investigate faith as a "universal feature of human living," a psychologically describable, structured process of meaning-making in terms of whatever the individual construes to be his or her "ultimate environment," the most comprehensive reality defining the limit conditions of human existence.[11] This approach to faith has the great virtue of making that theological category inclusive rather than the property of one privileged religious tradition. At the same time, the equation of faith with meaning-making raises the foundational question: Just what is "the meaning of meaning?" Here we suggest that it is within contemporary psychoanalytic thought, rather than structural developmental theory, that one comes closer to a phenomenological account of the origins of the experience of "meaning."[12]

Arguably the most profound discovery, and the most radical insight of the object relations theorists, is that whatever it is we mean by meaning, we must look for its *fons et origo* in the basic psycho-social processes whereby human beings come to be constituted as selves, separate and yet bound, distinct and yet related. The meaning that matters for human beings, whether negotiated in the coinage of religious symbolic language or in drafts on secular speech, has to do with satisfying the fundamental human hunger *to be*—which for human beings means to-be-in-relationship.

This crucial insight derives from the clinical observations of these theorists, and in particular from the painful experience of sitting in therapy with fellow human beings whose earliest life experience has deeply wounded them in their sense of being real. The presenting plaint of such persons is that they experience a pervading sense of being empty, disconnected, and somehow out of contact with either their own interiority or the world of others around them. One of the early British clinicians of this school, Harry Guntrip, summarized the matter in these words: "An absence, non-realization, or disassociation of the experience of 'being' and of the possibility of it, and along with that an incapacity for healthy, natural, spontaneous 'doing' is the most radical clinical phenomenon in analysis."[13] Such a phenomenon is radical in the original derivation of the word (radix = root) because it points to the very root problematic and paradox of human existence. The hunger for meaning is the innate desire (we might even say "preadaptive readiness") to experience ourselves as vitally alive, that is, as a center of consciousness capable of soliciting emotionally satisfying recognition and response from our world. Yet this experience of aliveness is not something that an individual can simply give to himself. It can only be the gift of the patterned interactions with the others into whose company and care the child is born. What Erikson called the tension between basic trust and mistrust accurately condenses the core issue of human development: Is the ultimate environment in which I show up (which in the first instance is an interpersonal environment) trustworthy to receive, respond, and mirror my initiatives and readiness to give and receive love? The shape of an individual's faith reflects his or her unique personal history of that struggle. That faith is primally carried forward as a preconceptual, somatic experience of the quality and character of one's own bodily being-in-the-world. It is this sense that constitutes the "inarticulate feelings of reality" that are potentially the deep structure of religious representations, symbols, and beliefs.

Two additional theoretical points should serve to illustrate the religious representational process and its roots in religious experiencing. For both of these points we are indebted to the work of Eugene Gendlin.[14]

The first point is that it is misleading to talk about feelings of either meaningfulness or meaninglessness as though the capacity to feel and the experience of meaning were separable psychic processes. Gendlin argues that feeling or our "felt sense" of how it is with us at any given time is already, in his words, "implicitly meaningful." This is because "feeling is how we are alive in the environment and therefore we feel is a bodily way the whole context of our living.''[15] Consequently and by contrast, it is precisely the lack of a capacity to live out of one's feelings that is linked to the haunting sense of meaninglessness.

The second point is made in response to the question of why we should even be concerned with religious representation or symbolization (James' ''translations of a text into another tongue'') if it is the inarticulate, prethematic experience or feeling that is most primary and determinative. In answer, Gendlin argued that while there is always a surplus of meaning in our feelings (i.e., the sense that we know more than we can say), the drive to render that feeling articulate in metaphor, image, or concept is crucial. This is so because when an image or concept is found that most accurately completes and captures our felt sense of our life situation, we experience what he terms a ''felt shift.'' A felt shift is best defined as a deep but subtle bodily signal that tells us we have appropriately symbolized what we know at the level of our embodied selves. It is this full process of feeling translating into expression that we experience as meaningful, regardless of the content of that articulated self-awareness. It is also the condition for a movement of self-transcendence that propels an individual beyond the psychic position he or she occupied before this articulation. Gendlin describes this movement: ''When an individual expresses accurately for the first time how he is, just then and in precisely so doing he is no longer that way. The accuracy which he feels so deeply—the physically sensed release of the words which feel exactly right—this very feeling is a feeling of change, of resolution, or moving a step forward.''[16]

It is possible now to bring together our earlier discussion of faith as meaning-making with Gendlin's model of affective experiencing. Our argument proceeds on three assumptions:

1. If our faith is descriptive of a total reaction to life as it comes to us, a relationship taken to our ultimate environment

2. If ''we feel in a bodily way the whole context of our living''

3. If that bodily sense of the whole only becomes available for genuine transformation and self-appropriation in a relationship that permits it to cross the thin line into language

Then what we may look for in life in general and psychotherapy in particular are the circumstances under which an individual's faith or felt-sense of the context of being comes to articulation in metaphor, imagery, and symbol. While we may be more directly interested in this process when it involves recognizable symbols of a particular religious tradition, the logic of this argument requires us to identify this as a process of religious experiencing regardless of the symbols used by the client.

In the following case, we shall see that the breakthroughs in empathic understanding on the part of the analyst occur precisely at the points at which she intuits that her clients' idiosyncratic religious representations are the expression of a profound faith struggle, an effort to maintain some sense of aliveness. It should also be apparent in this material that psychic restructuring occurs as the subject is gradually enabled to express that faith, that is, to articulate both verbally and in a series of drawings "how it is for her" in relationship to what she hopes may be ultimately trustworthy in life but fears may not be.

IN THE HANDS OF THE LIVING GOD: BACKGROUND OF THE CASE

For the purposes of making this discussion as accessible as possible, we have chosen a highly unusual piece of clinical material—a carefully documented presentation of a course of psychoanalysis that lasted nearly sixteen years. The analyst was Marion Milner, a highly original and creative contributor to what is sometimes referred to as the "independent tradition" in the British psychoanalytic tradition.[17] The case, published in 1969 under the title, *In the Hands of the Living God*, is a detailed account of the analytic treatment of a young woman named Susan who entered therapy in 1943 at the age of twenty-three and finally terminated in 1959 at the age of thirty-nine.[18]

This is a lengthy analysis by almost any standards and likely contains much that many in the field would find problematic, both by way of technique and theory. Yet for that very reason, the account itself is the fascinating documentation of Milner's own growth and education as an analyst.[19]

We see Milner over those sixteen years tacking into the heady intellectual high winds of the psychoanalytic debates in Britain, trying to incorporate the work of Melanie Klein and her followers while constantly running up against the limitations both of that paradigm and of traditional drive theory. In the end, however, when theory conflicts with the actual data of the analysis, it is usually the voice of Susan and Susan's experience that wins out, and thus it is Susan who eventually teaches Milner to be a healing listener. This is perhaps why British analyst Masud Khan, in commenting on the first draft of this book, observed, "This is not really an account of an analysis, but of a research into how to really let oneself be used, to become the servant of a process."[20]

Milner's humility and patience before the slow unfolding of Susan's process of healing, the emergence of Susan's true self, is so great that Milner presents the material of this process with much of the highly metaphoric and poetic untidiness, confusion, and paradox with which Milner was herself entrusted with that self-disclosure. In consequence, it must be said that *In the Hands of the Living God* strains the patience and taxes the empathy of the reader in many of the same ways that sitting for four or five hours a week with Susan for sixteen years must have challenged Milner as the analyst. For the reader not involved in such a process, however, the book offers a rare vicarious participation in the endlessly complex expressions of the unconscious in analytic work.

Milner's first words in her book are: "This book is about a patient who came to her first session saying three things: that she had lost her soul; that the world was no longer outside her; and that all this had happened since she received

E.C.T. [electroconvulsive therapy]."[21] The ECT treatment Susan referred to occurred during an inpatient hospitalization three weeks prior to her entering therapy with Milner. One might well summarize the whole of the sixteen years of analytic treatment as about Susan's recovery of soul, her rediscovery of a world outside of herself by the reconstitution of an inner world, and the slow understanding on the part of Milner, if not of Susan, as to why Susan's decision to receive ECT had the devastating meanings that it did for her.

SUSAN'S FAMILY HISTORY

The reconstruction offered here of Susan's family history is one that was complete only after many years in analysis as Susan slowly and painfully allowed herself to discover her own life history within the often-tested security of her relationship with Milner. Susan's mother was found at six months of age in the arms of her own eighteen-year-old mother who had died of malnutrition. This woman (Susan's maternal grandmother) was herself the illegitimate child of a London barrister who for unknown reasons was unable or unwilling to save his daughter from starvation. Susan's mother was then taken in and raised by an elderly aunt and uncle who were grudging in their affection and basically unsympathetic to the orphan. It is appropriate to posit that this child, deprived of love and support from birth, would herself quite likely become one of those narcissistically wounded human beings who then must look to their own children for the affirmation and nurture they themselves never received and in so doing continue the cycle of narcissistic injury.[22] That in fact does appear to be exactly what occurred.

Susan's mother was subject to bitter depressions and would often walk out of the house and leave Susan and her older sister by four years, Carol, in order to wander around the town. During these periods of depression, the mother would not speak to her children for days and Susan remembers how she would cling to her mother and not bear to be separated. Susan recalled at one point in therapy that her mother would ask her, "Do you love me?" to which Susan would reply, "I love you the whole world"—an apt statement from a young child for whom the love of the mothering other does indeed constitute "the whole world." The oral deprivation and intense neediness of Susan's mother is underscored by the fact that although there was seldom enough to eat, Susan's mother apparently would criticize her for being "greedy." In that same vein, the mother frequently would blame her troubles and difficulties on the fact of Susan's birth and imply that it would have been better had Susan never been born. Yet for all this negativity there was, inconsistently to be sure, evidence of some intermittent nurturance. Susan's mother also communicated to Susan that she had great expectations for her and that Susan would do something spectacular some day. She would write her daughter when she was away from home and call her "O Moon of my delight." She would also teach Susan poetry and declare her to be her favorite child.

If Susan's mother was emotionally unavailable in any consistent fashion, Susan's father was even more mysteriously absent. The man who Susan grew up believing was her natural father, a man they called "Pop," had abandoned Susan's mother and older sister Carol when Susan was still an infant. There was another man, alleged to be a boarder named Jackie, an alcoholic former soldier, who lived with Susan's mother on and off during most of Susan's youth. In the second year of her analysis, Susan was finally told what she had occasionally suspected, that Jackie was indeed her natural father. This odd family unit grew up in the most embarrassing poverty and disorder due to the meager support sent by Pop and to Jackie's bouts with drinking.

The mother's inconsistency and inability for empathy with Susan was perhaps nowhere more decisively evident in Susan's youth than during a period of sexual abuse that became a central and troubling memory in her analysis.

When she was about four, an old man next door would expose himself at the lavatory window and beckon to her. She went to his house, and he gave her bread, jam, and other sweets as bribes so he could masturbate against her. He would make toys for her doll house, which was something that Jackie would never do. For a long time she continued going to see the man, although she felt terrible about it. Eventually she managed to tell her sister, who did not believe her. When she tried to tell her mother, the mother replied: "Don't tell me—it will kill me!" As a result she kept silent, but when her mother asked her later to tell, she found she could not.

At this later point, when the mother tried to force Susan to recount what had happened, Susan was only able to stand blushing, with her head bowed. Blushing, which Susan said became horrible at that point in her life, remained one of those involuntary physical reactions that plagued Susan into young adulthood.

This family pattern briefly sketched is perhaps already all too familiar in its general features to those who have worked with the victims of child sexual abuse and emotional neglect. It is the interactional pattern that is also the dynamic condition for the development of what D. W. Winnicott called the schizoid or "false self" structure.[23] Susan, like all human beings, does "desire to be desired by the one she desires," but what she must settle for is to make a precocious adaptation to a desperately needy mother who recruits her to her own care and her own mirroring.[24] The result is the death, or more accurately, the live burial of Susan's own desires and all the vital creative energies associated with that desiring. It is telling that one of the earliest dreams Susan shares with Milner is the recurrent dream of a baby that could not be born.[25] Deprived of the reflective mirroring of an appreciative, responsive, "good enough" parent, she lacks the internalized sense of being connected with a source of spontaneous agency and creativity within, or with a world outside of herself that is safe and welcoming of her own explorations and initiatives. It is unsurprising that at the age of ten, her only effective way of negotiating the world of school and play was to develop an elaborate and demanding set of obsessive rituals to ensure that nothing of what was spontaneously her would be active in the world.

RELIGIOUS SYMBOLIZATION AND THE CAPACITY
FOR PLAY

What gradually becomes apparent for Milner through the course of her work with Susan, and what must be regarded as one of Milner's most important insights, is that there is a direct relationship between the impoverishment of the inner representational world and the inability to make genuine contact with a living world around one. It is not the case that a child, faced with a dissatisfying and disconfirming "external world" is automatically able to withdraw "inside" to find solace and comfort from some essentially private but richer interior reality. On the contrary, the capacity to have an inner world or, in Winnicott's words, the capacity to be alone, is itself a developmental accomplishment and the gift of the Other.[26] It is the Other that secures the place of a tolerable and solacing solitude. The late Paul Pruyser in his last book described aptly that the major achievement of the capacity for illusion, including illusionistic religion, is to make available to an individual this capacity to be alone:

If one can be alone with the internal representation of a benign object, human or divine, that grants the exercise of autonomy and a spirited use of the imagination, the fantasy can be productive, inventive, happy and potentially creative. But if one is saddled with a haunting introject, human or divine, one cannot be happy while alone and is doomed to engage in rather morbid, repetitive fantasizing, beset with fears and worries.[27]

Although Susan's fantasy life gives abundant evidence of the negative introjects of which Pruyser speaks, the presence of such introjects apparent in dreams and eventually in doodle drawings is not the same thing as having access to a usable symbolic imagination. On the contrary, one of the distinctive features of Susan's cognitive defenses, which early frustrates Milner's efforts at making standard analytic interpretations (themselves a species of metaphor), is Susan's defiant insistence that none of it made any sense. "A thing is what it is and not something else!" she would angrily insist.

In this sense, Susan presents rather like a child at the mythic-literal stage of cognitive development, unable to accept that a symbol always points beyond itself to a yet-more with which it is not identical. She is like such a child, but with a critical difference. In health, the mythic-literal child is likely to have a universe populated with literally interpreted imaginative productions that can be befriended and made available for solace and companionship. The condition for such an interior world is that the interpersonal universe has been rendered safe enough to permit the relaxation of vigilance and the active play of the imagination. This is what Susan emphatically lacked. Milner's statement of this insight is so striking it deserves to be quoted in full:

It was here that I came to wonder whether there was not a paradox in this area, whether this inability to accept a duality of symbol and thing symbolized, was not partly related to the insecurity of her childhood, the constant need to keep a watchful eye on the world, which thus starved her of the very state of reverie, of absent mindedness, in which the distinction between fantasy and actuality can be temporarily suspended. Here I found myself beginning to think of the role of illusion in symbol formation and the fact that she had often told me how she could not, in childhood, tolerate anything that was "not real".... When I thought of the conditions of her childhood—of needing to be constantly on the alert for danger from her drunken father and her parents' quarrels—of having to be the person who kept an eye on the outside world, doing it for her mother, instead of her mother doing it for her, like having, as she said, "to help my mother across the roads", I wondered if it had not produced an extreme and excessive concentration on logic and outer things at the expense of both reverie and fantasy.[28]

The healing that happens over the course of Susan's therapy involves the recovery of a genuine ability to play. The possibility of play is sufficient basic trust to allow oneself to freely and spontaneously symbolize without the risk of making "a mess"—for symbolic play requires tolerating ambiguity, chaos, and the undifferentiated. That basic trust, which we have earlier linked to faith, is a felt-sense of inner safety which may or may not be carried by a representation of the divine. Where this is the case, however, that representation of God is available to be the guarantor and protector of play and not one more demanding and unpredictable figure to be watched. One of Winnicott's analysands originally made just this point in a wise and wistful observation, "Some people use God like an analyst—someone to be there while you play."[29] At the beginning of their work together, Susan is not able to have reliable and consistent access to such a representation or to the underlying somatic experience that it might convey. As such it is Milner who in effect must be the mediator of such a God. What Milner must learn to do, and she does only after experiencing much frustration and making many mistakes, is to create the "holding environment" that assures Susan that Milner will neither abandon her nor be destroyed by either Susan's rage or intense neediness. But that requires Milner herself to learn to tolerate not knowing, to give up the impossible demand of Susan that Milner as therapist produce neat, logical, clear, and incisive interpretations. Milner must find a way not to rob her patient of her own creativity by offering anything that Susan is not ready to produce herself. In effect, Milner must herself be able to play in order to permit that emergent possibility in Susan. Milner must be the one to tolerate chaos and the void. She does this by learning to attend to the play of her own symbolic imagination and to listen to the deeper knowing of her own pre-verbal felt-sense as it makes its way across the threshold of speech.

One way Milner manages this is by paying attention to the lines of poetry that would come spontaneously into her head during the analytic hour. It was in this fashion that Milner one day came upon the words from a poem by D. H. Lawrence that gave her the title of the book and that alerted her to the fact that what Susan was missing in her life was an ontological certainty about the fundamental trustworthiness of existence:

It is a fearful thing to fall into the hands of the living God,
But it is a much more fearful thing to fall out of them.

Although it took Milner a long time to understand the significance for Susan of these lines, her eventual reconstruction of their meaning is central to our thesis. After the ECT, there had been a loss of some essential part of Susan's unconscious memories of her mother's hands and arms, which had been holding, protecting, and sustaining her, and without which she would have died. This would have been a God-like experience, both as a God-like merciful "other" sustaining her, or in moments of no differentiation, a feeling of herself as "being God." Milner sees this good aspect of experiences as an infant with her mother as the earliest form of the God she believed in before ECT.

What Susan is in quest of, I believe, is what Christopher Bollas describes as the "unthought known," or "the transformational object." What he means by that is "an identification that emerges from symbiotic relating, where the first object is 'known' not so much by putting it into object representation, but as a recurrent experience of being—a more existential as opposed to representational knowing."[30] This mode of existential knowing Bollas explicitly identifies with the origins of the religious and aesthetic sensibility in human culture.[31]

In light of the above, we might formulate the task of therapy as the restoration of Susan's felt-sense (existential knowing) of the essential security of Being, in effect, to renew her faith in the felt-meanings that cohered to her earlier representation of God. Although it would be beyond the scope of this chapter to trace the process of that therapy over its fifteen-year duration, its essential elements are found in the reconstruction of the actual events that immediately led up to Susan's entry into therapy. Indeed, it was the disclosure and working through of the trauma of those events in the interpretation of the transference over the years of the therapy that encapsulates the entire therapeutic process.

FALLING OUT OF THE HANDS OF THE LIVING GOD

Recall that when Susan first entered Milner's consulting room, "a tall slim girl with a walk like Garbo in 'Queen Christina' and a remotely withdrawn madonna-like face," she had three presenting complaints: "that she had lost her soul; that the world was no longer outside her; and that all this had happened since she received E.C.T." To understand what these complaints signified, it was necessary for Milner to reconstruct the four years of Susan's life immediately prior to the breakdown that put her into the mental institution where she received the shock treatments. In so doing, Milner came to appreciate that the trauma of the ECT had to be understood in the light of Susan's own experience of those four years, including the several weeks in the mental institution immediately prior to the ECT, as a period of "breakthrough"—a fragile but existentially powerful period of personal spiritual development for Susan.

At the age of nineteen, Susan left her mother's chaotic home to go to London and live on her own. There she met a gifted and sophisticated young woman who had the same first name as her mother's erstwhile lover and Susan's natural, though consciously unknown father, Jackie. This young woman, Jackie, aggressively took over Susan's life and taught her many of the things she never learned at home. At the same time as Jackie bullied Susan, she also took an active interest in Susan's welfare and when World War II broke out, she brought Susan to live with her on a farm in rural England.

At that farm, working in the fields, Susan began for the first time in her life to develop a feel for her own body and its sense of place in the world. She had previously been awkward, uncoordinated, and easily disoriented outdoors as though she had never developed a sense of body-self that could judge boundaries and distances. Years later, as Susan reflected on these moments, she described them as "mystical". During her four years of farm work, she became aware of every muscle in her body. Milner notes that one of the methods for beginning training for mystical experience is to learn to become aware of the parts of one's own body, from the inside. She thinks Susan perhaps stumbled into an experience of mystical consciousness, on a precarious basis.

Perhaps because of the relative psychic safety of the farm and the maternal preoccupations of Jackie with Susan, these new body sensations began to open up for Susan a sense of interiority and the beginning of a sense that she might have a valuable inner experience that is in some relationship with an outside world. Susan said of this time later in therapy that during those days on the farm she understood for the first time the passage in scripture, "and she pondered all these things in her heart." Susan recalled that during this time on the farm she felt she was "breaking down into reality," "in the world" and inhabiting her body for the first time as well.

Unfortunately, the farm ultimately proved a very unreliable holding environment and a series of unfortunate abandonments occurred that re-created earlier traumata. Jackie's mother, Mrs. Dick, was a semi-invalid who developed paranoid fantasies that Susan was after her husband, in spite of the fact that Susan alone of the entire household was good to Mrs. Dick. The elderly woman died of a heart attack, and it fell to Susan to find her sitting up in bed, dead. When Susan came out of the ECT, the image of the deceased Mrs. Dick was one of the first memories she recalled. The second blow occurred when a young sculptor came to live on the farm and appears to have developed a romantic interest in Susan. Immediately after Mrs. Dick's death, Susan had begun to develop severe somatic ailments that necessitated her mother visiting the farm. The mother in a highly inappropriate way made her own play for the young man in competition with her own daughter, and Jackie—perhaps out of jealousy, disgust, or grief— withdrew her interest in helping Susan and sent her away to live with another older woman. After only six weeks there, Susan's psychosomatic symptoms became so severe that she had to be admitted to a local mental hospital.

Susan's time at the mental hospital was intense and difficult to reconstruct and interpret. On the one hand she experienced for the first time in her life intense feelings, including agonizing feelings of hate that made her feel that she was "going to pieces." At the same time, she said that she also knew feelings of intense ecstasy, which she felt were the result of an "inner gesture of total surrender," a surrender she felt was somehow to God. The totality of these feelings, both the frightening and ecstatic ones, were tremendously important to Susan and it took many years in analysis before she would trust Milner with them. Susan said of these experiences, "I had so much, I felt so many things."

During the first week of this hospitalization, Susan developed an intense relationship with a female psychiatrist, Dr. F., upon whose short and erratic appointments she became very dependent. Susan nevertheless felt that she could not trust Dr. F. enough to speak of her intense experiences. When she did try to speak of her feelings of hate and urge to make some sort of restitution or reparation, Dr. F. dismissed her with glib assurances that Susan experienced as an effort to subvert her conscience. After several weeks, Susan concluded that only a priest might understand what she was going through and made an effort to talk with someone at a local Benedictine monastery. The monks unfortunately did not seem to know what to make of this mental patient showing up with talk of surrender to God and could only recommend that she talk with her parish priest. As a sometime Protestant, this advice was no help at all to Susan.

Dr. F. began to urge Susan to accept a course of ECT treatment with the warning: "If you can't accept what we have to offer you, then you must leave." Susan was scared but resistant, saying that she felt she was getting somewhere without such treatment and in any case felt it was somehow wrong because, as she put it, she "believed in God." Eventually, Dr. F's threats to discharge Susan prevailed, along with a feeling Susan had from looking at persons recovering from their convulsions that they were peaceful and must somehow have received something good. With mixed feelings, Susan agreed to undergo the treatment. Her last conscious thought before experiencing the first shock was, "There goes all that beauty." When Susan came to from her experience of ECT, Dr. F. completely withdrew from her case and soon after had Susan discharged anyway.

INTERPRETATION AND CONCLUSIONS

A number of years ago, at the beginning of my graduate study of religion and psychology, I was present at an intake conference at a community mental health center during which the attending psychiatrist made an offhand observation of a patient's psychotic decompensation, "I think she may be having an ox-hunting experience but lacks the language or context to understand it." The psychiatrist's reference was to the famous series of Zen paintings depicting the hunting of oxen as a metaphor for the experience of enlightenment that includes the experience of nothingness or void at the center of life.[32] Though it was one of those remarks that may have been offered only half-seriously, it stayed with me and returned while wrestling with understanding this case. What it suggests is that an individual like Susan in the months preceding her ECT treatment and particularly in the weeks of hospitalization immediately preceding that treatment may indeed have been undergoing something of the sort of movement of consciousness that can be called "religious experiencing" in the sense earlier described. It is worth considering just how this might be true, and why it is an experience that ultimately cannot be psychically sustained, both for reasons particular to Susan's developmental deficits and for the failure of both medical and religious professionals around her to understand and work with her in terms of that experience.

Christopher Bollas, writing of the adult search for the transformational object, says: "Thus in adult life, the quest is not to possess the object; rather the object is pursued in order to surrender to it as a medium that alters the self, where the subject-as-supplicant now feels himself to be the recipient of enviro-somatic caring, identified with metamorphoses of the self."[33] We would suggest that Susan had something of the experience that Bollas describes. For reasons perhaps related initially to the relatively nurturant environment of the farm or of the relationship with Jackie, her felt-sense of that "background of safety" originally there in her life had been uniquely reawakened and permitted her to begin to experience a wider range of real affect than she had hitherto risked. Unfortunately, she was desperately overdrawn psychologically in attempting to integrate such an experience or sustain it against the other events in her life: the withdrawal of Jackie, the rivalry once more of her mother, and finally the betrayal by Dr. F.

Engler has made the point in his writings on a spectrum model of psychological development that the experiences of ego loss described in the religious literatures of the world mystical traditions universally presume that the individual has achieved sufficient self-structure to undergo a form of its deconstruction. Put more simply, one must have a self in order to lose a self.[34] Sadly, it is just such a requisite self that Susan lacked. Susan's internal world made her tremendously vulnerable to fragmentation and the defensive splitting. One can begin to reconstruct how this might have occurred.

The death of Mrs. Dick and the reappearance of Susan's mother must have mobilized for Susan the feelings she had that her own "greediness" was responsible for depleting and destroying her mother and that her dependence was intolerably bad and wrong. Although she tried to stave off that sense of being a bad self, the somatic illnesses are a signal that it is a losing battle. The behavior of Dr. F. is the culminating blow. Here is a mother figure who threatens Susan that she will be thrown out if she refuses the only good that Dr. F. has to offer, and Susan contemplating the possibility of E.C.T. is made to feel both ungrateful and greedy at the same time. When Dr. F. in fact abandons Susan after the treatment it is only a confirmation of what Susan must most secretly fear—that her intense desiring destroys—and so the only way to live safely in the world is to be possessed by "the devil," the image for her of self-sufficiency and isolation.

The long road back to sanity and human communion for Susan led through a relationship in which one party traced the deep structure of Susan's religious discourse back to its source in the unspoken cry for ultimate meaning and connection that could not be heard in the hospital. This involved feeling as well as thinking the prethematic meanings that were and are invested in Susan's religious language. The invitation of a case such as *In the Hands of the Living God* is for us to reflect with Milner on the listening perspectives on religious representations we continually must invent in order, like her, to be "servants of a process."

NOTES

1. The observations of University of Chicago theologian Langdon Gilkey are relevant here if we make the further extension of his remarks by recognizing that "ordinary" or "contemporary" experience includes more than what can be publicly shared or even consciously known.

Theological symbols, explicated without reference to ordinary experience, have meaning only "eidetically" in terms of their inherent structures or intentional meanings . . . but one must not confuse an understanding of their eidetic meanings with the religious meaning for us of these symbols in our contemporary situation. That meaning is possible only when these symbols are united to the experiences in our actual contemporary life which they symbolize.

See Langdon Gilkey, "The Problem of God: A Programmatic Essay," in George F. McLean, OMI, ed., *Traces of God in a Contemporary Culture* (New York: Alba House, 1973), p. 18.

2. Ana-Maria Rizzuto, *The Birth of the Living God* (Chicago: University of Chicago Press, 1979). See also John McDargh, *Psychoanalytic Object Relations Theory and the Study of Religion: On Faith and the Imaging of God* (Lanham, Md.: University Press of America, 1984).

3. D. W. Winnicott, *Playing and Reality* (New York: Basic Books, 1971). Following Winnicott, Rizzuto argues for the lifelong value of "illusory" mental creations, in a word, for culture. Thus she writes:

It [i.e., religion] is an integral part of being human, truly human in our capacity to create nonvisible but meaningful realities capable of containing our potential for imaginative expansion beyond the boundaries of the senses. Without these fictive realities human life becomes a dull animal existence. Without unseen atoms, imaginary chemical formulas, or even such fictive entities as id, ego and superego, the entire domain of culture becomes a flat, irrelevant world of sensory appearance. (p. 47)

4. Rizzuto, *Living God*, p. 88.

5. Eugene Gendlin, *Focusing*, revised edition. (New York: Bantam Press, 1981). Christopher Bollas, *The Shadow of the Object: Psychoanalysis of the Unthought Known* (New York: Columbia University Press, 1987).

6. Rizzuto, *Living God*, pp. 47–48.

7. Paul Pruyser, *Between Belief and Unbelief* (New York: Harper and Row, 1974). For a critical review of recent works on religion from a psychoanalytic object-relations perspective, see also Daniel Merkur, "Freud's Atheism: Object Relations and the Theory of Religion," *Religious Studies Review*, 16 (1990): 11–18.

8. The term "religious experiencing" is adopted from the recent work of John Shea, who has shown that James anticipates the research of existential psychologist Eugene Gendlin, who similarly emphasizes the primacy of "experiencing" as a "primary, present

and felt phenomenon which can be directly referred to.'' Rizzuto also has been concerned to speak of the representational process rather than of object representations as static and reified psychic entities. Nevertheless, the language of feeling of experiencing may more successfully emphasize that we are concerned with a dynamic process in which the very activity of naming one's experience advances and changes that experience. John Shea, *Religious Experiencing: William James and Eugene Gendlin* (Lanham, Md.: University Press of America, 1987), p. 80.

9. William James, *The Varieties of Religious Experience* (Cambridge, Mass.: Harvard University Press, 1985), p. 67.

10.

Faith is deeper, richer, more personal. It is engendered by a religious tradition, in some cases, and to some degree by its doctrines; but it is a quality of the person, not of the system. It is an orientation of the personality, to oneself, to one's neighbor, to the universe; a total response; a way of seeing whatever one sees and of handling whatever one handles; a capacity to live at more than a mundane level; to see, to feel, to act in terms of a transcendent dimension.

See Wilfred Cantwell Smith, *Faith and Belief* (Princeton, N.J.: Princeton University Press, 1979), p. 12.

11. James Fowler, *Stages of Faith: The Psychology of Human Development and the Quest for Meaning* (New York: Harper and Row, 1981), p. 14. The other significant theological influence on Fowler's approach to faith has been the work of H. Richard Niebuhr. See James Fowler, *To See the Kingdom: The Theological Vision of H. Richard Niebuhr* (Nashville, Tenn.: Abingdon Press, 1974).

12. Fowler himself more recently has turned to the research of Daniel Stern and others into early childhood development for a more adequate account of the foundations of faith in the formation of the prelinguistic sense of self. See Fowler, ''Strength for the Journey: Early Childhood Development in Selfhood and Faith,'' in Doris Blazer, ed., *Faith Development Early Childhood* (Kansas City, Mo.: Sheed and Ward, 1989).

13. Harry Guntrip, *Schizoid Phenomena, Object Relations and the Self* (New York: International Universities Press, 1969), p. 255.

14. A student originally of Carl Rogers, Eugene Gendlin based his work on the one hand on a sophisticated philosophical argument regarding the nature of experience and on the other hand on the long-term research conducted at the University of Chicago on psychotherapy outcomes. It was the latter that identified one variable that seemed to predict significant positive change in the course of therapy irrespective of the modality employed: the client's capacity to attend to and find ways of articulating what Gendlin came to call the ''felt sense'' of his or her existence in the present moment. The philosophical background of Gendlin's work is presented in *Experiencing and the Creation of Meaning* (Toronto: Free Press of Glencoe, 1962). Gendlin's more practical and clinical applications are found in a popular text, *Focusing* (New York: Bantam Press, 1981). The significance for spiritual formation of Gendlin's theory and method of teaching the cultivation of one's ''felt sense'' of life has been noted by a number of current spiritual directors. See, for example, Peter Campbell and Edwin McMahon, *Biospirituality: Focusing as a Way to Grow* (Chicago: Loyola University Press, 1985).

15. Eugene Gendlin, ''Existential Explication and Truth,'' *Journal of Existentialism*, 16 (1965): 135.

16. Gendlin, ''Existentialism and Experiential Psychotherapy,'' in Clark Moustakas,

ed., *Existential Child Therapy: The Child's Discovery of Himself* (New York: Basic Books, 1966), p. 227.

17. Gregorio Kohon, *The British School of Psychoanalysis: The Independent Tradition* (London: Free Association Books, 1986).

18. Marion Milner, *In the Hands of the Living God: An Account of a Psycho-analytic Treatment* (New York: International Universities Press, 1969).

19. Milner's contributions to psychoanalytic work have been recognized by the recent publication of her collected papers in the New Library of Psychoanalysis series, *The Suppressed Madness of Sane Men: Forty-Four Years of Exploring Psychoanalysis* (London: Tavistock Publications, 1987). Marion Milner appears to have been something of a maverick even within British psychoanalytic circles, which were in those early days less medically dominated than the U.S. institutes, though no less given to fierce internal intellectual disputes. She took seriously the religious dimensions of the analytic process, was extremely interested in a highly personal way in problems of creativity and self-expression, and wrote about her own experience in this area with a candor and directness rare among working analysts. One of these books, published originally in 1936 under the name of Joanna Field, has recently been republished, *A Life of One's Own* (Los Angeles: J. P. Tarcher, 1981). This book is a description of a period of self-analysis prior to Milner's formal analytic training. Interestingly, it initially involves free associating to the word "God."

Milner's own path to analytic work was a circuitous one that led through work with juveniles, industrial psychology, a period of study under Elton Mayo at the Harvard Business School in the late 1920s, and finally in the late 1930s, the discovery of the work of Melanie Klein, Susan Isaacs, and the beginning of training in 1939. She was supervised in her analytic work by Melanie Klein and Joan Riviere and knew both David Winnicott (who wrote the preface to *In the Hands of the Living God*) and Anna Freud, who wrote an introduction to her book, *On Not Being Able to Paint* (London: Heinemann, 1950).

20. Milner, *In the Hands of the Living God*, p. xxxi.

21. Milner, ibid., p. xix.

22. For an account of this transgenerational process see Alice Miller, *The Drama of the Gifted Child: How Narcissistic Parents Form and Deform the Emotional Lives of Their Gifted Children* (New York: Basic Books, 1981).

23. D. W. Winnicott, "Ego Distortion in Terms of True and False Self," in his *Maturational Structures and the Facilitating Environment* (New York: International Universities Press, 1965), pp. 140–52.

24. Catholic theologian Sebastian Moore, in writing of his search to articulate the "one universal human desire without some satisfaction of which our life would be unendurable and total satisfaction of which would be perfect bliss," says that he concluded: "That we all desire to be desired by the one we desire is the one uncontested human proposition." See *The Fire and the Rose Are One* (New York: Seabury-Crossroads Press, 1980), p. xii.

25. Milner, *In the Hands of the Living God*, p. 24.

26. D. W. Winnicott, "The Capacity to Be Alone," in his *Maturational Structures*.

27. Paul Pruyser, *The Play of the Imagination: Toward a Psychoanalysis of Culture* (New York: International Universities Press, 1983).

28. Milner, *In the Hands of the Living God*, pp. 40–41.

29. D. W. Winnicott, *Playing and Reality* (New York: Basic Books, 1971), p. 62.

30. Bollas, *The Shadow of the Object*, p. 14.

31.

In adult life, therefore, to seek the transformational object is to recollect and early object experience, to remember not cognitively but existentially—through intense affective experience—a relationship which was identified with cumulative transformational experiences of the self. . . . The search for symbolic equivalents to the transformational object, and the experience with which it is identified, continues in adult life. We develop faith in a deity whose absence, ironically, is held to be as important a test of man's being as his presence.

See Bollas, *The Shadow of the Object*, p. 17.

32. Interestingly, one finds in Milner a fascination with this same series of paintings, particularly the one that is simply a circle symbolizing the "blankness" from which creative understanding emerges. Marion Milner, "Some Notes on Psychoanalysis Ideas of Mysticism," in *The Suppressed Madness of Sane Men*, p. 260.

33. Bollas, *The Shadow of the Object*, p. 14.

34. Jack Engler, "Therapeutic Aims in Psychotherapy and Meditation," in Ken Wilber, Jack Engler, and Dan Brown, eds., *Transformation of Consciousness: Conventional and Contemplative Perspectives on Development* (Boston: Shambhala Press, 1986), pp. 17–52. See also John McDargh, "The Life of the Self in Christian Spirituality and Contemporary Psychoanalysis," *Horizons*, 11 (1984).

Chapter 2

The Capacity to Forgive: An Object Relations Perspective

John Gartner

In beginning a chapter on the topic of forgiveness, one must immediately justify why the topic is of psychological importance. More specifically, one must speak to the suspicion that many readers may share, namely, that such a topic is only important to those who, because of their own religious agenda, wish to call attention to religious concepts like forgiveness. Perhaps beginning on this defensive note reveals my paranoia, but as paranoia is the underlying topic of this chapter, such parallel process may be expected and perhaps even forgiven.

A review of the psychological literature on forgiveness reveals that there is very little literature on the topic and with some exceptions,[1] what does exist is published in journals that focus exclusively on psychology and religion[2] or in books aimed at the popular religious market.[3] Unfortunately, many of these books and articles demonstrate a lack of psychological sophistication.

Yet the neglect of forgiveness by mainstream psychologists strikes one as a startling discrepancy, given that an increased capacity to forgive is widely acknowledged as a hallmark of successful psychotherapy. Quoting from the *Comprehensive Textbook of Psychiatry*, Hunter explains:

It is notable that in most successful analyses, and indeed psychotherapy, there is a marked reduction of bitterness and resentment on the part of the patient towards the persons whom he had previously blamed or held responsible for his sufferings. "Frequently towards the end of an analysis a patient recalls some positive memories about the parental figures he has consistently maligned."[4]

It appears, therefore, that, though the capacity to forgive represents a telos or developmental goal for both religionists and psychotherapists, for reasons that are probably obvious to those who have witnessed the long history of conflict between religion and psychology, no one has applied psychology's recent advances in clinical theory toward understanding it.

Recent developments in psychoanalytic thinking labeled object relations theory provide a unique perspective for understanding forgiveness. It is my contention that the inability to forgive marks the operation of primitive defenses, in particular splitting, as described in detail by Klein[5] and refined by Kernberg.[6]

According to Klein, at the age of approximately four months, the infant passes through a stage of development that she called the "paranoid-schizoid position." During this period, the infant has two conflicting experiences of the mother's breast. It is both gratifying in the food and comfort it supplies, which mobilizes erotic feelings; and at other times it is frustrating in its unavailability, which mobilizes aggressive feelings in the infant. Through the primitive defense of splitting, the infant experiences the gratifying and frustrating breast as two separate objects sometimes referred to as the "good" and "bad" breasts. According to Klein, who accepted Freud's dual-instinct theory, the fundamental human anxiety is the ego's response to aggressive feelings, as these feelings constitute an expression of the death instinct. The fundamental nightmare is that hate, death, evil, and destruction will overwhelm and destroy the loving libidinal, gratifying, and good aspects of the self and the breast. The infant must find some way to reduce the anxiety inherent in hating the object that gives him life.

The infant does this through splitting and projection. Through splitting, the infant maintains the false view that it is not the idealized good breast that frustrates him but some other devalued "bad breast." Further, through projection, the infant rids himself of his own aggressive feelings by attributing them to that same bad object, thus preserving the experience that both self and the primary other are good.

There are two primary costs of these defenses. First, the accurate perception of reality is compromised, and unless the infant progresses beyond this stage, there will be long-term difficulties with reality testing. Second, the infant has created a world of persecutory bad objects from which he now perpetually fears attack and retaliation—thus the paranoid nature of this stage.

Under conditions of optimal development the infant gradually develops a more integrated and realistic view of himself and others. Gradually he reowns or reintrojects his own projected aggression, leading to feelings of guilt for his newly acknowledged hate and aggression toward the mother, a stage that Klein called the "depressive position." Further, the infant sees the mother in a more realistic fashion as having both good and bad aspects. However, if the early experiences of aggression and deprivation are too intense, it may never feel safe to bring good and bad experiences of self and other together in an integrated fashion, and the result will be severe psychopathology and a continued reliance on primitive defenses.

Kernberg has criticized Klein in a number of ways, but has for the most part accepted her views on primitive defenses, especially splitting, and the role of aggression in development.[7] Integrating Mahler's developmental sequence, he has placed the period of splitting in the second year of life during the period of separation-individuation, after the separation of self and object representations has been established. Further, Kernberg has clarified the nature of self and object representations by positing the existence of good self, bad self, good object, and bad object representations, where the distinction between self and object representation can appear blurred in Klein. He has also postulated that there is always a specific connecting affect between each self and object representation (for example, contemptuous mother feels disgust for worthless child). Finally, he has expanded these ideas to account for the psychology of severe personality disorders, making the use of primitive defenses in conjunction with the maintenance of reality testing, the operational definition of character pathology. Perhaps the key point for this paper is that Kernberg has outlined richly and clearly that the dividing line between character pathology and higher-level neurotic functioning lies in the integration of good and bad object representations. To understand and experience oneself and others as full complicated human beings with good and bad qualities is the road to health. Stereotyped and extreme devalued or idealized views is the mark of illness.

With this background, we are free to explore an operational definition of forgiveness. I contend that mature forgiveness is definitively not the replacement of negative hateful feelings with loving feelings, as is commonly believed. Mature forgiveness is an integrated realistic view that contains both good and bad aspects of self and others. Forgiveness allows us to absorb the full impact of the evil that men do while not losing sight of their humanity. Forgiveness is a both/and affair. In Kernbergian terms, the grammar of forgiveness would look something like:

Someone has behaved destructively toward me (bad object representation), stimulating feelings of hate (connecting negative affect) in me (bad self-representation). At the same time, I know that I have at times behaved in ways which are at least remotely similar (bad self-representation). The other person is not a devil, but a human being with hopes, virtues, wounds, and struggles (good self and object representation) whom I can empathize with (connecting positive affect).

Diagramming the sentence structure of forgiveness in this way makes clear that the failure to forgive is a manifestation of splitting, for it only contains the first sentence of the above paragraph: "Someone has behaved destructively toward me (bad object representation) stimulating feelings of hate (connecting negative affect) in me (bad self-representation)." Thus, the view of the other is a caricatured "all bad" one.

Where there is splitting, projective mechanisms cannot be far behind. The bad self-representation (the self who feels hateful) is sure to be projected. The grammar of those propositional statements is, "I feel hate but . . . that person is making me feel hateful feelings. It is his evil influence. The badness comes from him."

As we recall from our discussion of Klein, the price paid for this cognitive distortion is the experience of being persecuted by the devil one has created, namely paranoid anxiety. The only author who has appreciated this aspect of unforgiveness is Hunter, who has stated that "the development in the individual of the capacity for forgiveness should be seen in relation to its polar opposite, the fear of retaliation and paranoid anxiety."[8]

Those who have worked clinically with borderline patients will easily recognize the application this has to the borderline's experience of the world. Borderlines perpetually misperceive others, who may be laboring heroically to help them, as persecuting, depriving, and belittling them. Although initially they may idealize their helper, after frequent minor disappointments they experience them as persecutory demons who are causing all the badness in their life and "making them feel" a variety of negative affect states.

Is unforgiveness always a manifestation of splitting? The most challenging example, of course, is unforgiving survivors of experiences such as the Holocaust. To accuse unforgiving survivors of character pathology appears the worst example of blaming the victim one could imagine. Even to suggest it is itself an outrage. Yet, without stigmatizing victims, we find in Klein a ready explanation for such phenomena. Klein argues that even in those who have advanced beyond the paranoid-schizoid position, primitive defenses remain a part of the psychological apparatus and can in moments of regression be reactivated. The explanation for some individuals' fixation at a level of primitive defensive operation, according to both Klein and Kernberg, is that frustration, abuse, or constitutional factors make the experience of aggressive feelings so powerful that they cannot be integrated with positive feelings and thus splitting is maintained. Therefore, it is logical that experiences of catastrophic abuse later in life will also mobilize aggressive feelings that are too severe to be integrated and reactivate splitting. We all have our breaking points (those who know me personally will assure you mine is comparatively fragile), beyond which we cannot help but say, like Tevya, "There is no other hand." Nonetheless, as someone who lost distant relatives in the Holocaust, what is most frightening to me about the reality of that tragedy, as was perhaps best illustrated by the movie "Shoa," is that the majority of Nazi collaborators were not demons. They were human beings who, in a moment of cultural madness, submitted to the banal evil impulses that live inside us all.

Closely related to the problem of unforgiveness is what might be called immature forgiveness. As Hunter has said, the word "forgiveness" can sometimes have an "unctuous or smug quality as though the forgiver is possessed of an astonishing and irritating virtue."[9] Those who have traveled in religious circles are no doubt familiar with this brand of false compassion.

The explanation is clearly that religious language is at once being used to express the very process of splitting that it is being invoked to alleviate. For the essential structure of the split is maintained: The forgiver is good, and the forgiven one is bad. Indeed, the forgiver's very act of forgiveness serves to reinforce his or her moral superiority.

This brand of forgiveness usually reveals telltale signs of reaction formation. The believer will contend that he has been "healed" by God of his hateful feeling and given new loving feelings in their place. Note that hateful feelings are not integrated with additional loving feelings but replaced by them, an almost textbook definition of reaction formation.

Yet the hostility has not disappeared. It finds expression in the intrusive superior nature of the forgiveness dispensed. Often, the forgiven one feels insulted rather than reconciled with, understood by, and accepted by the forgiver. On one hand, he or she has been maligned as the target of the forgiver's negative projections; on the other, she or he has been "forgiven"—certainly the ultimate backhanded compliment.

Typically, such acts of forgiveness are socially sanctioned in tight-knit religious cultures that can best be characterized as paranoid systems. Outsiders and unbelievers are the target of negative projections and experienced as persecutory objects. They are experienced as "hating God's children," "corrupting society," "slaves to the devil," and so on. Once again, splitting, paranoia and unforgiveness go hand in hand.

Having clarified the capacity to forgive, how then does one achieve it? From both the psychological and theological vantage point there can really be only one answer: through the experience of being forgiven.

Of course, man's need to be forgiven by God is a central part of the Judeo-Christian tradition as old as the Bible itself. However, the need for forgiveness by an object outside of the self is more than theological dogma; it is a psychological necessity as well.

Tillich has argued that self-acceptance in a vacuum, without the mediation of a forgiving other, is logically impossible. The same self cannot at once seek absolution for guilt and possess the moral authority to grant absolution. That would be like a criminal pardoning himself.

How can you accept yourself? This is the ultimate question. But then the answer is: You cannot accept yourself because you are guilty. . . . Nobody will believe this act of forgiveness if he forgives himself. . . . Otherwise, it is simply saying, 'I am a good man'; but that is just the opposite of what forgiveness means. . . . Otherwise, it is simply a self-confirmation in a state of estrangement.[10]

More central to our current discussion is the developmental understanding that object relations theory provides; namely, that all self-representations are formed through the experience of a relationship. It is in the dyadic matrix that we discover who we are. In this tradition, self-forgiveness in a vacuum would be as psychologically impossible as it is theologically impossible to the religionist.

To be consistent with the logic of our discussion, self-forgiveness must involve the integration of good and bad self-representations, in the same way that forgiveness of others involves the integration of good and bad object representations. The nature of both the religious and therapeutic process is to hasten this integration.

No better illustration of this therapeutic action can be found than the ministry of Jesus. Jesus made two complementary interventions in his society that were both shocking and radical. He aggressively confronted the hypocrisy of the Pharisees, the religious hierarchy of his day, who declared themselves righteous. In turn, he found value in the prostitutes, tax collectors, and sinners who by all standards were considered depraved. Like a good family therapist, he made full frontal assault on the splitting of ancient Israel. When asked to summarize his own ministry, the great evangelist John Wesley said simply, "To comfort the afflicted and afflict the comforted." The spiritual adviser must make the person they are counseling aware of the self-representation, good or bad, that is split off from awareness.

In our role as psychotherapists, we perform very much the same function. This seems most dramatically illustrated in the treatment of borderline patients who so vividly display splitting. The initial phase of this treatment inevitably involves active confrontation of the patient's projections. The patient accuses her therapist of depriving, belittling, and persecuting her (most borderlines in treatment are female), and the therapist replies that it is just the opposite. The therapist helps the patient see that it is she who is behaving in an aggressive and destructive fashion. As one might imagine, sparks do fly, just as they did when Jesus confronted Pharisees. Yet the second phase of therapy, which is far less dramatic but no less important, is the gradual realization by the patient that, indeed, although she has behaved like a first-class bitch, the therapist has not given up on her. She still comes to sessions, still attends to her inner and outer world, and perhaps most importantly, still likes her.

This is forgiveness. (Indeed, these exasperating patients are in need of forgiveness.) It allows the patients to reintroject the split-off negative self-representations without their overwhelming or destroying the good self-representation. "I was a bitch, but Dr. Gartner liked me anyway. That gave me hope"—I have heard more than one of them say in one form or another. That means that splitting is no longer needed. It's finally safe to admit who one really is.

In one sense this might sound similar to the notion that the "real relationship" of warmth and caring between therapist and patient provides a "corrective emotional experience"[11] (Alexander and French, 1946), a theory that Kernberg for the most part has not endorsed, stressing instead the power of interpretation, confrontation, and limit setting.[12] I believe Kernberg has underestimated the importance of therapist warmth and involvement for positive treatment outcomes with borderlines and would agree with authors, such as Buie and Adler, who argue that love of one's borderlines is part of the cure.[13] In turn, what Kernberg's critics fail to recognize is that it is both an act of love and a corrective experience to tolerate and contain the borderline's aggression without retaliating or withdrawing. As Waldinger and Gunderson have written:

Kernberg's view of treatment is most classical and least concerned with corrective experiences. Yet even he writes of the importance of the therapist "holding" the patient, that is tolerating the patient's expressions of intense ambivalence. As the patient sees the therapist does not crumble under the patient's aggressive onslaughts, the patient's fears about his or her own impulses diminish and the integrative ego functions are strengthened.[14]

The ability of the therapeutic relationship to endure hate and aggression serves as a living contradiction to the notion that either the patient or the therapist is "all bad." It is this living witness to the reality of ambivalence that makes the capacity for forgiveness possible.

God's forgiveness operates in the same way. No matter how bad our sin, He has the capacity to love us, find value in our goodness, and ensure that our destructive impulses and behavior will not prevail against the newfound spirit within.

What forgiveness ultimately achieves is to give us back ourselves, by eliminating the need for splitting and projection. Jung, who argued that psychotherapy is "built on the practice of confession,"[15] wrote:

The inferior and even the worthless belongs to me as my shadow and gives me substance and mass. How can I be substantial without casting a shadow? I must have a dark side too if I am to be whole; and by becoming conscious of my shadow I remember once more that I am a human being like any other.[16]

Once having received the experience of being forgiven, one can afford to forgive others in the same spirit of generosity. Most importantly, having eliminated the need for splitting and projection, one no longer needs to create persecuting devils; one can have a friendly relationship to the world and recognize even those who have committed evil against us are "human beings like any other."

Having outlined my basic theory, below is a summary of the case that helped teach me about the principles I am using it to illustrate:

THE WOMAN WHO HATED EVERYBODY

Without question the most difficult patient I ever treated was L. L. was a 28-year-old, single, white female. She was five feet tall, overweight, and had a jagged, mannish haircut. The most notable thing about her was that she seemed to stare right through you.

When I first met her, she stared angrily at me, refusing to speak. Finally, in an expressionless voice, she said, "I'm going to kill myself. It's only a question of when."

The patient had a long history of lethal suicide attempts, self-mutilation, and hospitalizations. She had been admitted for what would amount to a two-year-long stay in our long-term unit for the treatment of borderline personality disorder after burning her stomach and genitals over twenty times with a cigarette. She did this the day her therapist left for vacation.

In the unit, the patient would sit in the same chair all day every day (she was on restricted status because of her suicidal state) and silently stare at anyone who dared walk by. I found myself avoiding the unit unless it was absolutely necessary for me to stop in.

The patient began hurting herself at age five. She hit her arms and hands with hammers and tried to jump out of a moving car. Both of her parents were alcoholics who used to fight loudly and bitterly. The patient and her twin brother would often hide together in the closet when they became too frightened by the row. Her father beat her mother during these quarrels, often sending her to the hospital. Yet all of this was a family secret as father was an extremely wealthy and successful attorney. By age 21, Father had graduated first in his class from an Ivy League law school. Mother was verbally and physically abusive toward the patient, once holding her head underwater in the bathtub and screaming, "I hope you die." When the patient was eight, her father began sexually abusing her, forcing her to perform fellatio and intercourse. Despite this, the father was the patient's preferred parent. He called her "princess" and gave her outrageously lavish presents (for example, $1,500 life-size stuffed animals) and threw birthday parties for her at the most expensive downtown hotels. When the patient was 12, her father died of a heart attack while he was arguing with her. Mother's alcoholism rapidly worsened. She began beating the children and never left the home. By age 16, the patient began to physically retaliate, once pushing her mother down the stairs.

Throughout childhood and adolescence, the patient was severely withdrawn and depressed. Her only companion was a large sheep dog. By age 18, she had passed through several psychotherapies and been treated with a variety of medications by one of the nation's most prominent psychopharmacologists, with no response. When the patient was 18, her mother committed suicide on her own birthday with the patient's antidepressant medication.

The patient's twin brother settled the estate as best he could. Later, after his death, it would be discovered that the father's law partner stole most of the family fortune. The patient and her brother rented an apartment. However, she was forced to find her own apartment after he began abusing drugs and alcohol and beating her. Essentially, the patient spent the next ten years as a professional patient. She did not work, attend school or socialize. She lived in and out of hospitals after suicide attempts and drifted in and out of several unsuccessful outpatient therapies.

Therapy was a battle. Each session began with her silent stare.

"What's the silence about?" I asked.

No answer.

"I have the impression that this silence is your attack on me and your treatment."

Silence.

"Is that what you want?"

"Yes," she answered.

"What makes you want to do that?"

"I hate everyone."

"I assume everyone includes me?"

"I've suffered all my life, why shouldn't you?"

"Why should either of us suffer?"

"That's easy for you to say, little boy blue. You think you're a big shot, post doc at an Ivy League hospital. Too bad you look like a 16-year-old little prick. I bet you don't know that the patients laugh at you as you walk down the hall and the nurses think you're a little snob."

"Sounds like you're pissed off at me."

She narrowed her eyes and stared at me. "You know what I fantasize about doing? Sticking a knife in my throat and spattering you with my blood as I die. Fuck you!"

Never had I felt so defeated. Months of interactions like the above were punctuated only by constant complaints from the nursing staff that "my" patient was impossible. Yet I felt determined to penetrate this wall of hate.

"You know what you are?"

L. narrowed her eyes. "What?"

"You're a religious martyr. At first I wasn't sure, but you're definitely a religious martyr."

"What the hell are you talking about?"

"You know, those Buddhist monks who burned themselves to protest the murders in Vietnam. That's what you're doing to protest the horror perpetrated against you by your family."

"Oh yeah? Well, you're an asshole."

"Insulting me is part of being a religious martyr. Destroying your psychotherapy is part of the protest."

"Is calling patients names part of your treatment?"

I assumed a solemn countenance and stamped my feet as if marching off to a ritualistic sacrificial fate. "Got a light?" I asked, referring to the monks who set themselves on fire.

Suddenly, she burst out laughing. "You're the weirdest doctor I ever had."

"I guess that's why they laugh at me."

"They don't really laugh at you. I just said that because I wanted to get you."

"Don't you still?"

"No. . . . I don't know. . . . I mean . . . I guess I like you."

Indeed, the patient came to admit that she not only liked me but was in love with me. Every other member of the staff she vilified. In her estimate they hated her, which in fact was not completely untrue. Neither was it undeserved, as her abuse of them was relentless. The hate of all hates, however, was reserved for her dead mother. At almost every session, the patient chanted, "I wish my mother was alive so I could kill the bitch."

Being loved had its hazards, however. The patient seemed, uncannily, to know every move I made throughout the hospital. She was furiously jealous of everything I did apart from the sessions with her. For months, each session began with stony silence, insults, and vows to kill herself, which I would confront and interpret. Typically, they now ended with apologies and embarrassed declarations of her affection for me.

Gradually, it emerged that she felt humiliated and frustrated by her affection for me and experienced it as a form of torture instituted by me for the purpose of driving her crazy. The aggressive back-and-forth of her provocations and my confrontations was both a defense against this frightening vulnerability and an eroticized recapitulation of past sadomasochistic relationships.

Our relationship became more stable as she metabolized my interpretations of the dynamics described above. My role became that of coach rather than savior or devil, as we collaborated on her real-life problems. The staff started spontaneously saying they liked her better. We discussed her temptation to act out while I was on vacation, her usual pattern. I was pleased to find that while I was away, she was elected patient vice president!

One day I was surprised to find her status had been dropped. The nurses reported the patient had inexplicably and suddenly become suicidal and had asked to be restricted to the unit. She reported that she heard the voice of her dead mother calling her name.

In session, the precipitant to this incident quickly became clear. This was her mother's birthday and, more importantly, the anniversary of her suicide. L. indeed seemed psychotic.

"The bitch is still trying to kill me. Dragging me into her grave. Get away, bitch! Get away!"

L. was put on neuroleptic medication, and over the course of the week, the hallucinations and agitation diminished in intensity.

The next week, L. seemed sad: "I still hear the voice calling me but it's softer now. I can ignore it if I want to."

"But you're not sure you want to?"

"I don't know. . . . That doesn't make sense."

"I've often wondered . . . do you ever miss her?"

At that moment her face went blank and I became frightened. What had I said? Would she attack me? Walk out? After a few seconds that felt like hours, she burst into tears—the first time I ever saw her cry in a year and a half. Over the next few months, she recalled for the first time positive things about her mother. For the first time, she began to express some empathy for her mother's experience. She began to question aloud whether the mother's alcoholism had caused her mother to do and say things she wouldn't have without the addiction. She started wondering what sort of mother she could be, fearing that she would likely be just as sick and destructive.

At this time, the patient did something rather remarkable. For the full year and a half she had been on the unit (indeed, for most of her life), she had had no friends and spent most of her time glaring from her chair. Out of the blue, she "adopted" one of my adolescent female patients. The girl she befriended was the loudest, most outrageous, but nonetheless charming patient on the unit. The two of them were quickly nicknamed the "giggle sisters" as they repeatedly interrupted unit meetings and disrupted hall decorum by laughing uproariously over virtually anything. The two became inseparable to the point that the staff was wondering how to tame their enthusiasm! I would frequently bump into them in the hall. They would chime, "Hello, Dr. Gartner," and burst into laughter.

Over the next few months, L. appeared to make steady progress until I announced that I would be leaving both the hospital and the area. At that time she regressed, it seemed, to where she had been at admission. She became totally negativistic, refusing to speak except to promise suicide. Nothing I said or did appeared to have any impact. The staff became quite discouraged, as did I. As the months before my termination turned into weeks, I secretly became quite anxious. Never had I felt so hopeless as a clinician.

One day during my last week at the hospital, she showed up at my office with a large drawing of us waving goodbye.

"I've been thinking a lot lately," she said. "I really hate you for leaving me. I have to admit I don't really understand how you could do it. Maybe it's easy for you because you can do anything you want, but it leaves me with nothing. That makes me want to hurt you and kill myself. But I can't forget what you've done for me. I know I gave you a hard time (laughing) . . . a *real* hard time, but you didn't give up on me, even when the other staff wanted to. I think it's shitty of you to walk out on me but . . . I guess I can forgive you."

After this incident, our final few sessions were spent discussing our termination, her program, and her plans. We said goodbye warmly. From what I heard the patient had difficulty, but was successfully discharged to a halfway house and outpatient treatment.

Forgiveness and its role in this treatment could be understood either as a product or as a precipitant toward more integrated object relations. I believe this case illustrates that both are true. Tolerating increased ambivalence toward the therapist and, later, the mother was a necessary first step, without which any mention of forgiveness would have been absurd and the termination of therapy probably would have ended in another suicide attempt. The patient's act of forgiveness represented a culmination of this development and permitted her to progress by allowing her to feel both grateful and furious at the same person at the same time. No doubt, as a new developmental leap, this forgiveness was itself fleeting, a lesson that would need to be "remembered" over and over before it was stable. For that same reason, the appearance of the capacity for forgiveness heralded a dramatically new possibility for this patient—the possibility of not recapitulating the destructive relationships that had, like demons, possessed her and her family.

NOTES

1. R. P. Fitzgibbons, "The Cognitive and Emotive Uses of Forgiveness in the Treatment of Anger," *Psychotherapy*, *23* (1986): 629–33; R. Hunter, "Forgiveness, Retaliation and Paranoid Reactions," *Journal of the Canadian Psychiatric Association*, *23* (1978): 167–73; M. Kaufman, "The Courage to Forgive," *Israel Journal of Psychiatry and Related Sciences*, *21* (1984): 177–87; E. M. Pattison, "On the Failure to Forgive or Be Forgiven," *American Journal of Psychotherapy*, *19* (1965): 106–15.

2. J. Ashbrook, "Paul Tillich Converses with Psychotherapists," *Journal of Religion and Health*, *11*, 1 (1972): 40–72; J. Brandsma, "Forgiveness: A Dynamic, Theological and Therapeutic Analysis," *Pastoral Psychology*, *31* (1982): 40–50; T. Brink, "The Role of Religion in Later Life: A Case of Consolation and Forgiveness," *Journal of Psychology and Christianity*, *4* (1985): 22–25; H. Close, "Forgiveness and Responsibility: A Case Study," *Pastoral Psychology*, *21* (1970): 19–25; D. Donnelly, "Forgiveness and Recidivism," *Pastoral Psychology*, *33* (1984): 15–24; R. Sexton and R. Maddock, "The Adam and Eve Syndrome," *Journal of Religion and Health*, *17*, 3 (1978): 163–68; S. Spidell and D. Liberman, "Moral Development and the Forgiveness of Sin," *Journal of Psychology and Theology*, *9* (1981): 159–63; E. Todd, "The Value of Confession and Forgiveness According to Jung," *Journal of Religion and Health*, *24*, 1 (1985): 39–48; O. Walters,"Psychodynamics in Tillich's Theology," *Journal of Religion and Health*, *24*, 1 (1985): 39–48; K. Wapnich, "Forgiveness: A Spiritual Psychotherapy," *Psychotherapy and the Religiously Committed Patient*, special issue of *Psychotherapy Patient*, *1* (1985): 47–53; W. Wilson, "The Utilization of Christian Beliefs in Therapy," *Journal of Psychology and Theology*, *2* (1974): 125–31.

3. D. Augsburger, *The Freedom of Forgiveness* (Chicago: Moody Press, 1973); D. Augsburger, *Caring Enough to Forgive. Caring Enough Not to Forgive* (Pelham, N.Y.: Herald Books, 1981); D. Donnelly, *Learning to Forgive* (Nashville, Tenn.: Abingdon, 1982a); D. Donnelly, *Putting Forgiveness Into Practice* (Allen, Texas: Argus, 1982b); L. Smedes, *Forgive and Forget: Healing the Hurts We Don't Deserve* (New York: Harper & Row, 1984).

4. Hunter, "Forgiveness," p. 168.

5. M. Klein, "Notes on Some Schizoid Mechanisms," *International Journal of Psychoanalysis*, *27* (1946): 99–110; M. Klein, "On Identification," in his *New Directions in Psychoanalysis* (London: Hogarth, 1955).

6. O. Kernberg, *Borderline Conditions and Pathological Narcissism* (New York: Aronson, 1975); O. Kernberg, *Object Relations Theory and Clinical Psychoanalysis* (New

York: Aronson, 1976); O. Kernberg, *Internal World and External Reality* (New York: Aronson, 1980); O. Kernberg, *Severe Personality Disorders* (New Haven, Conn.: Yale University Press, 1984).

7. Kernberg, *Internal World*.

8. Hunter, "Forgiveness," p. 167.

9. Ibid., p. 168.

10. Ashbrook, "Paul Tillich," p. 54–67.

11. F. Alexander and T. M. French, *Psychoanalytic Therapy* (New York: Ronald Press, 1946).

12. O. Kernberg, "The Psychotherapeutic Treatment of Borderline Personalities," in L. Grinspoon, ed., *Psychiatry*, vol. 1 (Washington, D.C.: American Psychiatric Press, 1982).

13. D. Buie and G. Adler, "The Definitive Treatment of the Borderline Personality," *International Journal of Psychoanalytic Psychotherapy*, 9 (1982): 51–87.

14. R. J. Waldinger and J. G. Gunderson, *Effective Psychotherapy with Borderline Patients* (New York: Macmillan, 1987).

15. Todd, "Value of Confession," p. 44.

16. Ibid., p. 44.

Chapter 3

The Functions of Faith: Religious Psychodynamics in Multiple Personality Disorder

David G. Benner

As attested to by both this volume and a growing body of other recent psychoanalytic research, the traditional Freudian view of religion as monolithically pathological is much in need of revision. As a result of unresolved conflicts in his own personality (Vitz, 1988), limited personal and professional experience with religion, and the inadequacies of early drive theory, it is now quite apparent that Freud left us a rather incomplete conceptualization of religious experience.

Two recent and related developments have, however, begun to bring about the necessary revision in the psychoanalytic psychology of religion. The first of these was the development of ego psychology, particularly the work of Heinz Hartmann (1964). Following the trail suggested by Freud himself and first systematically explored by his daughter Anna, Hartmann shifted the point of psychoanalytic focus from the id to the ego, from instinct to higher-order psychological functions. His hypothesized conflict-free sphere of ego functions provided the basis for the conceptualization of religion in terms other than instinctual gratification.

The second development, object relations theory, also had its beginnings in Freud. Schafer identifies three main features of the embyonic object relations theory held by Freud: 1. our earliest involvement with family members has a lasting influence on subsequent relationships; 2. this influence is mediated by *imagos* of these significant people; and 3. these imagos may be transformed but never destroyed (Schafer, 1968: 220). Thus, it was not the idea of internalizations of significant object relations that was novel to the writings of Fairbairn (1952b), Winnicott (1965), and other object relations theorists, but

rather it was their systematic examination of the way in which these representations contribute to both intrapsychic and interpersonal functioning that most
extended Freud's work.

If ego psychology moved the psychoanalytic focus from the id to the ego,
object relations theory has built on this foundation by moving it even further
from the biological and impersonal to the psychological and the personal. Thus,
it is not surprising that object relations theory has generally viewed religion more
sympathetically than was the case with drive theory. This is obviously part of
the reason that the understanding of religion that is beginning to emerge from
applications of object relations theory is so revolutionary to orthodox psychoanalytic thought. Perhaps the best example of this is Winnicott's reinterpretation
of the role of illusion in psychic life and his demonstration of the ego-integrating
and ego-enhancing properties of the lifelong use of transitional phenomena such
as religion (Winnicott, 1971).

Recent investigations of the psychic creation, elaboration, and function of
individuals' representation of God by Rizzutto (1979) and McDargh (1983) also
give ample demonstration to the usefulness of object relations theory in the
development of a psychoanalytic psychology of religion. The work of Meissner
(1969, 1984, 1987) further illustrates fertile applications of this same theoretical
framework, his understanding of faith identifying the potential for psychological
growth and healing that is resident in religious experience.

These and other recent writings suggest the basis for the hope that many feel
that a more balanced and comprehensive psychoanalytic theory of religion may
be beginning to emerge. This possibility was noted by Loewald over a decade
ago when he wrote:

If we are willing to admit that instinctual life and religious life both betoken forms of
experience that underlie and go beyond conscious and personalized forms of mentation
. . . then we may be at a point where psychoanalysis can begin to contribute in its own
way to the understanding of religious experience, instead of ignoring or rejecting its
genuine validity or treating it as a mark of human immaturity. (Loewald, 1978: 73)

RELIGIOUS DYNAMICS IN PERSONALITY

One aspect of religious experience that has been made clear by recent psychoanalytic investigations is the fact that religious faith serves multiple and complex purposes in personality. No longer is it responsible to assert that religion is
either simply pathological or consistently constructive. For some individuals, on balance, it may be more a force of pathology than of health, while for others, the opposite
may be true. What is apparent, however, is that for most, if not all, people, religion
is a mixture of both constructive and pathological components.

A study of the function of faith in multiple personality disorder may assist in
understanding these complex dynamics in as much as the fragmentation of per-

sonality that exists in such persons provides a built-in degree of segregation of the major psychodynamic forces that are operative. In this disorder, aspects of personality that are usually fused are torn apart, thus providing unique and often valuable windows into the intrapsychic world. For example, one personality may be built around a core of guilt while another may be grounded in anger or pain, giving a relatively uncomplicated and often quite transparent view of these respective dynamics in the overall personality. The dynamics of religious functioning that are more intertwined in non-multiples may, therefore, be more easily teased apart in multiples, shedding light on the place of religion in personality.

Religion often seems to feature quite prominently in persons diagnosed with multiple personality disorder. Several authors have noted fundamentalistic religions to be a frequent characteristic of their family backgrounds (Coons, 1980; Boor, 1982; Stern, 1984; Higdon, 1986). Multiplicity now being well linked to childhood abuse (Kluft, 1985), it is also noteworthy that a significant number of children who develop multiple personalities encounter this abuse within the context of religious cults. It is not surprising, therefore, that religion often serves as a container for their pressing questions about good and evil and that one or more of the personalities of multiples are frequently quite religious, while many more often have strong cathexes to religious matters.

Noteworthy, however, is the fact that the burgeoning literature on multiple personality disorder contains only one study of the religious lives of persons with this disorder. Bowman, Coons, Jones, and Oldstrom (1987) report an investigation of the religious experience of seven female multiple personality patients, examining in particular the God-representations of the main personality and one alternate personality of each. They document a correlation between God-representations and parental representations and also between God-representations and general personality traits. They also noted several important differences between the God-representations of main and alternate personalities of their subjects: Main personalities generally are believers who hold quite ambivalent views of God, while secondary personalities are less likely to be believers but hold non-ambivalent views of God.

While this study is a significant beginning to the understanding of the religious experience of multiple personalities, its major limitation is the fact that in none of the subjects described were all the personalities examined. The research method involved only a single interview divided between the main personality and one alternate personality. While it furthers our understanding of God-representations and their relationship to other personality dynamics, it does not provide an understanding of the multiple meanings and functions of religion in the total personality system of persons with this disorder.

The purpose of the present chapter is to take a first step toward this larger goal. This will involve the analysis of a single case of multiple personalities and an examination of the religious dynamics of each of the personalities. I will first present the essential features of the developmental history and then describe the personalities. Discussion of the religious dynamics will follow the presentation of the case material.

CASE MATERIAL

The case I wish to examine is that of a thirty-nine-year-old divorced Jewish female whom I will call M. First diagnosed as a multiple personality at age twenty-nine, seventy-one ego elements were identified over the course of 450 hours of psychotherapy. Following the criteria suggested by Kluft (1984), fifteen of these elements are appropriately classified as personalities, the remaining fifty-six being less well developed and therefore designated as ego fragments. These fragments lacked either a sense of life history (that is, of their own existence) or a range of functions or emotional responses. Many served a special but limited function (such as balancing the checkbook or administering medication), most never participated in therapy, and none was in any way a full-orbed personality. Ego fragments are usually quite easily fused to related personalities and are not, therefore, usually the focus of much psychotherapeutic attention in the treatment of multiple personalities.

Overview of Developmental History

Born and raised in Poland, M.'s parents were both survivors of World War II Nazi concentration camps. Married but childless before the war, they were reunited in 1947 and M. was born three years later. Her mother was very sick throughout the pregnancy and died of a brain tumor when M. was three months old.

After the death of his wife, M.'s father coped with his grief by emotional withdrawal and escape into his work, which involved considerable travel and frequent and extended periods of absence from the home. M. was looked after by a series of babysitters until her father married one of these women a short time later. However, M.'s stepmother proved to be a seriously disturbed woman, subjecting the child to repeated acts of physical violence. These included burnings, beatings, locking M. in a cage in the attic, and burying her alive in the yard.

When she was four, her father began to worry about his daughter's emotional isolation and retreat into silence and took her to a psychiatrist. This consultation evidently opened the father's eyes to at least some of what was going on at home and he immediately changed employment in order to be at home more and took over most of the responsibility for the care of M. The abuse seemed to terminate during this period of paternal interest and M. became very close to her father. Unfortunately, he died of a heart attack in less than a year and her stepmother placed her in an orphanage at this point. She remained in this orphanage for five years, during which she suffered much persecution as one of the few Jewish children in the institution.

At age ten, M.'s stepmother, now remarried, took her out of the orphanage, and the family moved to the United States. Her stepparents were very active in a satanic cult and over the next few years she was deeply involved in cult activities, being forced to witness and participate in human sacrifices and other ritualistic acts of violence. She was also repeatedly sexually abused by her stepfather and tortured by her stepmother. At thirteen, she became pregnant by her stepfather, who subsequently aborted the fetus himself, almost killing M. Then, in an attempt to ensure that she would have no memory of the event, he attached electrodes to her head and administered bursts of electricity. She again became pregnant by him at fourteen, this followed by yet another non-medical home abortion and a follow-up course of electroshock.

Despite the turmoil that continued at home, the remainder of M.'s adolescent years went somewhat better. She managed to do very well at school and through this won her ticket out of the home by means of a full scholarship to a university. Graduating with a major in psychology, she began a doctoral program in clinical psychology, completing one year of studies before dropping out. The apparent reason for this was her involvement with the Moonies. Her conversion to this religious cult was the occasion for a move to another part of the country, where she took up residence in one of their communes.

This was the context for yet another set of trauma. Under the direction of the leader of her commune, M. married a man she didn't love and who quickly showed himself to be abusive and sadistic. She had one child from this marriage but left this child and her husband when she escaped from the cult three years after her arrival. Her abandonment of the child was reluctant but was the result of her judgment that it was the only way she could get free of the cult and her husband. This act of abandonment was subsequently the conscious focus of much guilt.

After leaving the Moonies, M. converted to Roman Catholicism and applied to enter a convent. On being rejected for the novitiate, she moved to yet another part of the country and began to work in the social services field. Shortly after finalizing her divorce, she met and quickly married another alcoholic and abusive man, this time staying with him for only six months. At the time she came to me for treatment, she was in the process of her second divorce and had just joined a congregation of Jewish Christians in an attempt to reconcile her Jewish heritage with her new-found beliefs as a Christian.

The Personalities

M.'s host personality (the personality that has control of the body for the majority of the time) was, during the period of our work together, the original personality (the entity that developed first after birth and from which the others developed). As we will subsequently see, this was not always the case for her, as alternate personalities sometimes served as the host personality for extended periods of time.

The original personality of M. was dependent, depressive, and highly manipulative. The pattern of her manipulation was to identify other people's needs and then find some way of meeting them. This was the personality that had studied psychology and worked as a social worker. The helper role was a standard way by which she endeared herself to those whom she needed and subsequently manipulated. Her chronic depression had been the focus of much of the approximately ten years of previous psychotherapy she had received, none of it identifying or correctly diagnosing her multiplicity. Unable to express anger directly and deeply burdened by layers of neurotic guilt, this personality was highly ineffectual in coping with life.

Two other features of the original personality are particularly important in understanding her religious dynamics: her tendency to guilt absorption and masochism and her delusions of grandiosity. This personality was plagued by deep and pervasive feelings of guilt and shame. She felt herself to be an awful person and viewed her life's problems as a continuing confirmation of the fact that she deserved punishment. Not surprisingly, this lead her to view God as judge and to relate to him with considerable ambivalence. Although she affirmed that God was all good and loving, she wished that he would show this love by punishing her in a way she felt she deserved. Thus, it was not God's love but rather his punishment that she found most attractive. She felt herself to be so guilty and so deserving of punishment that only God could give her what she deserved.

The grandiosity revealed in this sense of badness is even more clearly evidenced in a network of religious delusions held by this personality. She felt herself to be in possession of a stone that had been brought by Moses from Egypt and that gave her a unique relationship with God. She wore this stone on a ring to which she attached a number of magical expectations that strained reality contact. One of these was that she believed this stone marked her special status in religious history as the one who was to become the mother of a messianic figure. This child, she believed, would be fathered by Jesus, whom she viewed as her husband. These religious delusions were the only evidence of psychotic process in this personality and were well contained, even if quite fixed. She shared them with only a very small number of people, her reality contact being sufficiently good as to afford her the awareness of how incredible her beliefs would be to most people.

God, for the original personality, was both transcendent and imminent. The pain she experienced in the face of what seemed to be his frequent abandonment of her was relieved by the sexualization of her relationship with him, making him an object of great intimacy. However, even in this intimacy, God was less an object of love and devotion than of fear. She retained conscious memory of religious instruction at the feet of her Orthodox Jewish father, whom she recalled telling her of the goodness and utter trustworthiness of God. These teachings seem to have been internalized and were at the basis of her unswerving belief in God's existence. This she claimed to have never seriously doubted, her various religious conversions merely marking successive stages in her spiritual pilgrimage.

Alter 1 was two years old and seemed to be associated with an experience of M. being thrown down the stairs by her stepmother at this age. Emotionally hungry but frightened, this personality spent much of the time, when she was out, crying, sucking her thumb, and rocking. She was largely non-verbal, although she intermittently used both Polish and English words and phrases. While she could be engaged in play therapy, most of her communication came through alter 3, who was emotionally close to her and who was capable of and willing to communicate her experience to me. As would be expected by her age, she offered no religious material during the course of our work together.

Alter 2 was totally nonverbal. Communicating through art as well as through alter 3, she identified herself as three years old and seems to have been associated with the period of autism noted by her father at that age. This personality was discovered at a point of working through conflicts encountered by M. during her graduate work in clinical psychology, these precipitated by her undertaking a research paper on infantile autism. The decompensation that she experienced on undertaking this research was obviously an important factor in her decision to leave graduate school.

This personality was very hard to work with, and it took a long time to win sufficient trust to get any sense of her religious experience. She associated religion with her father and seemed to have no independent sense of God. She represented herself as Jewish, further reflecting her identification with her father and his religious practice.

Alter 3 was four years old and the warmest and most engaging of the personalities. Usually happy and optimistic, she refused to own any experience that was painful. Although she spoke continuously of her father, she was unwilling to discuss his death. She was the personality who absorbed the good experiences with him prior to his death, basking in his love and attention and denying or repressing all other negative experiences.

Although this personality could not face anything painful in her own experience, she could feel the pain of the other personalities. In fact, she displayed a good deal of empathy, particularly in relation to the infant personalities for whom she felt responsible. In addition to English, this personality spoke both Polish and Yiddish, neither of these languages being known by the original personality. She strongly identified with Orthodox Judaism. Her God was the God she met on her father's lap—loving, personal, and all good. She did not blame God for what had happened to M., leaving him out of those questions so as to preserve the good experience she had of him.

Alter 4 was a five-year-old girl associated with the death of her father. Deeply depressed and occasionally suicidal, she absorbed all the pain of this loss, seeming to have none of the good experience of her relationship with her father to counteract it. Claiming to believe in God, she was, however, deeply disappointed in him and didn't know how to reconcile this experience with her image of God. She desperately wanted to be able to trust God but felt cautious about trusting anyone after the loss of her father, the only person she ever really trusted. She also identified herself as Jewish.

Alter 5 was a six-year-old girl associated with abusive experiences in the orphanage. Angry and sullen, she distanced herself from anything soft and tender. She felt herself to be a misfit in the world of the other personalities, whom she experienced as all like each other and quite unlike her. She often asked me how she got "in there" with the others, claiming that she didn't belong and that it was some cruel trick of fate that had locked her inside this alien body with a strange family. She actively disidentified with Judaism and although Polish was her main tongue, she spoke only in English as a way of distancing herself from everything associated with her childhood.

This personality was the most anti-religious of all of the elements in the system. She felt religion made people soft, thus making it more difficult for such people to cope with the harsh realities of life. In her experience, life was tough, and she had no intention of allowing religion to distort this basic existential perception.

Alter 6 identified herself as twelve years old and was associated with teenage experiences in the satanic cult. Frightened and overtly compliant, she was at the same time passive-aggressive and highly manipulative. Seductive in her relationships with men, she also played out the sadistic aspects of her experiences in the satanist cult by acts of emotional cruelty to the men she encountered.

Alter 6 claimed to be a satanist. She said she originally had pretended to go along with the religious rituals of the cult out of fear but came to believe in Satan's power and subsequently made a pact with him for her soul. The bargain was that in exchange for her service and loyalty, he was to protect her from further hurt. Although she seemed to be disappointed with Satan (she felt that he had not kept his end of the bargain), she experienced too much fear of her God to even consider disbelieving in him or reneging on the commitments she had made to him. She defended against the guilt engendered by her imperfect loyalty to Satan by active proselytizing efforts on his behalf, in both the intrapsychic and extrapsychic worlds of relationships.

Alters 7, 8, and 9 were each associated with a single aspect of the pregnancies or abortions by her stepfather. Alter 7, describing herself as fourteen, claimed to be pregnant and was the happiest of the personalities. Displaying some psychotic symptomology, she harbored a fixed delusion of being pregnant. Continuously hopeful about the love her baby would return to her after its birth, this personality showed little conflict. She was, however, an important element in the overall dynamics of the personality and would emerge whenever things looked most desperate and hopeless. It is interesting to note that this personality had been the focus of some psychotherapeutic treatment received during the teen years, when she would tell people that she was pregnant and was referred for help because of what was perceived to be a pattern of chronic lying. Alter 7 claimed to be Jewish.

Alter 8, also stating her age as fourteen, was the most violent and angry of the personalities and was associated with the rage experienced at the abortions performed by her stepfather. This personality showed features of an antisocial personality disorder, most notably chronic kleptomania and lying and a disdain for conventional morality. She also reportedly hated men and showed a significant degree of homoerotic sexual orientation. She was the personality primarily involved in M.'s homosexual experiences and served in general as an outlet for M.'s aggressive and sexual drives. She claimed to be an atheist, having rejected the God she had been raised to believe and trust. This personality was also bulimic.

Alter 9, who also gave her age as fourteen, was associated with the grief occasioned by the abortions she experienced at the hands of her stepfather. This personality was the most depressed of all of the elements in the system, her depression being manifest primarily in terms of despair. She made several serious suicide attempts during treatment. Alter 9 deeply mourned the loss of her babies and strongly identified with the host personality in her loss of her child on leaving the Moonies. While wanting to get pregnant again, she was, however, filled with dread about what new form of loss she might experience if this were to happen.

This personality desperately wanted to believe in God. She envied the other personalities who were believers but felt she did not have the faith necessary to join their ranks. Her search for God was quite active and, as will be discussed later, she was the host personality at the point of a conversion to Christianity that occurred during the teen years.

Alter 10 was the intellectual element of the system. Giving her age as seventeen, she seems to have been the host personality for much of M.'s late high school years and for some of her undergraduate years at the university. She had discovered the possibility of escape from pain by retreat into the world of ideas and academic accomplishment, and her personality seemed to be largely configured around these interests. She read voraciously and expressed interest in returning to graduate school at some time in order to complete her doctorate.

In the early stages of therapy, Alter 10 spoke little of religion, indicating that it simply was not of much interest to her. She classified herself as a nominal atheist, her atheism being more associated with her desire for intellectual respectability than emotional struggles resulting from past trauma. Religious issues became more important to her as she became connected to other aspects of M.'s experience in the latter stages of therapy. At this point, her religious quest took on a distinctively intellectual tone and she became very interested in comparative religions and philosophical responses to the question of the existence of God.

Alter 11 was a committed Moonie who would not divulge her age. Having been the host personality for most of M.'s time with the Moonies, this personality was built primarily around her religious identification at this point in time. Quite suspicious and moderately hostile, she internalized the authoritarian style of life encountered in the commune and bossed the other personalities around. She was generally obnoxious in both her intrapsychic and extrapsychic relationships and had few friends in either world.

Alter 12 was one of the helpers of the system. Her responsibilities were for the management of several aspects of external life where M. had difficulty, most notably, finances and medications. She also did much of the driving of the car. This personality was most similar to the original personality in self-presentation (speech and mannerisms) and would often take over for the original personality if things got too rough for her, no one being aware that a switch in personality had occurred. She claimed to be twenty-four and described herself as Christian. She did not seem to share any of the religious delusions of the original personality. In terms of general psychological development, she was the healthiest of the elements in the personality, this reflected by her capacity for non-manipulative altruism, a well-developed sense of humor that was relatively devoid of hostility, and a value system that was based in her religious commitments and that seemed to provide drive regulation and integration of her personality.

Alter 13 held a number of executive functions in the coordination of the various personalities. Calling itself "Guardian," this personality claimed to be ageless and asexual. One of its major functions was the preservation of M.'s life history. Alter 13 was the only entity that had a relatively complete memory trace of her life experiences. This personality also chaired meetings of the alter personalities (which they called family council meetings), served as a peacemaker in disputes between the various ego elements, and held some degree of control over the switching of personalities. Viewed as an angel by some of the other elements of the system, this personality claimed to have been present from the first occasion of abuse.

Only very rarely taking control of the body, Alter 13 played out its role on the inner stage but kept in communication with me by letters and other surreptitious messages. These were the channels through which this personality fed me information about the psychological state of the host personality and of the inner system. In this regard, alter 13 functioned as a kind of co-therapist for much of this woman's treatment.

Alter 14 was a personality I met on only two occasions. She had an internal function that did not allow her much time to attend to the external world. She claimed that she spent all her time praying for the other personalities, praying that they would all be converted and come to faith in Jesus as their savior and messiah. Her presence was viewed with amusement and indifference by unbelieving personalities, with suspicion by Jewish, Moonie, and satanist personalities, and with comfort by those that were Christian. She gave her age as thirtynine, the same as that of the host personality.

DISCUSSION

Before embarking on a discussion of the religious psychodynamics in this case, we should briefly review the current state of knowledge about this complex disorder. Although the first case of multiple personality disorder was reported in 1817, between that date and 1970 only seventy-three additional cases were reported in the world's psychiatric and psychological literature (Greaves, 1980). However, between 1970 and 1980, fifty additional cases were reported, and since the inclusion of multiple personalities in Diagnostic and Statistical Manual (DSM) III in 1980, approximately 5,000 cases have been identified (Braun, 1986). Most of what we know about multiple personality disorder has been learned within the past ten years, a period that witnessed the publication of 95 percent of the present literature on the topic (see Boor and Coons, 1983 for a comprehensive bibliography, and Damgaard, Van Benschoten, and Fagen, 1985, and Kluft, 1987 for more recent updates).

The growing consensus on etiology is that the predisposing factors for the disorder are an inborn capacity for dissociation (this manifest by excellent responsivity to hypnosis) and repeated exposure to an inconsistently stressful environment (this usually involving physical and sexual abuse) (Braun, 1986). The precipitating event is usually a specific overwhelming trauma, this most frequently occurring before age six. The patient responds to this trauma with dissociation, the split in personality serving as a defensive strategy to contain the effects of the trauma.

The way in which this splitting relates to borderline and other pre-oedipal forms of splitting is at present quite unclear. Unlike the splits seen in borderline pathology, the fragmentation of multiple personalities is on some occasions repaired quite rapidly after abreaction alone. Although this does not occur in patients with the sort of polyfragmentation seen in the present case, the fact that it is possible at all even in the simplest cases suggests that these splits may be of a different sort than those seen in pre-oedipal conditions. In his excellent critical review of the psychoanalytic understanding of splitting, Pruyser (1975) notes that this seemingly simple term is much in need of conceptual clarification; nowhere is this more urgent than in the understanding of multiple personalities.

In the light of these questions about the nature of the splitting seen in multiple personalities, it is unfortunate that there are so few reported psychoanalytic studies of the disorder. Lasky (1978) and Marmer (1980) present the only case studies of the treatment of such patients by psychoanalysis, and a handful of other investigators report applications of psychoanalytic theory, most often object relations theory, to the analysis of the intrapsychic dynamics of the disorder.

Gruenewald (1977) argues that splitting in multiplicity is similar to that in narcissistic disorders, suggesting that the genetic antecedents of multiple personalities can be traced to the narcissistic phase of development. Greaves (1980) conceptualizes the disorder as a variant of borderline pathology, suggesting that multiple personalities may represent a higher level of ego development in that

Table 3.1
Summary of Personalities

Personality	Age	Dominant Characteristics	Religious Affiliation	Belief in God?
Original	39	guilty, depressed, delusions of grandeur	Jewish–Christian	Yes
Alter #1	2	emotionally hungry but frightened	?	?
Alter #2	3	autistic	Judiasm	?
Alter #3	4	cheerful, optimistic, & responsible	Judiasm	Yes
Alter #4	5	depressed	Judiasm	Yes
Alter #5	6	angry, sullen, & hard	renounced Judiasm	No
Alter #6	12	passive-aggressive	Satanist	Yes
Alter #7	14	happy & perpetually pregnant	Judiasm	Yes
Alter #8	14	antisocial, homosexual	renounced Judiasm	No
Alter #9	14	depressed	Christian	Struggling to believe
Alter #10	17	intellectual	nominal atheist	No
Alter #11	?	suspicious & hostile	Moonie	Yes
Alter #12	24	external world helper	Christian	Yes
Alter #13	?	internal world helper	Christian	Yes
Alter #14	39	one who prays	Christian	Yes

the splits form into relatively organized and internally integrated personalities. Benner and Joscelyne (1984) make the same argument, focusing on the process of object relations development in both disorders. However, drawing on Winnicott to suggest that trauma thwarts the integration of the self, they place more emphasis on the failure of ego integration as opposed to splitting. Grotstein (1984) extends this analysis by suggesting that splitting in multiple personalities serves as a defense against the confusion of ego boundaries.

A recent and noteworthy application of Winnicott's theory to the understanding of multiple personality is reported by Smith (1989), who argues that multiple personalities can best be understood as a complex, false self-formation that has its origins in the failure of the development of the psyche-soma unity. Noting that an absence of "good-enough mothering" can lead to a failure to develop ego boundaries that overlap with those of the body, he suggests that multiple personalities may be a retreat from the body (which is associated with pain) to the mind, which becomes an entity in itself.

This cursory literature review makes quite obvious how tentative our present understanding is of this complex disorder, particularly with regard to the nature of the splitting, which is so foundational to its dynamics. We proceed to a discussion of the specifically religious dynamics of the present case with caution, recognizing that the uncertainty that remains about the psychodynamic foundation of the disorder demands that interpretations of specific dynamics, religious or otherwise, be quite tentative.

In general terms, the religious dynamics of this case are consistent with the pattern reported by Bowman et al. (1987). These authors noted that the original personalities of their subjects all believed in the existence of God and were quite confident about this belief. Their views of God were, however, highly ambivalent. In contrast, alternate personalities in this study were less likely to believe in God but more likely to hold a non-ambivalent God-representation. M. was a firm believer in God and, in fact, claimed to never have had any serious doubts about this matter. Her view of God was, however, highly ambivalent, as she viewed him with both fear as the supreme judge of the universe and yet with sexual attraction as her lover. Alternate personalities were more variable in their belief but their views of God were clear-cut. Alter 3, for example, viewed God as a cosmic teddy bear, this representation having its roots in an all-good paternal representation, while alter 6 viewed God as evil and dangerously powerful, her God-representation having its roots in an all-bad representation of her stepfather. The God-representations of the alternate personalities were unambiguous and relatively simple, even if at the same time they were characteristically quite divergent from each other.

A central feature of the religious dynamic in M.'s original personality was her tendency to guilt absorption and moral masochism. Her guilt was consciously associated with the abandonment of her child in the cult but obviously had its roots much deeper than this. She felt she deserved punishment, and religion supported this conviction by providing her with a God that could be shaped into an image of the Grand Inquisitor.

This personality's guilt and masochism seem to be grounded in a defensive effort to ward off bad parental object representations. Fairbairn (1952) argues that this defense of guilt is based in our need for good relationships with objects. This need is so desperate that if our objects are not all good (which they never are), then we prefer to purge them of their badness, taking this badness on ourselves and thereby making them good and ourselves bad. We subsequently feel guilty and judge ourselves to deserve punishment. Fairbairn describes the reason for this process by drawing on a religious metaphor. He states:

It is better to be a sinner in a world ruled by God than to live in a world ruled by the Devil. A sinner in a world ruled by God may be bad; but there is always a certain sense of security to be derived from the fact that the world around is good—"God's in His heaven, All's right with the world!"—and in any case there is always a hope of redemption. In a world ruled by the Devil the individual may escape the badness of being a sinner but he is bad because the world around him is bad. Further, he can have no sense of security and no hope of redemption. The only prospect is one of death and destruction. (pp. 66–67)

The defense of guilt worked very well for M. Finding it more tolerable to regard herself as conditionally (i.e., morally) bad than to regard her parents as unconditionally (i.e., libidinally) bad, she was thus able to maintain a sense of security through the preservation of justice and order in the world. Guilt also helped her defend against her bad objects. It supported repression of the internalized bad-parent representation and simultaneously supported idealization of the internalized good-parent representation. And through this sequence of manipulations of internal object representations she was able to gain a good object relationship, if not in the external world, at least in the internal one. Religion supported this defensive use of guilt, and her God-representation was largely determined by these dynamics.

Religion also supported her grandiosity. Not content to serve as a mere worshiper of God, the sexualized relationship she felt herself to have with God and the unique role she saw herself destined to play in religious history quite transparently reveal an attitude of omnipotence as a defense against early narcissistic injuries. As noted by Fairbairn (1952b), such grandiosity and feelings of omnipotence are often well contained within certain spheres of personality. This is particularly clear in M.'s case, the omnipotence and grandiosity being exclusive to the original personality. Religious delusions thus also helped her defend against early narcissistic injuries by providing a context for her grandiosity.

Religion functioned in the original personality by helping her regulate her sexuality and begin to repair her relationship with males. Each of the personalities managed her sexual conflicts differently. The original personality did so, in her words, by "saving herself for Jesus." This is, of course, a long history of celibacy combined with religious devotion, and this was undoubtedly part of what suggested the religious life to M. when she attempted to gain admission to the convent. Sexual relationships had invariably been the cause of much pain for her, and she vowed to forsake sex with men and wait for her cosmic lover to come to her. He, she knew, would be gentle with her in a way no man had been or, she imagined, could be. Her sexuality was therefore repressed, but most importantly, it was for the first time connected to love. Her love for God was, as already noted, ambivalent. But her relationship with Jesus was a container for both sex and love, the integration of these two experiences being unique and ultimately therapeutic for her.

One final noteworthy aspect of the religious experience of the original personality is the fact that it was capable of faith in God at all. Throughout all of her experiences of trauma, she had remained a believer. How was this possible? It had not been for many of the alternate personalities.

The fact that the original personality had some positive experiences with her father probably provided the psychological basis for her belief in God. Belief in God was also made more possible because this was the personality that had been the recipient of her father's religious instruction. Through her father, she learned of God and she experienced love and acceptance. Although she felt herself to be unworthy of this love, it did provide a basis for her belief in God. Her internalized God was a composite of the all-good paternal representation and the punitive stepmother representation. She longed for a good and loving God, but, because of the defense of guilt, saw herself as deserving nothing better than a harsh and punitive God. Had she only experienced the cruelty of her stepmother, it is unlikely that she would have believed in God. Or, if she did, he would have been much more like the evil and dangerous God of alter 6.

Bowman et al. (1987) note that dissociation may also make belief easier for the original personality than for many of the alternate personalities. In the present case, it was the original personality who experienced the dissociation, depriving her of most of the memory and affect associated with the abuse and leaving her more free of rage. Thus, the very fact that she was a somewhat depleted and hollow personality made it easier for her to continue to believe in the existence of God.

The original personality was one of the least psychologically healthy of all of the personalities in M. With her focalized psychotic processes contained within a basically borderline personality organization, it is not surprising that religion served primarily pathological and defensive purposes for her. However, even here, religion was also at work as a constructive force, primarily in her sexuality and in the repair of her object relationships with males. One aspect of her representation of God was as gentle husband, something she had never known in reality. However, clinging to the hope of this as a possibility in a relationship was a reparative force in her personality.

Religion functioned in quite a different way in alter 3, (alters 1 and 2 offered no religious material for analysis). She was the little girl who had received the devoted attention of her father for the year after he became aware of her autistic behavior and before he died. Her God-representation was not well elaborated; neither did it differ very much from her father-representation, the latter being highly idealized. Her faith supported the perpetuation of this idealized father, and her spiritual quest reflected the deep longing for a perfect parent that Fairbairn described as the basic human drive. Her faith in God can also be seen as supporting her self-esteem. One of the most secure of the personalities, her self-esteem was buoyed by her experience of being valued and loved by her father/ God. This was the basis of much of her optimism and emotional resiliency.

Religious faith in alter 4 was primarily in the service of the repair of her capacity to trust. Her God was good but limited in power. She felt let down by him when he allowed her father to die, and she was not sure that she could ever again trust him or anyone else. Her faith in God's existence was quite strong, but the God she believed in was weak. Consequently, she felt no security in her relationship with him.

This very much shaped the transference relationship that developed in treatment. She viewed me as well meaning but powerless, holding little hope that I could be of any help to her or the others in her world. She observed me from the safety of her intrapsychic vantage point for a long time before communicating with me and came to trust me only very slowly. However, her capacity for such trust was grounded in her relationship to her father and to the God she met on his lap. Her slowly developing trust of me enhanced her trust of God, and her trust in God also enhanced her trust of me. The security she came to experience in the therapeutic relationship ultimately helped her reconcile her faith to her experience of loss.

Although alter 5 was overtly anti-religious, her unbelief served a clear religious function. This personality, associated with the abuse experienced during the years at the orphanage, rejected religion, which she saw as a futile effort to escape from the cruel realities of life. Her rage was more focused on God than on those who had hurt her during those years. It was grounded in what she perceived to be the unfairness of life, not merely her own pain. Unbelief was a scapegoat for this rage, which, being of cosmic proportions, needed to be projected onto something of similar proportions. God was ideally suited to the task. Her religious commitment was thus her denial of God's existence.

Alter 6 represents an interesting study in religious psychodynamics. This was the personality that identified herself as a satanist, claiming to have made a pact with the devil for her soul during the years of involvement in this cult. Her God-representation seems to draw principally on the all-bad stepfather representation. Her stepfather served as a high priest in the satanist cult and was thus easily identified with the devil. Her God was evil and very dangerous. He could not be ignored or trusted. But by means of the Freudian mechanism of identification with the aggressor, she could align herself with him and, she hoped, thereby protect herself. This was what she sought to do in her pact with the devil.

It is interesting to note that what she sought from this pact was not so much gratification as safety. This is reminiscent of Fairbairn's comments on a case of demon possession in which he noted that the basis of the individual's pact with the devil was not wine, women, and song but rather the privilege of being a child of Satan. He described this as follows: "What he sold his eternal soul to obtain, accordingly, was not gratification but a father, albeit one who had been a bad object to him in his childhood" (Fairbairn, 1952: p. 71). Similarly, what alter 6 sought was a relationship with her bad stepfather; she wanted to align herself with him and do whatever she had to do to receive his love and protection rather than his wrath. Religion was for her, therefore, a way of attempting to work out a bad object relationship, her relationship with her stepfather.

Religion was of little significance to alter 7, the personality destined to be eternally pregnant. Identifying herself as Jewish, alter 7's God-representation was neither well developed nor an object of significant cathexis for her.

Alter 8 needed a God to reject, and religion served purposes similar to those described for alter 5. Her rage was focused on her stepfather and was associated with the abortions he performed on her. God had not been there to protect her from these horrifying tragedies and she therefore felt that he did not exist. Her atheism was her religious commitment, and it supported the expression of her rage.

Alter 9, the personality associated with the grief over the abortions of early adolescence, evidenced more religious struggle than did any of the other personalities. She had experienced the hope of M.'s pregnancies and, in the face of her unwanted abortions, felt not only loss but utter hopelessness. She claimed to still believe in God but received little comfort from that belief. Her God had not protected her or her babies, and she struggled to understand how he could have done this to her. She wanted to believe in his goodness and his ability to take care of her but felt instead only doubt, sadness, and anger.

This personality's exposure to God seems to have been through her strong identification with the other personalities who had experienced significant losses, that is, the original personality and alter 3. Both of these personalities employed faith in God as a way of dealing with their loss, and this was where alter 9 met God. However, she related to God with more emotional honesty than did either of these personalities. God was a central reference point for her in her struggles, and prayer became her most important source of catharsis. She blamed God for what had happened to her and was not prepared to let him off the hook as some of the other believing personalities had done. Her faith was shaky, and her feelings toward God were ambivalent. But she kept talking to him throughout her struggle. Religion thus served as an anchor for her, an anchor that over time was more and more a central integrating reference point in her personality.

It is not surprising that alter 10, the primary intellectual element of personality, approached religion more cognitively than did any of the other personalities. Religion became the primary focus for her basic existential questions, which were not addressed as systematically by any other element of personality. She questioned the existence of God, the possibility of knowing him if he did exist, and the morality of his actions (or lack of the same) in the world. She examined the answers provided to these questions by philosophy and comparative religious studies and in so doing opened up important avenues of dialogue between the various religious factions of M.'s personality.

Faith served alter 10 by enhancing object relations development. God, for her, was originally no more than a theoretical hypothesis. But he came to be a focus of trust, commitment, and even devotion. In her relationship with God, she came to discover these non-intellectual elements of her personality, and they first received expression in her religious life. Alter 10 brought the intellect into relationship with faith in the total personality system and thus was an important point of integration of ego functions within personality.

Alter 11, the Moonie, found security and moral guidance in religion. Her faith gave her a comprehensive set of rules to be obeyed and the belief that if she obeyed these to the letter, all would eventually be well. She clung to this formula with a rigidity that matched what she had experienced in the cult. While religion thus served to aid repression and reinforce a harsh and punitive superego, it did provide her with a basis for the hope that there was order, meaning, and purpose to life, and this was the foundation for her sense of security.

Although alter 11's God was harsh and punitive, he was not capricious. Her God-representation was built on that of the leader of the cult and borrowed elements from the stepparent representations. However, it was also shaped by the religious instruction she received in the Moonies, and this allowed her to view many of her traumatic experiences as acts of redemptive discipline. God therefore could be experienced as having her best interests at heart. Because he loved her, he disciplined her. The painful experiences he allowed her to have were allowed for her good. This she firmly believed. She experienced herself not primarily as a victim of tragedy but as someone in the hands of a loving, if stern, God. This religious conviction further supported her faith in the intelligibility of life.

Alter 12 spoke of God much less than did most of the other personalities. However, her faith was obviously very important to her. Her God-representation was largely based on the all-good paternal representation and was very influenced by the religious instruction she received from him. Her God was good and was in control of everything that happened in life. Although his ways were often mysterious, they could be trusted because he could be trusted. This belief gave her personality a degree of stability that was in marked contrast to the more volatile nature of most of the other personality elements. Her faith therefore appeared to aid her affect management, which, while based primarily on intellectualization, served her well.

This personality was also the most altruistic of the personalities, and her capacity for love seems to have been enhanced by her religious faith. She was a helper, both by role assignment and character structure. Although her capacity for empathy allowed her to experience the pain of other personalities, she did not carry any of M.'s trauma. This made it easier for her to give and receive love. Although several other personalities spoke of God's love, only alter 12 seemed to actually experience this love, and this seemed to facilitate her giving love to others.

Alter 13, the internal world helper, provided little religious material for analysis. Viewed by some of the alternate personalities as a guardian angel, she made no effort to dissuade them from this belief, suggesting that she suffered from a fixed religious delusion. Not enough is known about this personality, however, to understand the precise way in which religious belief functioned for her.

Alter 14, the one who claimed to spend all her time praying, was superficially quite religious in a narrow, pious sense. She seemed to be a rather underdeveloped personality who, apart from offering prayer on behalf of the other personalities, played a relatively minor role in the intrapsychic system. She did, however, bring hope to the system. She was the only personality to show no fear of integration, and, in fact, never lost hope that this could happen. Furthermore, she felt that her role in the system made a direct contribution to this end, it being her expectation that the religious conversion of the non-Christian personalities would aid the possibility of integration of all the personalities.

Although we have seen evidence of the integrative function of religion in the original personality (integrating love with sex) and in alter 10 (integrating intellect with affect), a discussion of the religious dynamics of separate personalities fails to illuminate the most important integrative function of religion in this case, which took place at the level of the personality system as a whole. By looking at the fragments, we can fall into the trap of taking the metaphoric language of "multiple personalities" too literally. There is, in reality, just one self, one ego, one personality, even if it is badly fractured. But in spite of this fracture, there is an underlying unity to the personality, a unity that does not negate the fragmentation but allows the person to function in spite of the fragmentation (Benner and Evans, 1984). And in this case, religion was integrally involved in supporting and enhancing this unity. To recognize this, we must look briefly at the role of the multiple religious conversions experienced by M.

For a long time, religion enhanced the disunity and fragmentation that existed among the various personality elements. Personalities that were split off from each other and from the original personality in order to isolate and contain specific affects and drives found communication and harmonious relationships with each other even more difficult by virtue of their religious differences. The Jewish personalities felt betrayed by those who had converted to Christianity and the latter felt deeply mistrustful of the satanist and Moonie personalities. Religion was, at this point, a divisive force in intrapsychic functioning.

The original personality described herself as an orthodox Jew until she joined the Moonies at age twenty-one. She subsequently converted to Christianity at age twenty-four, and at age twenty-eight, she joined a group of Jews who accepted Jesus as their messiah. But this personality was not, in fact, the first to convert to Christianity. Alter 9 was the host personality for most of the time during the period between ages fourteen and sixteen, and at some point during these years, she converted to Christianity. Other personalities knew of this conversion, but the original personality did not. (The original personality had no knowledge of any of the alternate personalities even though all of them had knowledge of her and most had knowledge of the others). Thus, when the original personality returned to the host personality role somewhere around age sixteen, she did not know that there had been a conversion to Christianity within the personality system. She had to make this pilgrimage herself, and it took her another eight years to do so.

Over time and one by one, each of the personalities converted until all professed faith as Jewish Christians. I became aware of this unfolding process on the inner stage only as it was reported to me or as I saw evidence of changes in some of the personalities and inquired about this. For example, the decrease in suspiciousness in alter 11 was a quite visible indication of her conversion, as was the muting of anger in alter 5. These changes were not instantaneous; neither were they always permanent. But they were significant and noticeable.

As the various personalities united in faith, they came to have more of a basis for relating in other ways. They spoke of getting along better together, and this internal cooperation led to more stability in the psychic functioning of the original personality. M. only became aware of what was happening within her when the alternate personalities finally agreed to partially reduce the one-way amnestic barrier that had blocked her consciousness of their experience, giving her her first glimpse into a world she had previously heard of only through others. This did not automatically lead to integration of the personalities but was an important step in this direction.

In summary, although this analysis of the religious dynamics in this case is far from exhaustive, it does illustrate the multiple and complex ways in which religious faith can function within an individual. Across the various personalities, religion was employed both in the service of pathology and health. While it supported psychotic delusions, it also served as an aid to object relations repair and integration of fractured ego functions. This integrative function of religion was even more clear at the level of the personality as a whole.

Freud gave us the tools to understand the pathological elements of religion, but it was the object relations theorists who gave us comparable tools to understand the more constructive features of faith. Describing these health-enhancing aspects of religion, Meissner describes faith as a disposition of the psyche that integrates the diverse functions and various levels of the mind into a unified and organized whole (1969: 50). It is, according to Meissner,

a transforming process that touches all parts of the psychic structure and reorganizes them into a pattern that is different and integrates them into a more mature and effective level of functioning. Faith has, therefore, an integrative function in the psychic economy. True faith is thereby restorative, recuperative and effectively maturing. (1969: 70)

At its best, religion is capable of being a powerful force for healing of brokenness in personality. But at its worst, it can become entangled with pathological dynamics and be more a part of the problem than a part of the solution. It is thus a two-edged sword, and for most people, as is true in the present case, it probably cuts both ways.

Chapter 4

God-Representation as the Transformational Object

Edward P. Shafranske

Representations of God play a major role in a person's spiritual and religious life. Such representations express the nature of an individual's relationship to what he or she regards as personally sacred. This chapter presents an understanding of God-representations as the expression of an individual's desire for or acknowledgment of psychological, spiritual, or physical transformation.

It is proposed that contained within religious faith and within the background of all God-representations lies the transformational object. This psychoanalytic model of the transformational object suggests that moments of transformation within infancy are indelibly etched into the deep psychological structure of an individual's consciousness. The striving to locate anew the transformational object is expressed in a variety of human endeavors and in relationships with those psychological objects imbued with the potential to be transformative. Religious faith, and in particular, God-representational processes, are well-suited contexts in which the search for the transformational object ensues.

Within this chapter, the model of the transformational object is specifically applied to God-representational processes and to religious experience. In suggesting that these psychological dynamics are the mainspring within religious motivation, theistic faith is apprehended within the domain of all human enterprise that promises transformation and transcendence, such as, for example, aesthetic expression.

This model is seen to complement the theoretical and clinical contributions of a number of psychoanalysts, notably Ana-Maria Rizzuto, who have identified

the important role transitional phenomena play in God-representational processes.[1] This approach attempts to describe psychological phenomena that predate
and may in fact set the stage for the appearance of God-representations within
the transitional space. This chapter commences with an introduction to the context
in which God-representations are approached by a psychoanalytically oriented
psychology.

INTRODUCTION

A moment of personal recollection of one's own religious experiences or a
glimpse at a penitent in prayer, eyes raised to a cruciform or other religious
icon, may be enough to suggest the power and significance God-representations
possess. Such representations not only evoke awe, rapture, courage, or fear in
a solitary person but may also give rise to potent social or cultural movements
as witnessed throughout human history. It was not lost for example on John the
Baptist that Jesus chose to use the familiar term *Abba* to signify a unique personal
relationship with the transcendent, with Yahweh. The revelation of such a God-
representation was a startling confrontation to those at the baptism and foreshadowed the establishment of a new religious faith based on this novel form
of relationship with the sacred.

Expressions of one's personal cosmology through God-representations describe the nature of an individual's relationship with what appears as the embodiment of the source of all otherness. An individual's representations, for
example, a personal God, an impersonal force, or an absence of a meaningful
Other, reflect the rudimentary psychological foundation on which the forging of
a sense of place within the cradle of the universe will be carried out. The
significance of an inquiry into God-representation therefore goes beyond the
study of religion to an analysis of an individual's stance toward relational existence. Embedded within one's God-representations exists a personal statement
of one's relationship with all of existence. Harry Guntrip put this notion well:
"Since religion is preeminently an experience of personal relationship, which
extends the personal to the *n*th degree, to embrace both man and his universe
in one meaningful whole, the integrating nature of fully developed personal
relationship experience, is our most solid clue to the nature of religious experience."[2] Beyond Guntrip's seeming optimism in this exposition lies the possibility as well that one's religiosity may convey a negative sense of self and a
disharmony within existence. One's God-representations may in fact appear as
persecutory or bereft of concern for the person or, for that matter, an absence
of an Other. If one's creator is a malevolent force, one might wonder how this
bodes for any expression of human relationship. This is not to suggest that God-
representations are necessarily unidimensional, all good or all bad caricatures
along the motifs of a child's fairy-tale protagonists, but rather to point out that
such representations may serve to support or to deride the individual. God-
representations are viewed as highly personal expressions relevant not only to

one's religiosity but also as statements of one's relationship within the universe of significant psychological objects.

Representations of God are not simply abstract conceptions born of zealous faith or figurative, literary symbols summoned to put flesh on the insights of intellectual discernment. Psychoanalytic study informs us that these representations are far more complex psychological gestalts of conscious and unconscious processes. They are conceived to be amalgams of internalized parental imagos, fantasy, compensatory operations, and acculturation that serve a dynamic role in forwarding the psychological equilibrium of the individual. God-representations understood psychodynamically contribute not only to the religious sphere of human affairs but participate as well in the psychic life of all persons through their status as psychological objects within the representational world. By this is intimated that God-representations exist within the same field of influence as do other internalized objects.

God-representations in consort with all of other object relations form an internal relational matrix on which a primary sense of self is endowed and interpersonal relations are established. This internal relational matrix bears the imprint of all moments of relationality and provides an ongoing psychological context through which the vicissitudes of existence are apprehended and addressed. Everyday existence is shaped by past moments through the vestiges of the past, which are embedded within the objects of the representational world. God-representations as such play a significant role within the representational world and provide a relevant subject for study within psychoanalysis. This consideration of God-representational processes within the model of the transformational object serves as both an elucidation of the psychological constituents of religious experience and a contribution to the understanding of representational phenomena. A brief discussion of method in the psychoanalytic study of religion will establish the context for the presentation of the transformational object.

THE PSYCHOANALYTIC STUDY OF RELIGION

Any attempt to study religious experience commences with an appreciation of the utterly personal and idiographic character of the subject at hand. As illustrated in the works of William James, an examination of religiousness requires an inquiry into the shadows of another's personal subjectivity and a ferreting within the noetic, meaning-generating sphere of the individual.[3] Religiosity can be studied not only in terms of its sociology, that is, its institutional affiliation and practices, but also may be approached from the vantage point of a depth psychology. It is in reference to this domain that James pointed out that religion is on "its hither side a continuation of our subconscious life."[4] To attempt such a study of the "hither side" of religiousness, one must necessarily establish the lens and mode of perspective on which to record and place observations.

Psychoanalysis, as a scientific discipline and as a treatment regimen, claims as its domain of inquiry the subjective, intrapsychic life of the individual. Psychoanalysis provides a lens and perspective through which a psychology of religion that proposes to study representational processes may be established. This presentation of the transformational object as a heuristic model in the psychology of religion necessitates a brief review of the methodology utilized in psychoanalytic investigation and an acknowledgment of the theoretical contributions this study seeks to complement and forward.

Psychoanalytic investigation commences with the clinical case study. Within the clinical setting, verbal associations and observed behaviors of the patient as well as the private associations of the analyst become the data for inspection. These observations are disclosed within the explanatory frame of psychoanalysis. Phenomena that are exhibited within the consulting room become data only as they are comprehended through the use of the psychoanalytic lens. The refraction of psychoanalysis allows for psychological phenomena to be apprehended and to form an impression on the observer. As such, data are not recorded naively or purely phenomenologically but rather are captured within an enabling paradigm.

Spence has suggested that what is discovered in psychoanalytic investigation is substantively a construction of a narrative of the subjective life of the individual rather than a factual recording of historical truth.[5] Through disclosures and associations within the analytic partnership, a narrative that speaks to the subjective text of the patient is constructed. The data derived from clinical case studies in this view cannot be claimed as neutral, unbiased observations. Such data are collected through what Spence refers to as the analyst-researcher's "unwitting projection" within the intersubjective context of analysis and through the lens and perspective of the psychoanalytic paradigm. In light of this, all data are conceived to be theory-laden observations. Such an understanding has implications for the scientific verification of theoretical models that the clinical data purport to establish. The nature of the data that are collected has led some analysts to conclude that psychoanalytic investigation is best understood as a hermeneutic enterprise rather than a natural science.[6] Proponents of this view suggest that psychoanalysis contributes to human understanding as a unique discipline and recommends discontinuing attempts to justify its procedures within the natural science paradigm.

I have suggested in another work that although clinical case studies do not generally meet the canons of empirical science to establish the verification of theory; such studies are indispensable in the development of models that lend heuristic value and forward the development of continued research.[7] Clinical case studies provide for the discovery and illustration of hypotheses regarding the inner subjective life of individuals. Such data do not, however, provide verification that would elevate the theoretical model to that of scientific fact. It is important to remind readers of the delimitations of scientific verifiability concerning the subject at hand. This does not render the model insignificant but rather establishes parameters by which to assess its claims. This is particularly the case as a psychoanalytic model is presented that proposes to understand God-representational processes that lie on the hither side of consciousness and are hypothesized to originate in the preverbal life of the infant. The model of the transformational object in God-representational processes is delimited to the status of a model, that is, "an imaginative tool for ordering experience."[8] It is a provisional way of describing what is not directly accessible to observation.

A second consideration concerns the interpretation of data derived from the clinical case study. A cardinal feature of psychoanalytic investigation is the reliance on reconstruction as a vehicle by which descriptions of earlier psychological states of mind are inferred. Peterfreund has noted the limitations of a scientific model and metapsychology based on the adultomorphization of infancy in which the subjective states of infants are inferred from the analysis of adults, often of severely disturbed patients.[9] Stern addressed the same limitation in drawing a distinction between the "clinical infant," a creation of metapsychology, and the "observed infant."[10] It is important to keep in mind the limits of our ability to infer the developing consciousness of the child from clinical data derived from the observation of adults.

The study of mental states and subjective experiences of adults, much less infants, is methodologically problematic. Attempts to fathom the inner life of the individual are necessarily open to criticism and skepticism in light of the difficulties and delimitations briefly noted. Such is the case in approaching the present study of God-representational processes. Attempts to scientifically investigate religious experience in terms of subconscious process, as James considered crucial in understanding religiosity, are problematic. In placing the focus of investigation on the subconscious experience, we are struck, as Nina Coltart has reminded, by the "sheer unconsciousness of the unconscious."[11]

Having delineated the above limitations and difficulties inherent in conducting a psychoanalytic study of God-representational processes, a query might be posed: Upon what basis does the present study assert its relevance? The usefulness in the application of the model of the transformational object in God-representation is found in its ability to offer a conceptualization that incorporates empirical research findings from developmental psychology and various theoretical constructions of representational processes. It offers, in my view, a heuristic that leads to a narrative of subjective inner experience that resonates within the ongoing dialogue both within the consulting room, among psychoanalytic theoreticians, and among all those involved in the study of religion. It offers arguments that convey from a developmental perspective a cogent model with which to approach religious experience.

This study owes its impetus to many contributions within psychoanalysis. Freud's application of psychoanalytic concepts to the study of religiosity provided a unique perspective upon which to discern the dynamics of faith.[12] Freud's view of God-representation as a projective process vested in the identification with the oedipal father elucidates certain aspects of religious fervor. Jung's analytical psychology interwove psychological and religious dynamics within the process of individuation.[13]

With the advent of object relations theory, God-representation could be more cogently addressed as a psychological object in its own right. Ana-Maria Rizzuto initiated a refocusing of psychoanalytic inquiry to pre-oedipal factors in the formation of the God-representation in her seminal work, *The Birth of the Living God*.[14] In this text, she proposed that the formation of the image of God is an object-representational process that originates within the transitional space and that occurs, shaped by ever-present psychodynamics, throughout the life of the individual. Rizzuto's understanding goes beyond Freud's in asserting that the God-representation is "more than the cornerstone upon which it was built. It is a *new* original representation which, because it is new, may have the varied components that serve to soothe and comfort, provide inspiration and courage— or terror and dread—far beyond that inspired by the actual parents."[15] Through its creation by means of memorial, fantasy, and conceptual abilities, the God-representation comes to exist as a virtual object for the believer.

This discussion draws its impetus and theoretical foundation from the insights gleaned by Rizzuto. The presentation of the transformational object as a model for certain aspects of God-representational processes does not discount or supplant the role of transitional phenomena in God-representation but rather suggests constituents of religious experience that have their origin in psychological events prior to the transitional period, prior to the child's more comprehensive grasp of the parents as psychological objects. This investigation of God-representational processes is conducted within the parameters inherent in psychoanalytic research and is established on previous clinical and theoretical studies that have focused on the role of transitional phenomena.

The central thesis of this chapter is that the God-representational process is rooted in the earliest period of an individual's ontogenesis and is based not only on its function as a transitional object but is also related to the infant's experience of what Bollas has termed the transformational object.[16]

THE INFANT'S EXPERIENCE OF THE TRANSFORMATIONAL

To state that the infant is an experiencing organism may seem a rather in-auspicious place to being our discussion of the development of the God-representations within the representational world. It is a starting point, however, that brings commonplace notions of infancy and everyday observations of children into dialogue with metapsychological conceptions of inaccessible psychological processes and inferences derived from clinical case material. To intuit that the infant possesses an experiencing self prompts the following questions: What then is experienced by the infant? What is the content of the infant's thinking? How does the infant come to create mental representations of the world? In what ways do experiences within this early period of human consciousness shape the development of object relations and color future relational opportunities?

Recent contributions from psychoanalytic developmental research provide answers to these questions.[17] Stern, in his review of the research literature, concludes that the infant commences the work of discriminating between objects and establishing object relatedness from birth.[18] The infant appears to possess a propensity to yoke across varying sensory modalities object-related experiences. This ability of amodal perception contributes to a budding, unified consciousness of objects. The infant takes visceral sensations, perceptions, conceptions, affects—in sum, all experience—and gradually orders this into "islands of consistency" on the way to fully articulated object representations.[19]

The integration of experience occurs through the readiness of ego functions available to the newborn. The infant's first objects of attention are contained within moments of arousal in which the child's state of being is altered. Sandler and Sandler suggest:

The subjective experiences which register on the infant's sensorium are, in the first instance, predominantly feeling-states, although these are mixed with other sensations as well. The laying down of memory-traces and the organization of perceptual and memory structures gradually lead to the further development of the infant's representational world, which acts as the basis for the ongoing organization of the child's subjective experiences and motor activities. Naturally the *particular* interaction which he has with the external world, as well as his particular individual capabilities, will exercise a profound influence on the development of the child's representational world.[20]

Affect plays a crucial role in object formation in that feeling-states of pleasure and pain alert the infant to the subjective experience of being in the world. Such moments stimulate an arousal of consciousness from the repose of seemingly alert inattention and propel the child into the object world associated with pleasure and displeasure. The objects of the child's attention may be said to be the primary experiences of affect states rather than fully conceived whole persons. Through countless interactions, the infant comes to perceive invariants within clusters of affect-driven experience. Such moments, conjoined through memory and amodal perception, take form as the virtual self and virtual others on the way to the whole object formation. The understanding that moments of arousal may exist for the infant as nascent objects foreshadows our introduction of the transformational object. Such moments have import not only for the infant's developing perception of the object world but also for stimulating the discovery of the self as the subjective experience of being in the world.

Stern suggests that "the infant can experience the *process* of emerging organization as well as the result."[21] This means that the infant catches the actuality of his presence as a subject of experience. It is as though the infant comes upon existentially: "I think therefore I am." The experience of the emergent self within the world of objects is summoned particularly in moments in which the infant's experience of self and other is heightened. Such events are those in which intense or urgent states of arousal exist and in which an hedonic tone, that is, pleasurable or unpleasurable tone, is experienced. In such episodes of intensity, the object relational matrix, which always exists in the background of experience, is ushered to the foreground. In these moments, the infant experiences what Stern calls vitality affects.[22] Vitality affects alert the infant to his or her actual being in the world, existing as a conscious, emerging self.

On the way to more fully developed conceptions of self and others within the external world, the child experiences untold moments of vitality affect in which his or her physical and psychological states are transformed. Out of the circumstance of distress comes comfort, out of arousal comes calm, out of disquiet comes quiet, out of physical discomfort comes soothing, out of cold comes warm, out of wet comes dry, out of hard comes soft, out of empty comes full, out of hungry comes satiation. The infant experiences myriad occurrences of transformation that inscribe indelible impressions on the emergent self. These experiences forge into consciousness not so much the existence of a person per se but rather the presence of a process of transformation, which Bollas refers to as a transformational object.[23]

The presence of the transformative object is dimly perceived in the background of all interactions with the maternal object, as the mother provides a "background of safety"[24] and serves as the "background object of primary identification"[25] for the infant. Her presence is apprehended not so much as a conscious, well-formulated conception as what Bollas has characterized as the "unthought known." "While we do know something of the character of the object which affects us we may not have thought of it yet."[26] What is predominantly recorded is the event of transformation. With maturation, the experience will be more fully conceived within an object relational frame.

It is posited, however, that there exists a developmental period that is significant in the creation of one's inner subjective matrix in which *it is the transformations themselves that are objects of representation*. Before entry into the transitional space, the child creates representations that reflect his or her rudimentary conception of experience. This is in keeping with the natural endowment of ego function propensities. As summarized by Sandler and Rosenblatt:

The representations which the child constructs enable him to perceive sensations arising from various sources, to organize and structure them in a meaningful way. We know that perception is an active process by means of which the ego transforms raw sensory data into meaningful percepts. From this follows that the child creates, within its perceptual or representational world, images and organizations of his internal as well as external world.[27]

It is suggested that the infant constructs the percept of the transformational object in making meaningful the source of the transformations that are experienced. In presenting the transformational object, it is not suggested that the infant is totally unaware of the mother as object. However, the emphasis is placed on the integration of the experience of transformation, which occurs with limited reference to the external object. It is within this developmental context that the transformational object comes to exist within the budding representational world. Ogden's extensions of the work of Klein and others of the British school complement this discussion of a mode of object relations in which the object is not fully conceived.[28]

Ogden proposed that the infant occupies an autistic-contiguous position in which the mode of object relations is dominated by alterations in sensory contiguity. "The sensory experience," he noted, "*is* the infant in this mode."[29] Alterations or transformations of sensory states press on the consciousness of the infant. Objects apprehended within this developmental context are sensed or felt as shapes, only later to be conceptually known as persons. In proposing this as a position rather than a stage, Ogden is suggesting that this mode of experience is not transcended within the evolution of subjectivity, but rather that new modes of experience are built upon it.

Ogden's emphasis on the role of shifts in body sensation, together with Stern's observations regarding vitality affects, focuses attention on the significance that transformations of physical and psychological states may bear on the developing inner life of the infant. The nub of this argument is that the first class of registrations on consciousness are experiences of processes, events of transformation. From the vantage of an outside witness, such transformations in fact occur within an object relationship; however, such object distinctions may be somewhat blurred for the infant existing within the nursing couple, to use Winnicott's phrase.[30] Bollas writes:

Before the mother is personalized for the infant as a whole object, she has functioned as a region or source of transformation, and since the infant's own nascent subjectivity is almost completely the experience of the ego's integrations, the first object is identified with the alterations of the ego's state.[31]

The representation of the mother, which constitutes the first subject of internalization, is apprehended initially not so much as an object per se as a process. It is a given that the child experiences changes in physical and psychological states. The "good enough" mother serves as the transformative object in coaxing and aligning the environment to address the infant's needs. In such highly charged moments of alternations in ego states, the appearance of the mother as an object is foreshadowed by the experience of mother as a process of transformation.

It is akin to the child's experience of shadow puppetry, in which the hand that gives form to the dramatics on the screen is necessarily veiled in darkness but whose effect and presence is clearly felt and yet dimly known. The emergent self on the way to a core sense of self and other has been existentially touched by the transformational object. The trace of the transformative object (which will be more fully apprehended as mother) pre-eminently exists within the deep psychological structure of the self.

As the child matures and enters the transitional space, the transformational object is placed within more fully articulated, embodied objects. Bollas observes:

With the infant's creation of the transitional object, the transformational process is displaced from the mother-environment (where it originated) into countless subjective-objects, so that the transitional phase is heir to the transformational phase, as the infant evolves from experience of the process to articulation of the experience.[32]

It is through the consistent ministration of the mother and through the unfolding and expression of cognitive and other ego propensities that the maturing child comes to identify these transformations of ego states with the mother as a whole object. The dramatic altering of ego states in infancy, however, rivets into the budding subjective life of the individual a felt knowledge of the transformational. Such experiences constitute the deepest source of hope for and faith in transformation. The imprint of the transformational object can be felt in all human endeavors that at their heart bear the intent of transformation.

GOD-REPRESENTATIONS AND THE TRANSFORMATIONAL OBJECT

It has been proposed that experiences of transformation are apprehended, internalized, and fashioned to form the transformational object within the representational world. Such an object contains the vestiges of all moments of transformation. In being a representation formed prior to entry into the transitional realm, the transformational object serves as a precursor to more clearly fantasized and articulated transitional objects. The trace of the transformational object can be gleaned in all later-developed object representations that the subject imbues with the power to evoke transformation. This is suggested to be the case in God-representations, particularly in the instance of subjectively profound religious experiences that at their heart promise and may in fact evoke the transformation of the self.

God-representations, as understood by Rizzuto as transitional phenomena, may be viewed as more highly developed elaborations of the transformational object. Such representations of God reflect the maturing of the individual's ego functions and representational facility. Intrinsic to this conception of God-representational process is the assumption of a continuous developmental course. In the evolution of the representational world, archaically formed representations are built upon, and more complex representations are formed through the synthesizing function of the ego. Although God-representations of the transitional phase appear to supplant its precursor, the transformational is never entirely abandoned and continues to exist as an object. The notion of a developmental context for God-representations is in keeping with Rizzuto's observation that "object representations and self representations are compound memorial processes originating at all levels of development in time."[33]

God-representations of the transitional phase, which exist through the life course, may be viewed as sophisticated elaborations of the transformational object. Bollas has suggested that the trace of the transformative object may be found within many human expressions. He commented:

We have failed to take notice of the phenomena in adult life of the wide-ranging collective search for an object that is identified with the metamorphosis of the self. In many religious faiths, for example, when the subject believes in the deity's actual potential to transform the total environment, he sustains the terms of the earliest object tie within a mythic structure.[34]

Of particular substance here is that the God-representational process emanates not only from a distillation of qualities of past real objects but rather is the attempt ''to recollect an early object experience, to remember not cognitively but existentially, through an intense affective experience, a relationship which was identified with cumulative transformations of the self.''[35] The relationship that is sought is the relationship with the transformational object.

A supplicant in prayer addresses the embodiment of the transformational object in beseeching his or her God-representation for deliverance or transformation. Meissner contributes to our discussion in his description of prayer in terms of transitional phenomena.

In this activity, the believer immerses himself in the religious experience in a more direct, immediate, and personal way than in any other aspect of his religious involvement. . . . It is here that the qualities of the God-representation and their relationship to the believer's self-representation become immediate. The God he prays to is not ultimately the God of the theologian or of the philosophers, nor is this God likely to be in any sense reconcilable with the God of Scripture. Rather, the individual believer prays to a God who is represented by the highly personalized transitional object representation in his inner, private, personally idiosyncratic belief system. . . .

One might say that in prayer the individual figuratively enters the transitional space where he meets his God-representation. Prayer can become a channel for expressing what is most unique, profound, and personal in individual psychology.[36]

I concur with Meissner's articulate reading of the experience of prayer. In light of the present discussion, however, I take the liberty of paraphrasing his words to highlight the role the transformational object serves. In prayer, the individual does enter the transitional space, where he locates the transformational object in his dynamically created God-representation. Such experiences do express what is most unique, profound, and personal in individual psychology, that is, the relationship with the source of all transformation. The belief and articulation of God rests, as Meissner suggests, not on the works of theologians, philosophers, or even within Scripture, but rather derives from lived world experiences of the transformational. Such experiences take root in infancy within the context of a loving, attentive, care-giving mother who provides moments of transformation that are initially recorded as processes of transformation and exist within the representational world as the transformative object.

The transformational object, forged from moments of transformation in infancy, sets the tone for further elaboration as transitional God-representations that exist as virtual objects throughout the life of the individual. The trace of these moments provides the existential basis for hope and the trust that is placed in one's God-representation.

CLINICAL EXAMPLE

The search for the transformative in human affairs may prompt a mature religious faith, instill an appreciation of aesthetics, or lead to creative expression. For individuals who have attained more integrated object relations, the transformational object may be found within the transitional phenomena relied upon to bolster a cohesive self. To the individual living on the edge of more primitive object relations, the quest for the transformational in existence may bring emptiness and despair or prompt a manic course of behavior that may lead to our consulting rooms.

The following excerpt from a clinical case study depicts the search for the transformational object in a more primitive psychological setting in which the transformational had not been transfigured into a viable transitional object. In presenting this material, I am reminded of my earlier remarks regarding the usefulness of clinical case data in scientific verification of theoretical models. My inclusion of this case is offered in service of illustration of the application of the model of the transformational object rather than as evidence of its validity.

The patient was a twenty-four-year-old, single, college-educated man who presented himself as confused regarding his reason for seeking psychotherapy. His presenting problem was "a poor relationship with God and the need to turn away from a sinful life." This patient was skeptical of psychotherapy. He declared that his need was for spiritual guidance and insisted that I could be of no help to him. He came for counseling only in deference to the recommendations of his pastor. He said early in our first session that any concern I might show to him was "shallow and ingenuine" for "only the God of Israel can fully love." He spoke often in religious language, preferring to express his psychological distress, as "being in the desert, a horrible wretch, crying out to Yahweh." The tone within this first encounter with this patient could best be described as frenetic, disintegrating, a desperate quality. His descriptions of God and self exploded out of him in a staccato manner. In later sessions, I came to understand that these expressions were not so much declarations of belief or actual experiences as much as frantic attempts to hold onto some piece of a barely formed transitional God-representational object. This first session forebode the severity of this patient's psychological difficulties and the challenges that this case would pose.

In the second session he returned quite depressed and agitated. He spoke of betrayal, that God did not exist and that there was nothing more than emptiness in his life. It seems that the church that he had been attending had let him down;

the pastor was not available when he had called late one evening for consultation. What emerged as more significant in his disaffection with the church was the experience that "God was gone." His associations conveyed that God was gone because he no longer felt the visceral presence of God. It appeared that his God-representational object barely existed on the level of conception within the transitional space and was primarily an incorporation of body feeling-states. Such states were conjured through various religious rituals, services, and prayer consultations. He attended religious services as often as he could, sometimes three and four times a day, not for the religious "content" but rather for the visceral sensation that was his God-representation. Such sensations would well up during congregational singing, in the lighting of incense, or in a particularly dramatic homily. In the later instance, the patient could not recall what was preached but rather that it felt inspirational. Such experiences would fill him with a sense of awe and warmth; his emptiness was now filled up. His disaffection with the church and so many before and after it was based on the disillusionment and loss of feeling-states that momentarily transformed his empty state of self to one full of God. I came to learn, both within the transference and the continual challenges to the precarious therapeutic alliance, and through the unfolding of his history, of his life of manic searching for an object that would transform his being. He would search out and discover a religious congregation, most often one in which charismatic religious expression was supported, and would be touched by the transformational object in some visceral way. He would feel his body warm and would describe experiences that metapsychology would understand as losses of ego boundaries, depersonalization, and fusion states. God-representation was not conceived of but rather was viscerally known as a presence or felt form. Such experiences are characterized by Ogden as emanating from the autistic-contiguous mode of representation discussed earlier.[37] These moments of rapture were necessarily short-lived. God would literally disappear as the visceral sensations subsided with the close of the service. This would often prompt a manic search for another service or demand upon the minister for a special prayer session to cull the reappearance of the transformational object God. Another consequence might follow in which the patient would act out self-destructively in a fashion that he found debasing, for example, abusing alcohol, engaging the services of a prostitute, committing acts of vandalism. He would become the "wretch" he spoke of in search of a savior. He would inevitably find a congregation in which through a conversion experience he could touch, or rather, be touched by, his God. The multidetermined quality is to be noted in these acts: In addition to re-enacting the position of "the wretch crying out to be forgiven," he engaged in experiences that brought about momentary transformations of his depressed, empty self.

For this patient, the search for the transformative object had not yet fully evolved to the level of transitional phenomena. It might be conjectured that the primitiveness of this patient's psychological development did not allow for the viable functioning of a transitional object that could be maintained and counted upon to provide sustenance and cohesion through identification. It is significant that this patient rarely experienced God in private, solitary moments. Religious reading or reflection left him feeling empty, bereft of God. Rizzuto has spoken of the God-representation in terms of the child's teddy bear that can be taken off the shelf and that functions as a transitional object.[38] Such a figure, endowed with certain functions of the maternal object, can soothe and comfort. For this patient, it was as if he had no teddy bear to take off the shelf. His was a manic search to find such an object that would provide a sense of inner sustainment.

For this young man, who struggled to attain a sense of self, to create psychological cohesion, his quest for God was the expression of his search for the transformational object. In moments in which such a God was captured, he gloried in the relationship, although his grasp of the transformational object served only as a temporary haven from his emptiness. As these experiences did not bring about the lasting transformation of the self he became depressed and withdrew in fear, anger, and frustration. He would then begin again to search for the transformational object. No person or experience could maintain such a sense of the transcendent, to hold him over time within a transformative space in which he would feel warm, full, and alive. It seemed clear that his turning to God was a desperate plea for a transformational object to intervene, not as a whole object but rather as a source of rapture, to be seized out of his present existential state. As this patient experienced his inner emptiness and disillusionment with the interpersonal world of objects, he searched for a God-representation worthy to bear the weight of his psychological impoverishment.

This case study illustrates one dimension of the God-representational process that has its roots in events of transformation. It is proposed that the search for the transformational object is a constituent within more mature expressions of God-representation and exists for some as the sole experience of the God-representation. For most individuals, the expression of the archaic representation is overshadowed by the appearance of representations of a transitional nature. Rizzuto observed: "Those who are capable of mature religious belief renew their God representation to make it compatible with their emotional, conscious, and unconscious situation, as well as their cognitive and object related development."[39] The developmental quality of God-representational processes and religious faith can be extended to apply all appearances and psychological settings of God-representation. The God-representation of the patient presented above reflects and was a product of his object-related development.

SUMMARY

It has been proposed that a unique form of God-representation exists as the transformational object. Originating in the earliest period of an individual's ontogenesis, the transformational object is reflected in all subsequent, transitional phase, representations of God. The transformational object is the internalized representation of experiences of transformation that were impressed upon the nascent self. It is posited that certain aspects and forms of God-representation may be understood within this model. This understanding complements previous psychoanalytic scholarship that elucidated the role of transitional phenomena in God-representational processes. The model of the transformational object presents a conceptualization on which to bridge representational processes within the transitional space to an earlier period in the development of object relations. Further, the search for the transformative within a diverse range of human endeavors, including the religious, may be understood from the context of the representational world through the model of the transformational object.

NOTES

1. A-M. Rizzuto, *The Birth of the Living God* (Chicago: University of Chicago Press, 1979); Rizzuto, "Object Relation and the Formation of God," *British Journal of Medical Psychology, 47* (1974): 83–89; Rizzuto, "Freud, God, the Devil and the Theory of Object Representation," *International Review of Psycho-Analysis, 31* (1976): 83–89.

2. H. Guntrip, "Religion in Relation to Personal Integration," *British Journal of Medical Psychology, 42* (1969): 323–33.

3. W. James, *The Varieties of Religious Experience* (New York: New American Library, 1904/1958).

4. Ibid.

5. D. Spence, *Narrative Truth and Historical Truth* (New York: W. W. Norton, 1982).

6. Ibid.; see also: P. Ricoeur, *Freud and Philosophy: An Essay on Interpretation* (New Haven: Yale University Press, 1970); J. Habermas, *Theory and Practice* (Boston: Beacon Press, 1973).

7. E. Shafranske, "The Clinical Case Study Method in the Psychoanalytic Study of Religion: A Review and Critique." Paper presented at the annual meeting of the American Psychological Association, New Orleans, 1989.

8. I. Barbour, *Myths, Models, and Paradigms* (New York: Harper and Row, 1974), p. 6.

9. E. Peterfreund, "Some Critical Comments on Psychoanalytic Conceptualizations of Infancy," *International Journal of Psychoanalysis, 59* (1978): 427–41.

10. D. Stern, *The Interpersonal World of the Infant* (New York: Basic Books, 1985).

11. N. Coltart, " 'Slouching Towards Bethlehem . . . ' or Thinking the Unthinkable in Psychoanalysis," in G. Kohon (ed.), *The British School of Psychoanalysis* (New Haven: Yale University Press, 1986), p. 187.

12. See: J. Scharfenberg, *Sigmund Freud and His Critique of Religion*, tran. O. Dean, Jr. (Philadelphia: Fortress Press, 1988); and W. Meissner, *Psychoanalysis and Religious Experience* (New Haven: Yale University Press, 1984) for a review of Freud's work on religion.

13. C. Jung, *Psychology and Religion* (New Haven: Yale University Press, 1938).

14. Rizzuto, *Birth of the Living God.*

15. Ibid., p. 46. Emphasis in original.

16. C. Bollas, "The Transformational Object," *International Journal of Psychoanalysis, 60* (1979): 97–107; see also Bollas, *The Shadow of the Object* (New York: Columbia University Press, 1987).

17. Stern, *Interpersonal World*.

18. Ibid.

19. S. Eskalona, *The Roots of Individuality* (Chicago: Aldine, 1968).

20. J. Sandler and A-M. Sandler, "Object Relationships and Affects," *International Journal of Psychoanalysis*, *59* (1978): 291. Emphasis in original.

21. Stern, *Interpersonal World*, p. 45. Emphasis in original.

22. Ibid., p. 55.

23. Bollas, "The Transformational Object."

24. J. Sandler, "The Background of Safety," *International Journal of Psychoanalysis*, *41* (1960): 352–56.

25. J. Grotstein, "A Proposed Revision of the Psychoanalytic Concept of Primitive Mental States," *Contemporary Psychoanalysis*, *16* (1980): 479–546.

26. Bollas, *The Shadow of the Object*, p. 3.

27. J. Sandler and B. Rosenblatt, "The Concept of the Representational World," *Psychoanalytic Study of the Child*, *17* (1962): 132.

28. T. Ogden, "Instinct, Phantasy, and Psychological Deep Structure," *Contemporary Psychoanalysis*, *20* (1984): 500–25; Ogden, "The Concept of Internal Object Relations," *International Journal of Psychoanalysis*, *64* (1983): 224–27; Ogden, *The Primitive Edge of Experience* (Northvale, N.J.: Jason Aronson, 1989).

29. Ogden, *The Primitive Edge of Experience*, p. 31. Emphasis in original.

30. See A. Phillips, *Winnicott* (Cambridge: Harvard University Press, 1988), for an explication of Winnicott's contributions.

31. Bollas, *The Shadow of the Object*, p. 28.

32. C. Bollas, "The Transformational Object," in G. Kohon (ed.), *The British School of Psychoanalysis* (New Haven: Yale University Press, 1986), p. 85.

33. Rizzuto, *Birth of the Living God*, p. 54.

34. Bollas, *The Shadow of the Object*, p. 86.

35. Ibid., p. 17.

36. Meissner, *Psychoanalysis*, p. 182.

37. Ogden, *The Primitive Edge of Experience*.

38. Rizzuto, *Birth of the Living God*.

39. Ibid., p. 46.

Chapter 5

God-Representations in Adolescence

Mark R. Banschick

Adolescence is a particularly ripe developmental moment to consider the meaning and nature of God in one's life. This usually occurs because of the powerful amalgam of developmental factors that inevitably influence the adolescent's changing world. The growing adolescent experiences a great deal of change, both culturally and internally—more than can be accurately represented in this chapter. Yet among the various interrelated pressures toward maturity, three key developmental phenomena deserve particular mention in forming a God-representation during this period. The first is the cognitive leap of formalized operational thinking as outlined by Piaget (1969). The capacity to think abstractly brings about a natural questioning of the universe and one's place in it. The second, and related developmental task is the adolescent's re-engagement of his or her parents. The renegotiation of roles with parents occurs partly as a result of formalized thinking coupled with pubertal sexual and motor development, cultural pressures, and the adolescent's paradoxical experience of his or her own omnipotence contrasted with an increasing sense of vulnerability. Such struggles lead to the third developmental task, which can often involve an adolescent's experience of God—the formation of a consistent personal identity. Who am I? Do I believe in the God that I have been taught about in church or synagogue? What do I reject or, perhaps, accept? What is meaningful to me?

In my experience, with both healthy as well as with severely impaired young people, the experience of God can be an important organizing force during this developmentally fluid period. The adolescent's experience of God often may serve as a reflection of his or her internal state as well as a response to it.

ADOLESCENT DEVELOPMENT

The young person's cognitive apparatus achieves an important milestone during the first few years after puberty—the development of formalized operational thinking. This accomplishment (for those who achieve it) permits the adolescent to consider things and experiences in the abstract. He or she can reason from the particular to the general as well as challenge rules or ideas that had been presented as givens during earlier periods of life. Clearly, there are few ideas as abstract as the experience of God or one's place in the universe. The adolescent wonders about the world outside of his or her domain. Whereas during latency, the child had been fascinated by the rules of the concrete world of action, the adolescent becomes a philosopher in the rough. Existential questions can appear as real problems. What is the meaning of life and the origins of the universe? Where do I fit in the grand scheme of things? How does my church or synagogue fit into my life? Is "organized religion" irrelevant to what's really important to me or does it provide meaningful answers? While such questioning is important in and of itself, there are deeper developmental struggles that are often being addressed—by the very same questions—simultaneously and just out of consciousness.

The adolescent's struggle to define a working relationship (which can also be a rejected relationship) with his or her God or house of worship also serves the parallel but crucial function of engaging similar but more emotionally charged problems of a person's "fit" in his family. The attempt to define this fit can be dealt with as a reassessment of one's relationship to the beliefs and ideals of one's parents and teachers. The rejection of the Jewish or Christian God, for instance, is often replaced in early adolescence by the concept of "a force" that somehow directs things in the world. Such a theology maintains an ongoing relationship with a God experience while, in a safe way, rejecting parental beliefs. This common example of a renegotiated God experience demands abstract formal thinking as a prerequisite but more fundamentally serves the developmental issues of separation and identity.

Normative growth demands a re-engagement of parents and teachers as the child emerges with new-found intellectual, physical, and sexual prowess. These important biological developments, according to psychoanalytic theory, force the reawakening of the developmental self-object drama of earlier years. Blos (1967) characterized this time of life as the "second individuation process of adolescence." It is during these crucial years that the child catapults out of the quiescence of latency to experience, once again, separation and individuation, the oedipal drama—or both. How can the adolescent become independent despite powerful and regressive dependent longings? Should he or she submit to, challenge, or identify with the parental objects? Or with God? Can God be depended upon? Once again, the relationship with God, the ultimate object, can become a major locus for the engagement of developmental pressures, here in the processing of either individuation or oedipal dramas.

In the God-representation there are answers to the unanswerable. God can be adored, hated, ignored, idealized, or scorned, but nevertheless he remains a consistent, available object, separate from the young person's parents and therefore safe.

This brings the discussion to the third of the developmental forces in normative adolescence: the need to define a relatively stable identity. Adolescence demands much of a developing youngster: the awakening of sexuality, issues of autonomy, the oedipal drama, and preparation for true adult independence. It presents the youngster with myriad self-other experiences that often appear in contradiction with each other, such as observing the flaws of one's parents while remaining physically dependent on them or the common experience of new cognitive and sexual prowess combined with a nagging fear about failure in both. Erikson (1959) claimed that in order for the adolescent to successfully cope with this period, he or she needed to develop a reliable sense of self that was effective in a similarly coherent world. According to Erikson, a stable identity appreciates both the self and the world as generally consistent and effective. The experience of God usually represents the experience a person has of either himself or herself or of the world at large. A quixotic God often is appreciated from the standpoint of a confused self or unstable world; a grossly punitive God reveals latent fears of retribution either from an unkind world or from a destructive torturing superego. Thus, in normative adolescent development, a relatively available God, or even a rejected yet basically non-punitive God, can often be a worthy representation of a stabilizing identity.

GOD OBJECT IMAGES

A number of psychoanalytic thinkers, including Guntrip (1969), McDargh (1986), Meissner (1984), Rizzuto (1979), and Spero (1981), have addressed the meaning of God during the developmental process. These writers conceptualize the experience of God in the context of object relations theory. God becomes, within this theoretical framework, an object like any other, representing a blending of early self-parental relationships with an ongoing developmental experience of the world. The maturing child unconsciously assembles the residues of these early parental experiences, along with real and wished-for experiences, and assimilates these into his or her own internal object world. Therefore, God can be experienced in a wide variety of ways significantly dependent on the unique quality of each person's individual developmental process.

In my experience among relatively healthy adolescents, common God-representations include a generally accepting God, a rejected but not revengeful God, a mildly critical God, a unique personal God that clashes only moderately with parental faith, and often, a more impersonal God or "a force." These experiences of the ultimate other reflect well on relatively stable self-other representations of parents and peers. Among seriously disturbed adolescents, God-representations reflect a more chaotic or painful object world. The generally accepting God can be distorted, in the narcissistic or manic patient, into an omnipotent God with whom the youngster identifies in contempt of his or her parents. The rejected God becomes vengeful; youngsters sometimes report "demons" visiting, particularly at night just before sleep. Borderline teenagers commonly allude to a God who can become severely persecutory or radically nonavailable, despite being yearned for. These frightening God-representations, not uncommonly found on an adolescent psychiatric unit, are usually the expression of deeply distorted self-object representations. They warn of the possibility of serious disturbance in an adolescent's inner world.

THE DEVELOPMENTAL FUNCTION OF GOD

Whether or not God truly exists is a matter of debate for theologians and not for psychoanalysts. The God experience, in object relations theory, is generally considered to be among the various types of transitional phenomena that were originally conceptualized by Winnicott (1951). In the transitional experience, a person suspends strict reality testing in order to create a meaningful working-through of an important conflict. For the child struggling with fears of maternal abandonment, for instance, a blanket can become a satisfactory replacement for mother, serving the child's developmental demand to be self-soothed while mother is out of the room. When the experience of the blanket as a transitional object becomes internalized, the child has succeeded in his or her struggle toward autonomy. Other arenas of transitional experience in normative development include play, art, dance, creativity, and the experience of God. However, unlike other transitional objects—a blanket or a favorite toy—which a healthy youngster eventually abandons and mourns, the God experience as a transitional phenomenon, is never really abandoned and therefore never mourned. Certainly, one may lose meaningful interest in God at any point in development, either as a child or as an adult, but rarely because of the experience of his "death" or "loss." The ultimate other is an object that by its very nature can be rehabilitated, rejected, or engaged whenever a person's internal emotional circumstances require it. This leads to a most interesting conclusion, which has been convincingly argued by Ana-Maria Rizzuto (1979). God remains a transitional object that is available to a person at all points of life, as the person needs God and needs God to be.

The experience of God can therefore be extremely functional in the developing person. God can be a safe place like Winnicott's notion of a "holding environment," in which the adolescent can experiment with a variety of self-other relationships while not threatening the more highly charged parallel experience with his or her family. The God-representation can be rejected, devalued, or changed without—in healthy youngsters—serious retribution, while the growing teen-ager works through similar feelings with parental figures. The opposite can also occur, with God (sometimes the priest or rabbi as well) becoming idealized and the parents moderately devalued as the youngster separates successfully from parental dependency by becoming more devout.

However, the most common God-representation in my experience can be found in the lives of both normal and seriously disturbed children. It reaches back developmentally to another concept introduced by Erikson (1959), namely basic trust. The experience of God can evoke the earliest memories of basic trust, a comforting feeling that the world is basically a safe place to be in, like being held by mother. For normal people, this sense of trust is part of the day-to-day world, but for a disturbed adolescent, the experience of God in prayer may be the only place where such safety can be found. For the relatively healthy young person, art, music, relationships, or faith may all be helpful in re-experiencing basic trust during moments of confusion or anxiety. A neurotically impaired adolescent, for instance, can find a variety of ways to self-soothe when tense; listening to music or writing poetry can serve this purpose well in such people. But the more severely disturbed adolescent often has much fewer resources for self-soothing when under stress (thus, the high incidence of drug abuse).

The powerful internal pressures of aggression and sexuality in the more dis-organized teenager occurs often in a personal context of divorce, abuse, or neglect. Therefore, many of the severely character-disordered youngsters have little order in their inner world and often even less support externally. For these unfortunate young people, the world, both within and without, has become increasingly horrific and arbitrary. And unlike their healthier counterparts, they have characteristically little capacity to self-soothe. Yet for many such young-sters, whose relationship to organized faith is fragmentary and often hostile, there are still moments—often at night and just before sleep—when they may pray. More than half the hospitalized adolescents with whom I've had contact pray quietly at night in order to self-soothe. This kind of prayer is not particularly unique to frightened hospitalized youngsters; it's as old as prayer itself. The Psalmist, for instance, records a similar yearning for basic trust in an untrust-worthy world:

But thou are thee that took me out of the womb: thou didst make me hope when I was upon my mother's breasts. I was cast upon thee from the womb: thou art my God from my mother's belly. Be not far from me; for trouble is near; for there is none to help. (Psalm 22:10–12)

Many young people, including those with serious character pathology, retain a comparable access to basic trust in quiet prayer, particularly at night. The separation experience just before sleep can be frightening for a poorly defended youngster and prayer may organize—like the Psalmist notes—earlier object mem-ories of basic trust or ''hope'' on mother's breasts. Such prayer provides a sense of safety in an unsafe world.

JOHN: A CASE HISTORY

The patient, "John," was a fifteen-year-old boy when he was first admitted for psychiatric inpatient treatment. The early history is unusual because of the centrality of the religious experience in the development of this youngster's psychiatric disorder. John's parents converted to a fanatical Christian cult when the patient was three years old, leaving behind all family in California in order to move to a southwestern state in which the cult was headquartered. John was brought up in an unconventional home dominated by his father, who had become a minister in the church. His mother was a passive, dependent young woman who could not protect her son from a rageful and sadistic father. John's memories of her love proved to be enduring despite the horrific nature of the cult experience; beatings were commonplace in cult doctrine as well as in John's home.

What could be gathered from John's developmental history is that he was a bright and rather well-behaved child during his early years, and became more irritable and oppositional during early latency. It was at this time that the family cut off contact from relatives in California in an attempt to remove "unholy" influences from their new-found faith. John had been very close with his paternal grandmother, who had apparently aided in his upbringing; consequently, the youngster lost meaningful contact with this important person. Coexistent with this loss was the birth of a younger brother who became idealized by virtue of being born within the cult. These losses led to oppositional behavior that was poorly tolerated within the strict milieu of the cult setting.

Public education was scorned by the cult, and John was given the Bible to read for most of his formal training. Often, in the name of Jesus, this child was placed in solitary confinement for weeks at a time and subjected to physical beatings when belligerent or oppositional. At the age of thirteen, John burned down a home in the religious community in order to embarrass his father and express his rage. He secretly telephoned leaders of the cult and threatened in a disguised voice to murder or rape their wives.

By his fifteenth birthday, John was labeled as the devil by the community elders and excluded from the cult. He was abandoned by his parents and sent away to relatives in Washington, D.C., only to decompensate rather quickly in the public school setting. John was hospitalized because of violence in school and at home, drug abuse, and a history of torturing animals.

During the intake interview, it became apparent that religious belief was a very important organizing force in John's life. It would remain so throughout treatment. Surprisingly, this young man freely acknowledged that he very much believed in God and actively experienced him daily.

"I believe in God. Sure, I believe in God. That's why I'm a satanist," John said in his first interview. "Look, God's not very nice to us. He exists—that's definitely true. I have no problem with that, but it's not like he's led us to believe! God put us here to suffer. He is a sadist. He makes us kneel down to him, while at the same time he makes us suffer. It's a big lie, and God started it all!'' John went on to describe a variety of horrific God-experiences, including frightening ''visitations'' by ''demons'' at night.

Unfortunately, John had developed a pervasive and serious character disorder that was highly resistant to treatment. He evidenced severe narcissistic character pathology coupled with borderline and antisocial features. John's reality testing could be quite shaky at times, particularly when under stress—hence, the ''demons'' at night.

During the evening, just before sleep, this patient would appreciate a primitive, punitive self-object memory so characteristic of his experience of a hurtful and untrustworthy world.

John had identified with his persecutory father—identification with the aggressor. John's pathology was characterized by sadistic rage, poor impulse control, threatening behavior, and poor reality testing when under stress. He did have, however, a capacity to self-soothe. This he accomplished by writing satanic poetry that was as violent as his inner world, yet paradoxically soothing. In the horrific world of brutal poetry, John found some comfort. Why?

The experience of God as the devil served three important functions in John's inner world. First, by identifying with the devil, John rejected the God of his father and of the cult. Paradoxically, the devil became a ''good'' object for John precisely because it legitimized his rage and rejection of the parental world. Yet John remained symbolically attached to his parents by accepting the label he had been given. John was very resistant to treatment because of this problem. If he were to give up the devil identification, he would be without any relationship to his parents, for whom he still deeply yearned. Finally, as mentioned above, the sadism implicit in satanism provided John with a clear identification with his father while providing autonomy—however tragic—in the expression of this rage.

Despite the tragic nature of John's case history, it should be noted that his God-representations served an important organizing role. Satanic belief brought some meaning and consistency to an abusive and apparently arbitrary world.

Unfortunately, John's object world showed none of the flexibility commonly found in healthier youngsters. There was, for example, little place in John's world for a caring or quixotic God, an absent or even helpless God.

Within the hospital milieu, John recreated his painful and violent world with great vigor. He sadistically took advantage of the more vulnerable patients with whom he had contact. Within the first months of treatment, John behaved with great cruelty by inciting others to violence or psychosis and then blaming the staff for the problems that would ensue. The transference with his male therapist was powerfully charged with alternating self-object experiences of persecutor and persecuted. ''You know I've suffered and you'd like to see me suffer in jail for the rest of my life'' alternated with ''I'm a satanist and you're a wimp, and there isn't a thing that you're going to do about it.''

Treatment progressed and behavior improved when the focus of the therapeutic encounter left behind behavioral management and talk about the unit. This material was addressed actively in the milieu and through behavioral contracts. Individual therapy began to address John's transitional world, and satanic poetry served as a good vehicle in this process of engagement. Through poetry, John could describe his horrific inner world and his hope for change and a less violent world. This work, in a slow but fascinating way, moved from violent satanic poetry toward more standard biblical references. The Book of Revelations of the New Testament eventually became the focus of treatment, with both therapist and patient attempting to understand the significance of destruction and redemption. This process took many months and reflected a creative attempt, in John's transitional world, of working through to some experience of object constancy.

After close to a year in treatment, John was eventually discharged to residential care without meaningful contact with his parents but with a renewed connection to his extended family. John had dropped his satanic commitment but had not become a practicing Christian. However, his belief in an active, involved God remained strong. John's behavior had improved to a moderate degree, with a reduction in sadistic and antisocial involvement.

It is important to note that while this young man remained seriously disturbed, he improved in social functioning and showed higher-level defensive organization, with better reality testing and reduced splitting.

A compelling question arises from this case: Did the change in John's God-representation simply represent the developing change in his internal world or did it actually facilitate that change in his internal world?

DAVID: A CASE HISTORY

David, a seventeen-year-old Jewish male, was hospitalized because of long-standing school refusal, depression, schizotypal behavior, and poorly modulated aggression toward his parents. He was the only child in a household of practicing Jews. David's family history was significant for serious psychiatric dysfunction. His father had a disorder, most likely within the schizophrenic spectrum, that required maintenance on neuroleptic medications. David's father was an isolated man who worked the evening shift at the post office and required little emotional interplay with his wife or son. While generally docile and uninvolved, the father would on occasion erupt explosively—in a verbal sense—when frustrated and would occasionally experience paranoid decompensations that proved to be well managed with medication. David's mother was a depressed and quite dependent woman who essentially raised her son singlehandedly since the father could not tolerate the closeness of a family and spent most of his time either at work or sleeping. David's mother was quite "smothering" and had a poor sense of personal boundaries, making it difficult for her to allow her son to individuate in a healthy manner.

David was described by his parents as a bright and curious child in his early years, who had some minor separation difficulties. He was adored by his mother; her affection served a secondary purpose of distracting her from a disquieting marriage. The mother could describe her own parallel anxieties in David's steps toward autonomy, which very likely contributed to the problems of the child. He learned well but had few peers as friends. Teachers described David as somewhat isolated, but no psychiatric interventions were suggested.

During latency, David became quite close to his maternal grandfather, who was not a particularly religious man. He warmly remembers visiting his grandfather regularly, "fishing offshore" and "getting out of the house." This relationship had some real richness in it. It facilitated an identification with a healthier man while allowing for a more normative separation from the maternal bond. As David matured into early adolescence he visited his grandfather—a functional father—less frequently as he became immersed in the world of the orthodox yeshiva (religious school). The grandfather developed a slowly progressive dementia that led to his death just ten months prior to David's inpatient admission. This event was a clear precipitant in the decompensation that followed.

As David began the "second individuation process of adolescence," he found himself without a functional father, struggling in a hostile-dependent attachment to his mother. As his cognitive faculties matured, he could not come to terms with the relative deficits of his parents. David was a highly intelligent young man who was physically quite strong. Later treatment was to reveal that as he began to become aware of his father's real impairment and his mother's internal pain, he became acutely concerned about their fragility. While normative growth demanded renewed separation toward autonomy, David experienced this developmental push in an omnipotent and magical way. "If I left them," he would later say, "I thought that my father would go crazy and my mother would not go on [i.e., become suicidal]."

At the same time, this adolescent became enraged at the experience of being held back and "smothered." What in normal development would be a moderate regressive pull became for David too much to overcome. His rage increased as he withdrew slowly from healthy peer relationships and became increasingly homebound and depressed—dysfunctional like his mother and father. He was isolated in the family home in a hostile symbiotic attachment to his mother. Like his father, David's thought processes became blunted and schizophrenic-like, with magical fantasies and idiosyncratic religious beliefs. David was eventually hospitalized when he plunged a knife into his parent's bed after having withdrawn from school for a period of six months.

Prior to his grandfather's illness, David was a committed Jew who attended yeshiva with relish. As he decompensated, his religious life underwent a fundamental change. He began to believe that one of his teachers was the messiah. David believed that this man, in an omnipotent fashion, would save a handful of followers, himself included, from "going down the wrong path." Fueled by his own rage and poor reality testing, David maintained the belief that most Jews were "helpless idiots" who were actively being misled by wicked rabbis and the leaders of their congregations. In David's paranoid and grandiose world, responsible adults became liars who were "covering up the truth."

The messianic experience of God served a number of functions for this struggling adolescent. David's messianic God and leader served as an exaggerated experience of the "family romance" that Freud (1909) believed to be the fundamental psychodynamic mechanism behind the God experience. This young man urgently yearned for another family, one which could tolerate his sexual and aggressive urges. In the transitional world of the God experience, David could identify the deep flaws so painfully evident in his own parents by appreciating the Jewish adult world as either corrupt or incompetent. David's identification with an omnipotent leader and a messianic arrival also defended him against actively experiencing dependent longings. It also served to protect him from the shame of failing to remain at the yeshiva. Clearly, just as in John's situation, David's distorted God experience provided real meaning in a world that was crumbling, both internally and externally.

David was initially assessed to be quite depressed but not psychotic; the belief in his messiah could be challenged and was not fixed. He was thought to be struggling with unresolved grief at the loss of the grandfather in the context of evolving schizotypal personality features. Although religious beliefs were an important part of the presenting problem, interestingly, they played little role in David's treatment.

David's magical beliefs cleared soon after hospitalization, without any medication. In contrast to John's case, treatment for David was more along traditional lines, with few management issues to contend with. David went through the long process of mourning his grandfather and came to more realistic terms with both is mother and father. Religion became significantly less important in his life, as David no longer continued to be observant. Marital therapy occurred in parallel to David's progress. It became apparent that both parents, but particularly his mother, also struggled with unresolved grief. Progress in treatment was solidified when they were reluctantly able to "let go" of David in agreeing to a residential placement. The separation and individuation process occurred in the safety of the hospital setting, yielding a shy and somewhat over-intellectualized young man who clearly failed to meet any criteria for a schizotypal personality.

After nine months of treatment, David spoke about his messianic experience with embarrassment. He still very much believed in God, but that belief had become a less central part of his day-to-day life. He believed in a "force" that was essentially benign but unimportant for him at this stage of life, a God who could be rejected without being injured or becoming rejecting. This is, in my experience, a very common and healthy adolescent resolution, which, in David's case, reflected an ongoing attempt to forge a similar resolution with his parents.

DISCUSSION

The experience of God is clearly mediated through the complex mechanism of the human psyche. This ultimate object has characteristics that are unique to it as well as those that it shares with other objects such as parents and other important people in one's life. Unique to God is his ineffable nature: Humans are never really sure that he exists in the concrete world of action. As the Psalmist beautifully protests: "How long wilt thou forget me O Lord? Forever? How long wilt thou hide thy face from me?" (Psalm 13:1–2); or "My God, my God, why hast thou forsaken me?" (Psalm 22:1–2). Is God concretely knowable like a parent or a friend? Or is he perhaps just beyond grasp in a world unique to himself?

While important people and the experiences of them are internalized from a concrete source, one cannot with assurance make the same claim for God. Thus, God is never really experienced and never really lost, which gives Him a unique status among internalized objects. By definition, then, God is an object that lies in the unique arena of the transitional experience, like play, art or poetry, in which strict reality testing is partially suspended in order to permit the internal object world to be expressed and experimented with in a variety of ways, both in the service of health and in pathology.

In David's case, this process was in the service of healthy development; he was able to find a rather benign God within his internal world, perhaps reflecting earlier memories of a benign available grandfather. For this young man, the God who could be rejected while remaining unhurt and non-punitive represented a dramatic working through toward adolescent autonomy in the transitional world of the sacred. Like the blanket for the anxious toddler, David's God object facilitated the working through of a developmental conflict with his parents. David became increasingly aware that he and his family would "survive" his newfound identity as a young adult. This "new" God experience was adaptive to the adolescent developmental process in all three spheres, as outlined in the beginning of this discussion. While cognitively sophisticated, this benign but rejected God addressed both autonomous striving and identity formation in a helpful way.

Yet as Freud repeatedly argued in the Schreber case and elsewhere, religious beliefs can often lead to grossly maladaptive solutions to the conflicts of development. The contemptuous messianic God experience of David's decompensation proved to promote regression and illness. David, within the depths of illness, felt justified in his dysfunction because of his "special" relationship with God. The transitional experience can clearly have ill effects if it promotes a stabilization of regression. While this proved to be a temporary situation with David, John's story represents a less fortunate outcome.

John's satanic beliefs organized a massive resistance to treatment as he re-created again and again primitive sado-masochistic relationships that only served to re-enforce and stabilize pathology. John had access to a limited object world populated by persecutors and victims. It was a frightening inner world that made sense in the context of severe abuse and abandonment. Slowly, quieter voices emerged from the violent foreground of John's internal world—perhaps the helpless mother or traces of an earlier warmth with his grandmother. Yet time and again, John would become frightened by such yearnings and would act out with more violence and disruption. Although some real movement took place in treatment, it was limited because of John's poor ability to be flexible in the transitional experience. The world continued to remain as unsafe to John as was his experience of himself. Sadly, his experience of God helped to undermine healthier autonomous functioning, leaving him with a shaky identity in a shaky world populated by demons, ill equipped to handle the reality of abandonment and isolation.

CONCLUSION

The two case examples presented here were chosen because religious belief played a central role in the presentation of their respective pathologies. Both cases illustrate the various functions of the God-representation in adolescent development, both progressive and regressive.

For most adolescents, however, the God experience plays a more subtle role both in pathology and in healthy development. The God that a person experiences can yield important insights about that person's inner world and personality organization. As outlined earlier both in the review of normative adolescent development and the two case histories, the experience of the ultimate other can be a creative repository of data about basic trust, identity, relationship to parental objects, oedipal struggles, or the capacity to self-soothe. These insights are available both for the patient who has embraced his or her God object and for those who have rejected him outright. An inquiring therapist can know about this aspect of his or her patient's inner world only by asking.

This discussion has suggested that God is an object like any other, with a few unique features. The particular experience of one's God is therefore going to be deeply influenced by his or her developmental history with parents and important others during the early years of life. The God experience, by definition, is a transitional one, which lends it the functional power of both reflecting the internal life of a patient, and more importantly, of facilitating change and growth. Even when an adolescent rejects God, it is important to know the nature of the God object that is being rejected. What is rejected at any stage of development might be reworked, changed, or embraced later in life—or left on the shelf, never to be picked up again.

A wise psychotherapist, Paul Pruyser (1971), once noted that while therapists were quite comfortable asking their patients about the most private aspects of their sex lives, there still remained two real taboos left in the world of psychiatric care: money and religious belief.

Since Pruyser pointed out this strange anomaly almost twenty years ago, therapists have become quite willing to discuss the meaning of money in the treatment setting. It's time that the rich world of a patient's inner religious belief become a place where a psychiatrist—who, after all, is a "healer of the soul"— may go respectfully and in comfort.

Chapter 6

Psychoanalytic Treatment with a Buddhist Meditator

Jeffrey Rubin

Religion has played a seminal role in human history. Definitions of reality, wars, and visions of moral excellence have been part of its complex legacy. Religion has been involved in a variety of human activities, including prohibiting murder, extolling poverty and renunciation, distributing power, and regulating procreation (Pruyser, 1973). A history of religion might include accounts of compassion and persecution, wisdom and fanaticism. In our world, religion is Janus-faced: a progenitor of evil, spawning psychotic cults and unconscionable violence, and a midwife to transformation, facilitating psychological growth and trans-formation.

The relationship between psychoanalysis and religion has been fraught with conflict and misunderstanding. Religious issues have been avoided in much clinical diagnosis and treatment. Paul Pruyser (1971) notes that case records are "conspicuously devoid of articulate reference to religion" (p. 272). There is a "conspiracy of silence" about religion in "both diagnostic interviewing and in psychotherapy" (p. 272).

This selective inattention to religion on the part of clinicians is striking when it is juxtaposed with the 1984 Gallup poll that found that 99 percent of the U.S. public reports "a belief in God and a belief in prayer" and with the Group for the Advancement of Psychiatry's report (1968) that "manifest references to religion occur in about one-third of all psychoanalytic sessions" (p. 54).

Psychoanalytic clinicians, for the most part, seem highly uncomfortable with religion. In the words of William Meissner (1984), a psychoanalyst and a Jesuit, psychoanalysts "tend to regard religious thinking and convictions as suspect, even to hold them in contempt at times" (p. 5). According to Meissner, there is a "latent persuasion, not often expressed or even articulated . . . that religious ideas are inherently neurotic, self-deceptive and illusive" (p. 5).

Psychoanalysis has historically adopted a biased and restrictive perspective on religion, asserting, without always clinically demonstrating, that it is pathological and maladaptive. This anti-religious bias within psychoanalysis began with Freud's writings on religion. Critiques of religion in western Europe's Enlightenment antedated Freud, but it was his contribution to expose the parallels between an individual's personal history and the later configuration of his or her religious beliefs and practices (Lovinger, 1989).

Freud's interest in religion was evident throughout his work. Several recurrent themes dominate his disparate reflections on religion.

Freud saw himself as a destroyer of illusions. Writing to the poet Romain Rolland, a student of the renowned Indian saint Ramakrishna, he says, "A great part of my life's work . . . has been spent [trying to] destroy illusions of my own and those of mankind" (Meng and Freud, 1963: 341).

Freud called religion many things: a universal obsessional neurosis (1927: 43); a childhood neurosis (1927: 53); a form of masochism; a reaction formation against unacceptable impulses (1927); and a "delusion" (1927: 31). But above all, it was, for him, an "illusion" (1927: 30), an unrealistic belief that contradicts experience and reason. Illusion, for Freud, was not an error, but a "wish-fulfillment" (1927: 30–31). While he points out that illusion is not necessarily "false" and that "the truth-value" of religious doctrines does not lie within the scope of psychoanalytic inquiry (1927: 33), he nonetheless proceeds to condemn it as comparable to a "childhood neurosis" (1927: 53).

Two childhood wishes or psychological needs seemed to lead people to construct religious beliefs: the necessity of coming to terms with the complicated emotions of a child's relation to his or her father, and the child's sense of helplessness in the face of the danger of the inner and outer worlds.

Helplessness arouses the need for protection. Religious ideas, according to Freud, are born of the need to make tolerable the human sense of helplessness. They are designed to offer compensation, consolation, and protection for our existential vulnerability. Religion "allays our fear of the dangers of life" (1927: 33).

Freud believed that all sorts of "crimes" (p. 32) were committed in the name of religion: "When questions of religion are concerned, people are guilty of every possible sort of dishonesty and intellectual misdemeanor" (p. 32).

Freud hoped that humankind would surmount this "neurotic phase" and attain an "education to reality" (1927: 49). Like Lucretius, he wished to awaken humankind from the enchantment in which the priests held it captive (Gay, 1987). But Freud believed, to borrow a metaphor he used in contrasting psychotherapy with psychoanalysis, that only a select few are capable of replacing the superficial salve of religious illusions with the "pure gold" of psychoanalysis.

Freud explicitly acknowledged that his views on religion were his own and "form no part of analytic theory. . . . There are certainly many excellent analysts who do not share them" (Meng and Freud, 1963: 117).

Freud's knowledge of religion seemed confined to the Old and New Testaments, and the Greek, Roman, and Egyptian religions of antiquity. His theoretical writings on religion focused on Judaism and Christianity. His colleague and biographer Ernest Jones suggests that Freud did not appear to have "extended these studies to the religions of Indian and China" (Jones, 1957: 351).

According to Jones, Freud admitted that his study of religious belief was limited to that of the common man, and that he regretted having ignored the rarer and more profound type of religious emotion as experienced by mystics and saints (Jones, 1957: 360). In *Civilization and Its Discontents* (1930), Freud states that in *Future of an Illusion* (1927), he was

concerned much less with the deepest sources of religious feeling than with what the ordinary man understands by his religion—with the system of doctrines and promises which on one hand explains to him the riddles of this world with an enviable completeness, and on the other, assures him that a careful Providence will watch over his life and will compensate him in a future existence for any frustrations he suffers here (1930: 74).

Freud did not explore mature spirituality in general or Asian religion in particular. He buried religion alive.

Some aspects of Freud's work on religion—his anthropological speculations about and patriocentric explanations of the formation of God-representations—have met with skepticism and dismissal. But for the most part, his views on religion have, in the words of Saffady (1976), "held full sway in the psychoanalytic literature" (p. 292). Subsequent psychoanalysts have "tended to disagree with him in details more than essentials" (p. 292). Freud's own skepticism regarding religious beliefs and practices have been mirrored by the vast majority of subsequent psychoanalysts who have put further nails in religion's coffin.

The subsequent psychoanalytic literature has, for the most part, continued his predilection for pathologizing and dismissing religious experience.

Yet a small number of psychoanalysts (Pfister, 1948; Silberer, 1917; Jung, 1936; Menninger, 1942; Horney, 1945, 1987; Kelman, 1960; Fromm, Suzuki, and DeMartino, 1960; Milner, 1973; Rizzuto, 1979; Meissner, 1984; Kohut, 1985; Rubin, 1985; Winnicott, 1986; and Roland, 1988) have embraced psychoanalytic theory and technique while attempting to non-reductionistically explore religious phenomena. I shall provide a capsule summary of these thinkers before presenting the case material.

The Swiss psychoanalyst and pastor, Oskar Pfister, a close personal friend of Freud, was one of the first respondents to Freud's attacks on religion. Pfister concurred with Freud's observation that unconscious wishes may color the development of religion but believed this was insufficient to explain all of religion. In fact, he maintained that these motivations are more characteristic of less evolved forms of religion. According to Pfister, mature religious practices involved the exact opposite of the infantilism and self-centeredness so prevalent in its less evolved manifestations. Pfister (1948) believed that various theologies and religious traditions present different ways of lessening the inevitable human anxieties. Freud, according to Pfister, ignored religion's most essential features and "its . . . noblest utterances."

Silberer also detected a constructive dimension in religious experience. He distinguished between true mysticism and false mysticism. The latter is characterized by an "extension of personality," the former by a "shrinking" (Milner, 1973: 265).

Among psychoanalysts, Carl Jung was highly knowledgeable about Eastern religions. Jung had great respect for religion, a long-standing interest in Eastern thought, and respect for certain Oriental teachings.

For Jung, civilizational health, like individual health, was based in large part on balancing opposing aspects of life. Psychic one-sidedness, in Jung's view, may produce short-term gains of specialization but is, in the long run, emotionally detrimental. The modern West, in Jung's view, is one-sided. After having placed emphasis on the spiritual and intuitive side of life during the Middle Ages, the intellect has assumed a position of dominance in the modern world. Other aspects of human experience have been neglected and excluded. For Jung, we are too one-sided with our over-emphasis on intellect and the relative neglect of the intuitive. From the study of the East, the West could rediscover or resensitize itself to dimensions of life that have been neglected and excluded, such as intuition, feelings, and the inner life. While Jung admired the Eastern principle of inclusiveness and balance, he felt that Eastern thought had overstressed the intuitive at the expense of its sensitivity to science and technology.

Jung stressed that the West should not forsake science or the intellect. Many Eastern claims seemed, to Jung, ungrounded and illusory. The goal of egolessness is, for Jung, quixotic because it is a philosophical and psychological impossibility. Liberation can only be "partial."

Jung warned of the dangers for a Westerner of involvement in Eastern traditions. He felt that Eastern practices were unsuited to the Western mind. In "Yoga and the West" (1936), he says, "Study yoga—you will learn an infinite amount from it—but do not try to apply it, for we Europeans are not so constituted that we apply these methods correctly, just like that" (p. 534). Eastern practices would strengthen a patient's will and consciousness and thus perpetuate and further intensify the patient's split from the unconscious. This would further aggravate the already chronic Western overdevelopment of the will and the conscious part of the personality.

Another danger of uncritical adoption of Eastern practices is that many Westerners would become entranced by the exotic teachings of the East and thus avoid their own problems. Given the numerous sexual scandals reported in U.S. religious communities in recent years (cf. Boucher, 1988), this is prophetic.

Karl Menninger (1942) also took exception to psychoanalysis's exclusive emphasis on the neurotic determinants of religious belief. Agreeing with Freud's claim that transference, human infantilism, and egocentricity play an important role in the power of religious belief, he also stressed religion's adaptive aspects, such as its capacity to "control and direct aggression" and "foster life by inspiring love" (1942: p. 191).

Karen Horney first drew on Zen in *Our Inner Conflicts* (1945). Quoting from D. T. Suzuki, a Japanese scholar, writer, and interpreter of Zen to the West, she discussed Zen writings on sincerity and wholeheartedness. The goal of therapy, for Horney, was "wholeheartedness: to be without pretense, to be emotionally sincere, to be able to put the whole of oneself into one's feelings, one's work, one's beliefs" (1945: 242).

In *Our Inner Conflicts*, she referred to a "most interesting" paper by William James, "The Energies of Man," which discusses a number of examples of how spiritual training helped overcome illness.

Horney's concern with ultimate and spiritual questions and her interest in Zen and other non-Western religions grew toward the end of her life. She read from Aldous Huxley's *The Perennial Philosophy*, a compendium of major spiritual traditions, including Islamic, Christian, and Buddhist writings, almost every night during the last four years of her life (Quinn, 1987). Shortly before her death, she traveled to Japan with Suzuki to explore how Zen might reaffirm or complement her own psychoanalytic theories.

In a talk at Jikei-Kai Medical School in Tokyo, Horney suggested that there were a number of similarities between her ideas and those of Shomo Morita, the founder of Morita therapy, a treatment used in Japan that borrowed heavily from Zen. According to Morita, patients' problems resulted from their being captives of their own "subjectivity" and egocentricity. The cure drew on Zen and encouraged acceptance of things as they are.

In her posthumously published *Final Lectures* (1987), Horney discusses how Buddhism can enrich psychoanalysis. For Horney, as for the vast majority of psychoanalysts since Freud, the analyst's "attentiveness to the patient" is the basic prerequisite for doing sound psychoanalytic work. Attentiveness, according to Horney, is a "rare attainment" (p. 35), a "faculty for which the Orientals have a much deeper feeling than we do . . . [and] a much better training" (p. 18). Buddhism can train in what Horney terms "wholehearted attentiveness"—absorption in what one is doing. I agree with a recent biographer's reflections: "Had there been more time, there is no telling how Horney might have altered her views [on psychoanalysis] as the result of her new interest in Zen" (Quinn, 1987: 415).

Harold Kelman, a past president of the American Academy of Psychoanalysis, was a close associate of Karen Horney and served for years as editor of the *American Journal of Psychoanalysis*. Like Horney, Kelman felt an affinity with Eastern thought. In "Psychoanalytic Thought and Eastern Wisdom" (1960), he suggested that psychoanalysis carried to its logical conclusion is Eastern in technique but not in theory. The theories underlying psychoanalysis and Eastern thought are different, but the latter can enrich psychoanalytic practice. The way patients and analysts listen is, according to Kelman, very Eastern: Psychoanalytic patients are encouraged to say whatever comes to mind without judgment or censorship, which resembles Eastern meditative techniques involving non-judgmental attention to whatever is happening.

Erich Fromm, an existentially oriented psychoanalyst, also had a long-standing history of contact with Eastern thought. In *Zen Buddhism and Psychoanalysis* (1960), which he co-wrote with D. T. Suzuki and Richard DeMartino, a professor of religion, Fromm focused on how psychoanalysis can be useful to spiritual practitioners and how meditation can lead beyond the limits of psychoanalysis. Psychoanalysis can help meditators avoid "the danger of a false enlightenment (which is, of course, no enlightenment), one which is purely subjective, based on psychotic or hysterical phenomena, or on a self-induced state of trance. Analytic clarification might help the . . . [meditators] to avoid illusions." (pp. 140–41).

According to Fromm, meditation practice can extend the psychoanalytic vision of optimal psychological health. Meditation focuses not on the removal of symptoms—"absence of illness"—but on the presence of "well-being" (p. 91): being fully born, overcoming narrow views of the self, being completely aware of, and responsive to, the world. Well-being is a rare attainment that may go beyond the goals of psychoanalysis. The meditative vision of health, according to Fromm, extends and enriches the aim of psychoanalysis.

In "Some Notes on Psychoanalytic Ideas about Mysticism" (in 1973), psychoanalyst Marion Milner describes other constructive dimensions of religious experience. Although cognizant of the way religion, or what she terms "mysticism," can lead to "mental self-blinding, a dangerous denial of unpleasant truths, both in ourselves and the world" (p. 262), Milner also acknowledges the potentially "recuperative" and enriching dimensions of religion. She describes, for example, sitting in a garden, at a residential art school, wishing to paint but unable to find a subject. In order to deal with the tension she had

started a deep breathing exercise and had been astonished to find that the world around me immediately became quite different and by, now, exceedingly paintable . . . that turning one's attention inward, not to awareness of one's big toe but to the inner sensations of breathing . . . [had] a marked effect on the appearance and significance of the world. (p. 260–61)

In *The Birth of the Living God*, a ground-breaking empirical work on the origin, development and use of God-representations during the course of human life, psychoanalyst and Roman Catholic Ana-Maria Rizzuto (1979) has illuminated the complexity of religion and God representations. In contrast to Freud, who maintained that belief in God is based on a child's creation of a surrogate father figure to make tolerable a sense of helplessness in dealing with the universe, Rizzuto suggests that one's God-representation derives from various sources and is a crucial aspect of one's view of self, others, and the world.

In *Psychoanalysis and Religious Experience* (1984), William Meissner attempts to facilitate a meaningful dialogue between psychoanalysis and religion. Meissner contends that psychoanalysis has traditionally adopted a bias and reductionistic perspective in exploring religious experience. For Meissner, Freud's view of religion provides a distorted and fragmentary picture that precludes viewing religion in a more constructive light. Meissner, like Menninger, acknowledges that religion can embody pathological components while also stressing that it can amplify and deepen the quality of one's life. He hopes to renew an authentic dialogue between psychoanalysis and religion.

Heinz Kohut never produced a systematic and comprehensive work on religion, but references to religion are scattered throughout his writings. He maintained that religion was a "complex phenomenon" (1985: 261) with various meanings and functions. In a posthumously published interview, "Religion, Ethics and Values," he said that religion was "poor science" (in 1985: p. 261), sometimes a "crude mythology on the level of a fairy tale . . . in other words, primitive science" (p. 247). But he also felt that psychoanalysis had "underestimated" the "supportive aspect of religion" (p. 261), particularly its "civilizing influence." He maintained that religion could reduce "unmodified narcissism," offer constructive ideals, and curb destructive tendencies.

In "Meditation and Psychoanalytic Listening" (Rubin, 1985) I propose one way that psychoanalysis and Buddhism can be integrated. Freud defined the optimal state of mind for analysts to listen to patients as "evenly hovering attention" but he did not discuss, in a positive sense, how to develop it. He focused on what to avoid (censorship, prior expectations) but not what to do, that is, how to cultivate "evenly hovering attention." Buddhist insight meditation cultivates exactly this state of mind. Therefore, it can enrich psychoanalytic listening.

In his posthumously published *Home Is Where We Start From*, Winnicott (1986) asserts that participation in religion is an aspect of a healthy life. Healthy people, according to Winnicott, live in three worlds: (1) "life in the world, with interpersonal relationships"; (2) the life of the "personal (sometimes called inner psychical reality"; and (3) "the area of cultural experience . . . including the arts, the myths of history, the slow march of philosophical thought and the mysteries of mathematics, and of group management and of religion" (pp. 35–36). In Winnicott's view, religion—being part of the capacity to have cultural experience—is an essential aspect of health and healthy living.

Roland's (1988) psychoanalytic investigation of the self-experience of Indian and Japanese patients (some of whom were involved in non-Western religions) represents one of the few sympathetic approaches to non-Western religion in the psychoanalytic literature. Roland aptly notes that with rare exceptions, psychoanalysts have viewed religion in terms of "compensations and psychopathology" (p. 59). He recommends that psychoanalysts respect the unique meaning and purpose religion serves in people's lives.

The attempt to redress psychoanalytic reductionism and establish a meaningful dialogue between psychoanalysis and religion on the part of the psychoanalysts I have discussed has provided a crucial service to psychoanalysis. These efforts, however, have rarely been applied to Asian religion. Asian religion has been virtually ignored in the psychoanalytic literature.

The case study has a long and distinguished history within psychoanalysis, being the principal approach of the major psychoanalytic theorists (Stolorow and Atwood, 1979). It offers a unique means of elucidating the complex and multifaceted reality of both individual lives and the psychoanalytic process.

Clinical case studies of religion seem rare in psychoanalysis. As Pruyser notes, Freud never published a ''full fledged case study that focused on the dynamics of religion in the life of the person'' (Pruyser, 1973: 252). Neither, to my knowledge, have any subsequent psychoanalysts. There is a dearth of clinical data regarding religion within psychoanalysis, which this chapter attempts to begin to remedy.

In this chapter I will use the case study method and examine clinical data from a psychoanalytic treatment with a Buddhist meditator. These data, viewed through the template of psychoanalytic object relations theory and psychoanalytic self-psychology, will seek to demonstrate that religion is not inherently or monolithically pathological or constructive. Rather, it has multiple meanings and functions involving constructive, self-protective, and defensive components. It may

1. cultivate enhanced self-observational capacities and thus heighten self-awareness
2. express urgent wishes and aspirations
3. offer guidelines for morally acceptable behavior, provide a rationale for self-punishment, and reduce self-recriminative tendencies
4. enhance one's efforts to cope with difficulties or crises
5. protect, repair, or restore self-representations, that is, enduring images of self, which have been threatened or damaged
6. facilitate self-demarcation and enhance affect regulation and tolerance
7. impede awareness of disturbing thoughts, feelings, or fantasies
8. foster ''de-automatization'' of thought and action.

Object relations theory does not have a single comprehensive and agreed definition. It is the general term for a collection of psychoanalytic theories developed by Melanie Klein, Ronald Fairbairn, D. W. Winnicott, Harry Guntrip, and Masud Khan, among others, that focus on the impact of early relationships with significant others (especially parents) on personal and interpersonal development. It focuses on the ways that humans, from birth onward, seek and negotiate interpersonal contact and how they form governing images of themselves and others out of these experiences. In object relations theory, concern with the nature and capacity for attachment and intimacy replace classical psychoanalytic emphasis on conflicts over instinctual drives.

Briefly stated, what object relations theorists share, despite their theoretical and clinical differences, is a belief that people grow up in relation to "objects" or people and that these relationships become internalized and leave a kind of internal blueprint or template through which subsequent relationships are experienced and delimited. For example, the person who always assumes that he is being criticized by people in the present may be unconsciously attributing to others what he often experienced in an earlier relationship with a critical parent. Or the person from a violent and affectionless home may characteristically establish relationships involving struggle and violence because intimacy is unconsciously equated with strife.

Self-psychology also does not have a single comprehensive definition. It refers to the psychoanalytic school founded by Heinz Kohut in the early 1970s, that focuses on the primacy of self-experience; the nature of self-structure (including self-cohesion, temporal continuity and the affective coloring of self-experience); the importance of the empathic-introspective method as the cornerstone of psychoanalytic inquiry; the nature of self-development and the concept of self-object functions and self-object transferences such as mirroring, idealizing, and twinning; the role of significant others (parents, mates, friends) or valued systems of thought or culture in hindering or facilitating the maintenance and restoration of self-esteem and self-cohesion.

Self-psychology differs from object relations theory in its heightened emphasis on self, identity, and self-esteem issues and its explicit attention to self-object functions. According to the self-psychological perspective, people never outgrow the need for experiencing significant others or cultural creations (intellectual, religious, aesthetic, or philosophical systems) as either images of valued ideals or sources of psychological support and validation.

Although self-psychology has been virtually ignored in contemporary non-psychoanalytic examinations of religion, it provides a powerful tool for understanding the interface of psychology, spirituality, and religion. For example, it describes the strategies a person may use to develop, repair, and maintain a sense of identity throughout the life cycle by either seeking the approval of religious figures or merging with powerful and idealized religious individuals or systems of thought. Because of its capacity for understanding these strategies, self-psychology can illuminate some of the particular psychological meanings and functions of religious involvement.

Psychoanalytic case material is notoriously complex. In *Narrative Truth and Historical Truth* (1982), Spence has illuminated the inherent hermeneutical difficulties of the analytic encounter. The apparently "self-evident" data of psychoanalytic treatments are, in actuality, enormously complex and indissolubly connected to the theoretical frame of reference and clinical orientation of both patient and analyst. Reconstruction may often be a contemporary construction; acts of discovery may be moments of creation, and historical truth may be narrative fit.

In a compatible vein, Schafer (1983) notes that there is no single, comprehensive psychoanalytic life history of an analysand. Rather, there are various histories of the patient's past, shaped by the therapeutic environment, including the intersubjective context of the therapeutic relationship, the personal dynamics and theoretical orientation of both the analyst and the analysand, and the kind of approach that is utilized and the sort of questions asked. Thus we need to replace the notion of *the* single history of the analysand with the *multiple* histories of the analysand.

I shall confine myself to those details of the case material that illuminate the patient's relationship to religion.

I will be employing a strategy of discovery, not of proof (Smith, Bruner, and White, 1956). I hope to raise and spark new questions and suggest potentially promising lines of future research.

CLINICAL MATERIAL

Steven, a man in his mid-twenties, sought psychoanalytic treatment because of periodic bouts of mild frustration about his career, self-esteem issues, and as part of a more extensive quest for self-development and perfection. When he began analysis, he was attending graduate school and pursuing an advanced degree in the social sciences. Because he was involved in many academic projects, his ambition frequently exceeded his output. Although judged competent and successful by peers and students, he had anxiety about his capacities and often felt flawed and inadequate.

He usually became involved with women who were accomplished and "difficult." They turned out to be both full of potential and problems. He generally played the role of "caretaker," establishing an environment in which their needfulness was a central focus of the relationship. He often came to resent his role of "healing wounded sparrows."

He had several close male friendships and many acquaintances. His friends seemed bright, kind, and psychologically minded. The friendships involved sharing an interest in psychological, intellectual, and athletic pursuits. These relationships seemed substantial and enduring.

In graduate school, Steven became very interested in Asian thought. He read widely in Asian philosophy and psychology and meditated on a regular basis. At least once a year he participated in intensive, two-week-long residential meditation retreats in which he engaged in silent meditation for ten to fifteen hours a day. He followed traditional Buddhist ethical guidelines, such as refraining from killing, lying, stealing, sexual misconduct (defined by the school of Buddhism he was affiliated with as not being involved in adultery), and the consumption of mind-altering intoxicants. Outside of the retreat, he continued to abide by these principles.

He practiced *Vipassana* or insight meditation, the core technique of Theravadin Buddhism, a non-theistic ethical and psychological training system developed in India in the sixth century BC by Gautama Buddha, which served as a prototype for subsequent Buddhist schools such as Zen and Tibetan Buddhism (Goleman, 1977). This form of meditation has been well described in the classical (Buddhaghosa, 1976; Nyanaponika, 1962; Thera, 1941) and contemporary (Goldstein, 1976; Kornfield, 1977) meditative literature and has been largely preserved in its original form in contemporary Southeast Asia.

There are three interconnected dimensions to this practice: the cultivation of ethical purity, mental clarity, and insight and wisdom. Training in ethics is usually the first stage of this practice. Classical Buddhist texts maintain that unethical behavior is motivated by, and promotes, mental states such as greed, anger, and egotism, which disrupt the mind and interfere with developing mental clarity and insight. Adherence to ethical guidelines leads to mental "purification," in which counterproductive behaviors are gradually eroded and mental attentiveness and clarity are cultivated. Mental clarity facilitates the development of insight into the nature of selfhood and wisdom concerning oneself and the world.

There are two types of meditation practices: concentration and insight. Concentration meditation involves attending to the experience of one phenomenon, such as the sensation of breathing, until the mind becomes focused and concentrated. In insight meditation, one attends, without judgment, to the experience of whatever mental or physical phenomena—thoughts, feelings, sensations, or fantasies—is predominant in the field of awareness. This practice cultivates "mindfulness" or refined non-judgmental awareness of whatever is occurring, which leads to heightened perceptual acuity and attentiveness, increased control of voluntary processes, deepened insight into the nature of mental processes, selfhood and reality, the eradication of suffering, and the development of compassion and moral action.

Buddhism adopts a view of reality, consciousness, mind, selfhood, and health that is profoundly different from traditional Western psychology. The central tenets of Buddhism are that change, impermanence, suffering, and the ontological unreality of the self are the basic reality of existence. Suffering arises because humans become "attached" to what is inherently impermanent, especially to what Harry Stack Sullivan, in a different context, termed the "illusion of personality individuality"—the notion that there is a single, consistent self that is the thinker of thoughts and the generator of actions. The self, according to Buddhism, is like an automated teller; processes occur without someone performing them. Buddhism values non-attachment, voluntary simplicity, selfless behavior, and the cultivation of compassion and equanimity. The view of health underlying traditional Western psychiatry and psychology is, according to the Buddhist model, suboptimal. Buddhism claims that there are possibilities for health that exceed the limits of anything discussed in Western psychology.

Steven was initially enthralled with Buddhist philosophy and psychology. He felt that Buddhism's emphasis on self-awareness, honesty, and generosity was a welcome improvement over the materialism, selfishness, and hypocrisy of daily life.

He maintained that daily life, with its emphasis on individualism, promoted a merry-go-round of endless striving, stress, and emotional discontent. According to Steven, meditation encouraged seeing and appreciating other dimensions of existence, which led to deepened compassion and morality.

He valued psychoanalysis but believed that Buddhism offered a richer view of the workings of mental life than did Western psychology. Buddhist models of ideal mental health—enlightenment—particularly intrigued him. He maintained that this vision of health transcended the more restricted views of health in psychoanalysis. In his experience, Buddhist teachers embodied higher degrees of insight, morality, and wisdom than the psychoanalysts he had met or read about.

Steven was the oldest of two brothers in a middle-class family. His father was several years older than his mother. His parents, who were atheists, were in their late twenties when he was born. Steven was raised as a secular humanist.

He described his parents an intelligent people who related to each other in an affable but superficial manner. From Steven's account, childhood was a time in which he did well in school, had several close friends and was well-liked by adults and peers. He described himself as a sensitive child who spent hours playing baseball and touch football with classmates and neighborhood children and devouring biographies of professional baseball and football stars. He seemed to gain inspiration from the lives and training strategies of these sports figures.

As a child, Steven and his mother were quite close. Initially he described her as "kind" and "saintly." He remembered her as a sensitive and curious woman who valued him very much. He had fond memories of the time they spent together in his childhood.

In the course of analysis, he recovered childhood impressions that she was "controlling" and "infantilizing" and used him as though he was an extension of herself. She "wanted me to do what *she* wanted me to do. . . . Everything had to always be her way."

Their relationship changed for the worse when Steven was an adolescent. At that time, family life began revolving around the plight of his troubled and enigmatic younger brother. His brother was constantly in some sort of trouble, usually involving stealing or lying. When Steven was twelve, his brother stole his coin collection and bought candy with the proceeds. Steven remembered that his parents did not force his brother to make any sort of restitution.

His brother was subsequently thrown out of several schools, was sent to several psychiatric institutions and was in jail several times for non-violent crimes involving forged checks and stolen credit cards.

In the course of analysis, Steven's impression of his mother altered. He came to feel that she was an anxious, overly protective woman who was deeply concerned about the opinions of others and avoided conflict at any cost. He felt that she viewed him as if he were an extension of herself and demanded that he conform to her vision of what he should be. He expended a great deal of effort molding himself into the sort of person that would make her feel proud and successful as a parent.

Steven felt that she recruited him to assist her in handling his brother. Steven became the family "moderator," adjudicating between his brother's garbled explanations of his transgressions and his angry and baffled parents.

For his mother, he became a kind of a surrogate husband, providing advice and support about handling her youngest son and ministering to her emotional needs. As treatment progressed, Steven became aware of resenting that he had been cast in the role of family "redeemer." His parents and especially his mother had expected him to become accomplished and provide vicarious glory for her and the family so as to compensate for her sense of herself as a parental failure.

In Steven's view, this expectation led her to view him in an unrealistically grandiose light. When he was in high school, Steven recalled telling his mother that he imagined it would be a wonderful experience to participate in the Olympic marathon. Her response to him—an above-average quarter-miler on the high school track team—was: "Why *don't* you run in the next Olympic marathon? *You* can do it."

Steven felt he had a distant and unfulfilling relationship with his father, whom he described as a competent, critical, emotionally constrained and perfectionistic business executive with a bad temper. Steven and his father seemed to share very little. Their conversations revolved around professional sports and Steven's own athletic performance. Steven's father seemed to rebuff his son's attempts to establish a closer bond. After a while, Steven appeared to feel hopeless about communicating with him.

Steven feared that any affectively charged situation might ignite his father's temper. He described his father as susceptible to severe periodic emotional outbursts accompanied by loss of temper, yelling, and screaming. His father tended to become angry or panic when things did not conform to his rigid expectations. In one particularly traumatic incident when Steven was in elementary school, his father whipped him with a belt after learning that Seven had written some profanity on the back of a female classmate's class picture. Afterward, Steven made a secret vow that he would never lose his temper and become an "animal" like his father.

His father placed a great premium on performance. Steven presented various memories of his father criticizing and correcting his school work or athletic performance. Steven recounted with sadness that his father's only response after watching him play a nearly flawless game of baseball in junior high school in which he got several hits and made no errors was, "You played all right, but in the ninth inning you made a mistake." His father was like a "fun-house mirror"; whatever Steven did, the reflection was negative (Baker and Baker, 1987: 4). Steven felt that he could never please his father. He believed that if he was not perfect, his father viewed him a failure.

Although Steven hated his father's critical nature, he ultimately had a more difficult time deciphering his mother's intensely conflictual communications and actions. He felt that she expressed hostility under the guise of "sweetness," which, with her intrusiveness, masqueraded as caring and concern, and that pseudo-mutuality and interpersonal mystifications substituted for genuine emotional closeness. Steven felt that he had subordinated himself to his parents' demands to such an extent that he had sacrificed and lost touch with his own needs and goals. He felt periodically confused about his own goals and ideals and experienced an inordinate amount of self-doubt and self-blame. He had great difficult assessing his talents and abilities, alternating between his father's belief that he could do nothing and his mother's view that he could do anything. He strove to be super-successful so as to compensate for his brother's difficulties and his parent's sense of failure and win his father's approval. But his childhood and adolescence were pervaded by the sense that he had failed his entire family: He had not cured his troubled brother, redeemed his mother, or pleased his father. He never felt admired for his own accomplishments, which he kept essentially hidden so as not to threaten his brother's precarious self-esteem. He felt he would never live up to his father's ambitions for him, and that his father's emphasis on his improvement reflected a deep disappointment with him.

For the first several years in treatment he experienced his parents as moral exemplars, agreeing with their assessment that they were above moral reproach and essentially justified in criticizing the "mediocre" outside world. He accepted their view that many of his brother's difficulties with the law were due to prejudiced or rigid authorities. Their response, for example, after learning that their youngest son was arrested for abandoning a rented car in a different city was that "the car was a lemon."

In the course of treatment, Steven came to feel that his parents were hypocritical and self-serving. They seemed committed to not looking at their own responsibility for both his brother's behavior and its effect on Steven. Family life was permeated by half-truths and self-justifications. Given his own commitment to honesty and self-reflection, Steven felt increasingly alienated from his family and beset by self-doubts about the validity of his own goals and ideals.

Although he chose a life course very different from his family and had separated from them in certain ways, the impact of his family was preserved into his adulthood. In his relationships with women, self-abnegation and deference were assumed to be the best way to capture a woman's attention and to sustain her interest. Although he was able to draw on his considerable emotional and intellectual resources to create a meaningful life and achieve professional success, his divided loyalties to family members nevertheless complicated and undermined his self-esteem and his career. He felt intense conflicts between his own upwardly mobile intellectual ambitions and his deep loyalty to his imprisoned brother. He felt torn between the competing demands of not being successful and thus remaining loyal to his brother and his father's demands for perfection. Intellectual success raised the specter of separation, disloyalty, and danger.

In relation to his analyst, Steven was at first somewhat guarded and compliant.

Although he seemed to speak with a minimum of self-censorship and inhibition, he was fearful that his analyst would be judgmental, controlling, and intrusive, tacitly or covertly imposing his own agenda on Steven.

Above all, Steven wished, as he later put it, "not to rock the boat"—not to assert angry or oppositional feelings that would create friction between himself and his analyst. Steven alternated between fear that his anger would lead to his analyst attacking him (like his father) or crumbling (like his mother).

As his fantasies about these twin dangers were explored within the transference, his need for an idealized analyst whose insight and wisdom he could utilize and incorporate emerged. He also expressed an intense need for his analyst to be perfectly attuned to the subtlety of his thoughts and feelings.

As the analysis proceeded, material about Buddhism periodically emerged. At first, Steven treated Buddhism as a historic building in a changing neighborhood; he accorded it a kind of "landmark status" in which it was exempt from critical examination and the threat of demolition and preserved in its original form. Gradually, curiosity about Buddhism replaced veneration.

We treated Buddhism as a dream, examining Steven's associations to it rather than assigning it a standardized meaning. We attempted to illuminate its unconscious meanings and purposes rather than assume that it was either inherently pathological or unworthy of psychoanalytic scrutiny.

Various unconscious meanings and purposes emerged, and Steven's image of and relationship to Buddhism altered in the course of treatment. From our perspective, he developed a more nuanced and critical perspective on Buddhism. He found its vision of reality, a world everywhere beset by suffering caused by internal psychological attachment, to be an incomplete diagnosis of human suffering and worthy of critical scrutiny. He came to view Buddhism not as absolute ahistorical, transcultural truth but, as Schafer has termed in a different context, as a "vision of reality" (Schafer, 1976: 23).

Buddhism's vision of reality seemed, to Steven, to neglect intimate relationships, the body, the sociocultural causes of human suffering, the influence of the past on current behavior, and the way transference and resistance shape and delimit ordinary awareness and the quality of one's life.

He also felt that Buddhist goals such as complete liberation were unrealistic and psychologically enslaving. He believed that ideals such as complete awareness and total eradication of self-centeredness result in self-division and self-contempt.

Buddhism's unattainable ideals became, for Steven, further grist for the self-condemnation mill. He realized that seeking enlightenment was like playing baseball in front of his father: He could not win.

Dalbiez (1936) distinguishes between a system's doctrine or theories, and its method or operationalizable techniques (p. vii). In the course of treatment, Steven's interest in Asian psychology shifted from its theory to its method—the practice of meditation, the training of attentiveness, and the mind observing its own workings—rather than Buddhist viewpoints on such things as rebirth, the aetiology of suffering, or the possibility of completely transcending psychological conditioning.

He also began to de-idealize Buddhist teachers. Admiration rather than ideal-ization and subordination now characterized his relationship with them. He no longer viewed them as sources of complete insight and wisdom but as mortals whose commitment to self-examination and ethicality he respected.

DISCUSSION

We gradually came to understand that Buddhism had taken on constructive, defensive, reparative, and restitutive functions for Steven, simultaneously en-riching and limiting his life.

Cultivation of Self-Observational Capacities

Daily life is often pervaded by "mindlessness" or inattentiveness and auto-maticity of thought and action. Our typical mode of perception is

to an unrecognized extent, selective, distorted and outside voluntary control. We often operate on automatic pilot—reacting to a conscious and unconscious blend of fallacious associations, anticipatory fantasies, and habitual fears that make us unaware of the actual texture of our experience. (Rubin, 1985: 66)

In a previous publication (Rubin, 1985) summarized earlier, I described the way meditation cultivates increased mindfulness or attentiveness. In summary, I claimed that Freud defined the optimal state of mind for analysts as listening to patients with "evenly-hovering attention," but he did not discuss, in a positive sense, how to develop it. He focused on what to avoid (censorship, prior ex-pectations) and not what do, that is, how to cultivate "evenly hovering atten-tion." Since Buddhism cultivates exactly this state of mind, it can enrich psychoanalytic listening. Steven demonstrated a tremendous ability to access and describe nuances of his thoughts, feelings, and fantasies. Meditation practice seemed to cultivate this unusual degree of self-awareness.

Meditation Reduces Self-Recriminative Tendencies

This increased awareness facilitates greater access to formerly unconscious material. To cite one example among many, on several occasions while medi-tating, Steven became aware of the formerly unconscious hurt and rage he felt about the way his parents made him feel responsible for family difficulties and the extent to which they encouraged him to fulfill their own needs and goals.

His stance toward these feelings also changed. Non-judgmental attentiveness—the ability to experience thoughts and feelings impartially—replaced his perfec-tionistic father's criticalness. As his capacity for empathic self-observation increased, self-recriminative tendencies declined. Thoughts and actions that formerly provided ammunition for him to prosecute himself no longer tended to upset him. As he gradually experienced decreased self-criticalness and self-punishment, he came to feel more patience and compassion.

Self-Demarcation and Affect Regulation

Self-demarcation and affect regulation are two of the building blocks of self-organization and development. Margaret Mahler's seminal work highlights the crucial importance of the former, particularly the sense of oneself as a demarcated and distinctive person with a unique emotional life and a set of personal ideals and goals. Recent research in infant development in general and the patterning of early infant-caregiver interactions (Stern, 1985) have confirmed that affect regulation is of central importance in the development and organization of self-experience. For Stern (1985), affectivity is a "self-invariant," contributing during the first months of infancy to the development of "the core sense of self" (p. 69). "The rudiments of the infant's sense of self," Stolorow, Brandchaft, and Atwood (1987) note, "crystallize around its recurrent affect states" (p. 67). Significant caregivers play a central role in encouraging the development and consolidation of self-experience and the interactional context in which the development occurs.

Steven's parents had provided an environment inimical to the development of both of these capacities. Self-demarcation and affect integration had been derailed by their narcissistic use of him. Discovering his own goals and needs was difficult in an environment in which he felt compelled to become the sort of person that his parents demanded. As he gradually experienced decreased self-criticalness and self-punishment, he experienced less depressive affect and a clearer sense of his own thoughts, feelings, and goals. This was illustrated by both his emerging sense of his own ideals and aspirations and his changing reaction to negative thoughts and affects. He now had a greater capacity for self-soothing. He was able to acknowledge and tolerate painful affect rather than avoid it (like his mother) or panic or become enraged (like his father).

Express Urgent Wishes and Ideals/Self-Restoration

Inquiry into the origins and functions of his ambitions revealed that he was haunted by his failure to receive his critical father's approval, save his damaged brother, and redeem his mother. He had a deep fear that to abandon these strivings as compulsive necessities would be to lose forever any possibility of his being important and exciting to his parents (or anyone else).

His father's remoteness and volatility prevented him from providing Steven with an image of "idealized strength and calmness" (Kohut, 1984: 52) that Steven could utilize as a model for cultivating his own goals, ideals, and values. Consequently, this aspect of himself was underdeveloped. He became what

Kohut (1971) termed an "ideal hungry personality," seeking to identify with exemplary figures and exalted theories in the external world. In offering an image of, and a vehicle for, self-perfection, Buddhist meditation afforded him a substitute set of missing ideals and values, thus strengthening a dimension of himself that he needed to fortify to feel good about himself.

These ideals were restitutive and restrictive. Buddhist emphasis on self-purification and transformation had a dual unconscious function: It provided a means of attempting to win his perfectionist father's approval and atone for his unconscious guilt over his imagined crime of not saving, and wishing to destroy, his damaged brother. Perhaps if he were perfect, his father would accept him. Buddhism offered an opportunity to offset his sense of badness and repair the damage he felt he had committed. Buddhism thus became what Melanie Klein (1937), in another context, termed a vehicle for "reparation."

But it also became an agent of self-condemnation and self-inhibition. The quest for purity of action, like his father's demand for perfection, became one more ideal that he could never attain and thus one more occasion for self-condemnation. He periodically spoke of the guilt he felt when he was not meditating on a regular basis or not living up to Buddhism's ethical ideals.

Here Buddhism led to greater unconsciousness rather than increased mindfulness. Most humans, as Freud aptly noted, gravitate toward pleasure and away from pain. We feel better when we achieve our ideals. We feel badly when we do not attain our ideals. The seeds of self-deception and self-division are planted: Our need to feel good will lead us to ignore or bury feedback that we are not acting in accordance with our ideals. A situation is constructed in which non-ideal behavior becomes unconscious. Thus, instead of a meditation teacher utilizing the feeling of sexual attraction to a student as feedback about important personal and perhaps interpersonal phenomena, these feelings may be denied or acted out. It is no accident and not inconsequential that there have been so many incidents of sexual acting out in spiritual communities in the United States in recent years (Boucher, 1988).

Rationale for Self-Punishment

Steven was psychologically attracted to Buddhism's emphasis on non-attachment, or not being immersed in or negatively addicted to any phenomena, and its inherent asceticism for several reasons. It gratified what Freud (1926) in another context, termed his unconscious guilt and need for punishment for failing his father, mother, and brother. Second, it served as a rationale to not go beyond or have more than his imprisoned brother. A poignant example of this occurred several years ago, when Steven spent the Christmas weekend performing a self-created "meditation retreat" in his home. For several days, he turned off his phone, meditated throughout all his waking hours, and had no human contact. His later association to this event was that he had created a "cell." Fashioning his own "prison" was a way of punishing himself and remaining loyal to his incarcerated brother.

Asceticism—having little—also protected him from reliving the trauma of being robbed by his brother and unprotected and undefended by his parents. If he had few possessions, less could be taken from him than if he were wealthy and had a "large coin collection."

De-Automatization of Thought and Action and Enhancement of Capacity to Cope with Difficulties or Crises

In his studies of mystical practices and psychotherapy, Deikman (1982) emphasizes the centrality of "de-automatization"—an undoing of automatized, habitual thought and action. In cultivating perceptual acuity and attentiveness, meditation fostered awareness of and "de-automatization" from previously habitual patterns. This led Steven to feel an increased freedom of action, while also lessening the potential for the emergence of unconscious negative affects associated with danger to himself and his family. Being "de-automatized" minimized the chances of his being out of control like his punitive father. Thus there was less chance of his acting like an "animal" or anyone being "whipped."

Religion, according to Ludwig Feuerbach, the nineteenth-century German philosopher, is a form of human self-alienation. It gradually became evident that Buddhism's emphasis on cultivating "cool" rather than "hot" emotions—equanimity rather than passion (Kramer and Alstad, 1989)—inhibited him in certain ways, reinforcing his defensive passivity. In attempting to develop such qualities as equanimity and compassion, Steven focused on detaching from negative affects rather than experiencing them. This blocked the emergence of moral outrage against his parents for neglecting his needs and allowing his disturbed brother to dominate family life. The possibility of Steven being appropriately assertive or angry was thus unfortunately stifled.

CONCLUSION

From its inception, psychoanalysis has aspired to the status of science. In *New Introductory Lectures on Psycho-Analysis* (1933), Freud makes this explicit, asserting that science is psychoanalysis's *Weltanschauung*, or world view. Scientists have waged a long battle to obtain freedom from religious control. It is thus natural that religious matters would be suspect within psychoanalysis.

Numerous incidents in the history of religion, ranging from the Inquisition to recent scandals involving fundamentalist preachers and Buddhist teachers' sexually exploiting students, lend support and give us no reason to question Freud and psychoanalysis's interpretations of the pathological nature of religion. We may thus be tempted to dismiss religious phenomena as psychologically immature or irrational.

Challenges to psychoanalytic reductionism have often fallen victim to the opposite pitfall—accepting religious experience too uncritically. If Freud, as well as many subsequent psychoanalysts, precipitously dismissed religion, then much theological discourse and some non-psychoanalytic discourse that is sympathetic to religion's capacity to enrich human life tends to uncritically accept it. The complex conscious and unconscious processes by which people come to possess and use religious imagery are ignored in both approaches to religion (McDargh, 1989).

The problem is that not all religious involvements are inherently pathological or unequivocally constructive. Religion, like all psychic events, has multiple meanings and functions (Waelder, 1930).

Freud's revolutionary perspective on dream interpretation provides an indispensable starting point in illuminating these meanings and functions. The meaning of a dream, according to Freud, is arrived at not by translating dream material into the a priori meaning and "fixed-key" of a "dream-book" (1900) but by eliciting the dreamer's unique associations. The meaning of religious phenomena, it seems to me, is arrived at not by translating it, as so many analysts and theologians have done, into the "fixed-key" of the analysts' or theologians' "dream book" on religion but by elucidating a specific practitioner's unique associations.

What difference does it make to adopt this approach to religious material? First, one would approach the material by asking a different set of questions. Rather than asking what the pathological meanings and determinants of religion are, the clinician would think about its various unconscious meanings and purposes. The analyst might, for example, ask:

- Does religion facilitate or interfere with increased self-awareness?
- What wishes or aspirations does it express?
- What guidelines for acceptable behavior and what rationale for self-punishment are presented? Does religious involvement reduce or increase self-recriminative tendencies?
- Does religion enhance one's ability to cope with difficulties or crises?
- What effect does religion have on the patient's self-experience? Does it protect, restore, or repair self- or object-representations?
- Does it impede awareness of disturbing thoughts, feelings, or fantasies?

This is by no means a complete list of the questions that might be asked about religious phenomena. Other clinicians will undoubtedly discover other salient meanings and functions.

Such a strategy would help psychoanalysts and religionists avoid the twin dangers of unbridled reverence, which accepts religion without critical examination, or a priori pathologizing, which rejects it automatically. The picture of Buddhism that emerges from such an approach is that of a complex mosaic involving constructive, pathological, restitutive, integrative, and transformative dimensions.

It is fallacious to equate religious involvement with psychological immaturity or religious disbelief with psychological maturity. Each person's decision to participate in religion and his relation to it is unique and can be revealed only through detailed individual study. Religious involvement can best be understood neither by a priori pathological interpretations nor uncritical acceptance, but rather by examining its unconscious meanings and functions in a practitioner's life. The task of the clinician is to ascertain the unconscious meanings, functions, and motivational priority for a particular patient at a particular time.

Chapter 7

Transitional Space and Tibetan Buddhism: The Object Relations of Meditation

Mark Finn

The psychology of religion and object relations theory have become almost inseparable because any discussion of primary object representations cannot help considering religious representations, and no consideration of the psychology of religion can be separate from notions of primary relationships. The challenge has been to build a psychology of religion that is neither reductionist nor overly reverential. Noteworthy efforts have come from psychoanalysts writing within the Christian tradition (e.g., Rizzuto, 1979; Meissner, 1984). Recently several authors have joined the discussion from the perspective of Buddhist psychology (Engler, 1983; Aronson, 1985; Epstein, 1988). The thinking of these authors represents a maturation of the long relationship between Buddhism and psychoanalysis. Buddhism offers both intellectual and practical contributions to the psychology of religion, for in Buddhism a highly developed contemplative psychology has emerged out of hundreds of years of experience with actual meditative techniques. This technique of meditation has made the experience of Buddhist teachings readily accessible to many Western students.

There exist at least three views of the relationship between Buddhism and psychoanalysis. The first, which could be termed the classical, regards meditative practice as at best regressive if not frankly pathological (Alexander, 1931; Masson, 1980). This view categorizes meditative experiences as developmentally inferior to psychoanalysis. More recently, Wilber (1984) and Engler (1983) have turned the tables on this classical view and argued that meditative practice constitutes an advanced level of personality development that engages categories of development not conceived by psychoanalysis and superior to it. These authors think the pathologizing of meditation may derive from the fact that Eastern practices attract many disturbed individuals functioning at a borderline level of personality organization, and that these impaired meditators confuse their experiences of depersonalization and identity diffusion with "authentic" mystical attainment. Wilber and Engler recommend intensive psychotherapy of a traditional sort as a necessary remediation for such individuals prior to undertaking meditation. Wilber and Engler have made two important contributions to the discussion. First, they persuasively rescued advanced meditative states from uninformed pathological reductionism. Second, they have offered helpful clinical guidance on working with disturbed individuals who are failing to make important discriminations in their meditation practice. What is unfortunately lost in their position is the profound interpenetration of activities labeled psychoanalytic treatment and meditation. Epstein (1988) has been the most articulate theoretician of this latter third view. Epstein attempts, by separating types of meditation technique and clarifying such terms as ego and emptiness, to avoid reducing Buddhism and trivializing psychoanalysis. In other quarters, the technique of Buddhist meditation has been recruited without theoretical hesitation to the purposes of dynamic psychotherapy. It has been recommended to increase the patient's self-control (Walsh, 1980), to enhance the therapist's capacity for analytic listening (Rubin, 1985), and to increase psychological-mindedness in patients beginning dynamic psychotherapy (Kutz, Borysenko, and Benson, 1985). The latter authors cite Freud, who sought a technique to intensify the therapeutic process without the limitations of hypnosis, and suggest that Buddhist mindfulness-practice is such a technique. Because Buddhist doctrine is largely psychological and atheistic, it has been possible to present meditation independent of religious doctrine and iconography. Indeed, some authors, including Kutz, Borysenko, and Benson (1985), have explicitly advocated doing so. Although removing meditation from its religious context makes it more accessible for patients in clinical settings, the loss of the religious literature deprives us of the rationale of meditation, as well as of case examples from the primary texts that can illuminate the psychology of spiritual life. Furthermore, separating the technique from the tradition creates the impression that meditation is a completely solitary activity. While in a sense this is true, it is also true that in the Buddhist tradition, meditation practice is learned within a committed relationship to a teacher. This teacher is, in psychoanalytic terms, technically neutral: He is not evangelical but creates a frustrating situation for the purpose of uncovering self-deception and exploring hope and fear. Thus, it is possible to examine the accounts of Buddhist meditators and their teachers as representing a tradition of an "ethno-psychoanalysis" wherein a self-analytic technique is practiced within a committed relationship.

There is nothing original in describing Buddhism as a psychology as opposed to a religion. Zimmer (1951) states:

For though India in [Buddha's] time, half a millennium before Christ, was a veritable treasure-house of magical religious lore—to our eyes a jungle of mythological systems—the teachings of the Enlightened One offered no mythological vision, either of the present world or of a world beyond, and no tangible creed. It was presented as a therapy, a treatment or cure, for those strong enough to follow it—a method and a process of healing. (p. 467)

The ailment for which a cure is needed is that "one lives . . . enveloped by the impulses of various layers of one's own nature, woven in the spell of their specific atmosphere, to which one submits as to an outside world. The goal of the Buddhist Therapy is to bring this process of self-envelopment to a stop" (p. 471).

Until fairly recently, discussions of the relationship of psychoanalysis and Buddhism focused on Zen, perhaps because Zen, with its spare presentation, is appealing to those who find more florid religious forms repellent. However, Tibetan Buddhism unpacks the same essential practice and psychology as Zen in a more elaborated descriptive theory and more emotionally accessible bio-graphical literature emphasizing the relationship between teacher and student. And since the Chinese invasion of Tibet, Tibetan teachers and translators of their literature have become part of the Western cultural landscape. This chapter will describe the technique and rationale of Buddhist meditation, discuss some of the phenomena of meditation in terms of the concepts of object relations theory, and then present an actual "case example" from the Tibetan biographical lit-erature that exemplifies the interpenetration of the spiritual and the psycho-dynamic.

The technique of meditation basic to all Buddhist practice is that of mindful-ness. Whether in Burma, Japan, or Tibet, mindfulness meditation involves a posture that, according to Kalu Rinpoche (1986):

should be as straight as possible—not tense or rigid but erect and relaxed. The mind should not be tense or fixed in any particular direction. As long as the mind is at rest, simply dwelling in a state of clear transparent awareness without any thought, what rests and what experiences that rest is nothing other than mind itself. When a thought arises, the mind adopts some form of expression, takes some direction. In this technique we try to maintain awareness of the process by which thought arises and takes form; we try to understand the nature of the actual experience of thought arising in the mind. We should maintain a bare awareness of the nature of mind as it is, without any effort to force some particular state of consciousness, to continue a particular experience. (p. 121)

Instructions vary regarding on how the breath is attended to, but breathing in this approach is never manipulated. The breath is "followed": "When we inhale, the air comes into the inner world. When we exhale the air goes out to the outer world. The inner world is limitless and the outer world is limitless. We say 'inner world' and 'outer world' but actually there is just one whole world'' (Suzuki, 1970: 29).

One consequence of this practice that has interested psychodynamic clinicians is the phenomenon that has been described as follows by the Buddhist teacher Osel Tendzin (1982):

Meditation practice creates a neutral ground, where we can relate simply and directly with our body and our breath and our environment. In that neutral situation our mental world becomes quite vivid. We witness the newsreel of our lives, our mental autobiography, in memories, discursive thoughts and emotions. Once we begin to practice, we come home, so to speak. When we visit our family after a long absence, there is a great commotion. All our relations are very excited; they haven't seen us in years. Some of them cry; others seem very happy and relaxed; others are brooding—it's quite a show. Coming home in terms of meditation practice is the same. All of our relatives—our mental family of memories, dreams, hopes and fears, what we have been, what we are, what we hope to be—start to speak up, expressing their reaction to having us home. (p. 30)

The experience described here may be conceived of, in psychoanalytic terms, as the meditator's gaining access to what Winnicott (1951) calls the "transitional experience" between inner and outer worlds as well as to the interaction of primary and secondary process. Meditation, with its very simple instructions— sit up straight, relax, and pay attention—has generated a rich psychology. (Interestingly, psychoanalysis also begins with simple instructions: Lie down and say everything that comes to mind.) Arising from the ordinary but limitless profundity of meditation, an accompanying Buddhist psychology has developed characterized by a paradoxical logic which, like meditation itself, disrupts the tendency of the mind (also noted by psychoanalysis) to keep certain of its aspects separate and polarized.

The paradoxical logic of Buddhism is intriguing but confusing to Westerners, and has been subject to all kinds of misinterpretation. Let me attempt to paraphrase some teachings, which, after all, represent language reaching out toward the experience of silence.

The central assumption of Buddhist logic is the inseparability of the two truths: relative and absolute. Relative truth is the truth of conventional reality; it is the truth of categorized distinctions, cause and effect, and linear logic. Absolute truth is the truth of radical unity; it is the truth of no distinctions, no conditionalities. From the perspective of relative truth, there is a person standing in relationship to his environment; from the perspective of absolute truth, person and environment are one. This unity or absence of distinction is often rendered in translations of Buddhist texts as "emptiness." Few terms have generated as much confusion as "emptiness" or, as it is sometimes translated, "nothing." A typical symptom of an immature intoxication with Buddhism is a sort of nihilism based on the notion that Buddhism abolishes all distinctions, including that between good and evil. But this is incorrect. One cannot take absolute truth without relative truth, yet absolute truth is in fact absolute. Thus the relative psychological world and the absolute spiritual world are inseparable. Buddhist practice sets as its goal the collapse of such dualities as sacred versus profane, psychological versus spiritual, while recognizing the relative truth of the distinctions themselves. The Zen master, Suzuki Roshi (1970), in discussing the cross-legged seated posture of meditation, puts it this way:

When we cross our legs like this, even though we have a right leg and a left leg, they have become one. The position expresses the oneness of duality; not two and not one. Our body and mind are not two and not one. If you think your body and mind are two, that is wrong. If you think that they are one, that is also wrong. Our body and mind are both two *and* one. We usually think that if something is not one it is more than one; if it is not singular, it is plural. But in actual experience, our life is not only plural, but also singular. Each one of us is both dependent and independent. (p. 25)

The meditation instructions quoted earlier come from a tradition in Tibetan Buddhism called *Mahamudra*. The *Mahamudra* teachings posit that given the inseparability of the relative and absolute world, every gesture, however mundane, is an expression of absolute truth. From the more immediate psychological perspective of the meditation instructions, this may be taken to mean that in psychoanalytic terms primary and secondary processes are inseparable, and that developmentally in meditation, as in love and art, the most advanced aspects of personality have a paradoxical intermingling with earliest periods of human experience. Loewald (1976) argues for such a way of regarding experience when he suggests "a deeper meaning" for the terms primary and secondary process. Loewald states:

Mental and memorial processes are primary if and insofar as they are unitary, single-minded, as it were undifferentiated and non-differentiating, unhampered as Freud has described it, by laws of contradiction, causality, and by the differentiation of past, present and future and of subject and object, i.e., by the differentiation of temporal and spatial relations. mental processes are primary to the extent to which they are non-splitting to the extent to which they do not manifest or establish duality or multiplicity, no this and/ or that, no before and after, no action as distinguished from its agent or its goal or its object. The secondary process is secondary insofar as in it duality becomes established, insofar as it differentiates; among these differentiations is the distinction between the perceiver and the perceived. (p. 319)

The parallels between Loewald's "deeper" meaning for primary and secondary process and the Buddhist notion of relative and absolute truth become even more explicit when Loewald discusses time. Time, even everlasting time, for Loewald is contrasted with eternity, and the two ideas cannot be thought of independently of the other. Eternity, corresponding to the Buddhist absolute truth, "is not time that has no limit. The category of time does not apply except in contrast. In the experience of eternity time is abolished" (p. 63).

Winnicott (1951) makes a very similar point in discussing what might be called "relative and absolute truth" regarding the nature of transitional objects: The infant's thumb or teddy bear is neither a concrete aspect of external reality nor simply an artifact of inner life. Winnicott states:

My claim is that there is a need for this double statement; there is need for a triple one; there is a third part of the life of a human being, a part that we cannot ignore, an intermediate area of experiencing to which inner reality and external life both contribute. It is an area which is not challenged, because no claim is made on its behalf except that it shall exist as a resting-place for the individual engaged in the perpetual human task of keeping inner and outer reality separate yet inter-related. (p. 255)

Winnicott's conception of infant development follows the same logic as that suggested by Buddhist psychology: While in a certain sense external reality and internal wishes are separate, even opposed, growth occurs through our being able to experience these two realms as simultaneously separate and the same. For Winnicott, the transitional objects of infancy are the introduction to the realm of illusion on which human creativity depends. Illusion for Winnicott is not simple hallucination, but a complex, paradoxical, and vital aspect of experience, and, appropriately, it is the work of Winnicott that Meissner recruits in rebutting Freud's devaluation of religion as mere illusion. A classic Tibetan text, Gampopa's *The Jewel Ornament of Liberation*, asserts that what becomes absolute spiritual compassion arises from the relative experience of compassion between mother and child.

Growth for Loewald happens in a process he calls memorial activity, remembering, wherein non-dual primary memorial processes combine or recombine with secondary processes so "that we become free to create our lives anew." Loewald thus seems to be describing something quite similar to Winnicott's notion of transitional experience and to the "coming home" phenomena described by Osel Tendzin.

The memorial activity that produces developmental reorganization is, in Loewald's conception, precipitated by experiences of deprivation or satisfaction. However, Fairbairn (1924) argues that it is the recollection and return of bad objects that leads to growth. In analysis, this occurs when a patient is sufficiently secure in his relationship to his analyst that:

the goodness of the analyst as an object provides the patient with sufficient sense of security to enable [the patient] to tolerate the release of his bad objects from the unconscious and finally permit them to be exorcised. . . . [F]or it may be said of all psychoneurotic and psychotic patients that, if a true mass is being celebrated in the chapel, a black mass is being celebrated in the crypt. It becomes evident, accordingly, that the psychotherapist is the true successor to the exorcist. His business is not to pronounce the forgiveness of sins, but to cast out devils. (p. 113)

Fairbairn leaves an apparent tension implicit. Paradoxically, demons are driven out aggressively by the inviting security of the analytic relationship. Thus, Fairbairn, like Winnicott and Loewald, is attempting to explicate a zone of psychic life where, via complicated processes, past and present, good and bad objects, can play, recombine, and reorganize.

We turn now to a story from the life of the Tibetan Saint Milarepa, concerned with a turning point in Milarepa's meditation practice. In this account, a crisis and its resulting spiritual growth are described in ways very consistent with the processes Winnicott, Loewald, and Fairbairn described as psychological growth. The story is a vivid example of the inextricable intertwining of the psychological and the spiritual in a meditation practice conducted in the context of a committed relationship with a teacher.

Milarepa is the most famous religious figure of Tibet, a central figure in two key Tibetan texts. One recounts the story of his life (translated by Lhallungpa, 1982), and the other is a collection of spontaneous teaching poems, *The 100,000 Songs of Milarepa* (translated by Chang, 1977). Milarepa's biography is an extraordinary psychological document and worthy of an extended psychoanalytic consideration. Milarepa was born to a wealthy land-owning family. His father died when he was a child, and his aunt and uncle swindled him and his mother and sister out of their land. They were driven into poverty. His mother was desperate for revenge and threatened to commit suicide if Milarepa did not learn sorcery so that he could inflict retribution on his aunt and uncle. Reluctantly, he did so. Having mastered black magic, he caused a spell to destroy his aunt and uncle's house, killing their children. In remorse, he sought spiritual training from a guru named Marpa. Marpa is himself a remarkable figure. A strong-willed youth, he made several dangerous journeys to India to study with his own guru, Naropa, and translated the Indian Buddhist texts into Tibetan. A cantankerous individual who defied conventional expectations of how a holy man behaves, he was married with children and a successful farmer who used his wealth to finance his translating expeditions. Milarepa first encountered Marpa in a field without knowing who he was, and was encouraged by Marpa to drink beer. Milarepa had his misgivings but drank the beer down completely. (In the text it is noted that this was a good omen, indicating that Milarepa would take all of Marpa's teachings in without preconception as to what was spiritual.) Marpa's training was arduous, but eventually Milarepa was declared his spiritual heir. He left to practice *Mahamudra* meditation in solitude. What follows is an abridged version of "The Tale of the Red Rock Jewel Valley" from the Chang translation (p. 1–7).

The great Yogi Milarepa was staying at the Red Rock Jewel Valley, absorbing himself in the practice of *Mahamudra* meditation. He discovers he has run out of supplies and goes out to collect some wood. He gathers some twigs, but a storm arises and blows away his robe and wood. Due to weakness, he cannot withstand the storm and faints. When he awakes he sees his shred of clothing swaying from a tree. Struck by the futility of the world, he experiences a strong feeling of renunciation and he begins to meditate. Soon a cluster of clouds arises from a valley in the direction of the home of his guru, Marpa. He reflects that

Marpa and his wife are probably engaged in Buddhist practice, and a great, unbearable longing rises in him. He then sings a long song called "Thoughts of My Guru," recalling Marpa in detail. No sooner has he finished when the cloud reveals Marpa on a cluster of rainbows riding a white lioness.

Marpa asks, "Great sorcerer, why such deep emotion, why call me so desperately? Have you not faith in the Dharma? No matter what the course, you may be certain that we will never part."

Inspired, Milarepa sings another song. He returns to his cave, only to find demons with eyes as large as saucers. They mock him by giving sermons and tossing his books. Following his shock he thinks: "These must be local deities who dislike me because I have never given them offering as compliments." He sings them a flattering song and begs them to depart. They only advance further, grimacing and grinding their teeth. He tries to drive them out with incantations and sermons but they remain.

He finally declares that "through the mercy of Marpa, I have already fully realized that all being and all phenomena are of one's own mind. The mind itself is a transparency of voidness. What, therefore, is the use of all this and how foolish I am to try to dispel these manifestations physically."

Then he sings the "Song of Realization," which concludes:

Ye ghosts and demons, enemies of the Dharma, I welcome you today! It is my pleasure to receive you. I pray for you. Stay, do not hasten to leave. We will discourse and play together. Although you would be gone, stay the night. We will pit the black against the white Dharma and see who plays the best.

Before you came, you vowed to afflict me. Shame and disgrace would follow if you returned with this vow unfulfilled.

Milarepa moves on the demons with confidence. They swirl together and vanish.

As a consequence of this incident, Milarepa gained great spiritual progress and subsequently returned to the world and became a great teacher. His aunt even became a student.

My basic assumption in approaching this story is that it represents an illustration of unusual personality development that, like childhood or psychopathology, displays elemental aspects of human psychology in high relief. Throughout object relations theory, there is a subversive thread suggesting that conventional notions of functional normalcy are not a sufficient ceiling for human possibility. Winnicott is explicitly critical of "mere sanity" (in Davis and Wallbridge, 1981). Rizzuto also notes that the achievement of truly genuine relationship is no more "normal" than genuine religious accomplishment. The paradox noted by many authors is that these highest levels of development in love, art, or religion are related to yet qualitatively distinct from childhood and psychopathology. From the assumption that Milarepa's struggles, however violent and bizarre, represent not psychosis but something larger than "mere sanity,'' the story can be approached by looking at its two segments. The first part is Milarepa's despair and recollection of Marpa. His longing for Marpa attaches itself to the cloud. There is probably no phenomenon in nature that better captures the qualities of a transitional object than a cloud. It is as soft, fluffy, and impermanent as a beloved security blanket. It is also highly suitable for receiving all of our loving and hateful projections, as everyone who has gazed dreamily at clouds can attest. The cloud, like any good transitional object, joins Milarepa to the best object of his life, Marpa. Marpa confronts Milarepa with directness and asserts his complete internalization: "We are beyond parting." (In traditional Tibetan paintings, Milarepa is usually portrayed with his hand on his ear so as to always hear Marpa's teaching.)

Through the practice of meditation, Milarepa gains access to the transitional experience of Winnicott and the process of memorial activity described by Loewald. This memorial activity results in Milarepa's experiencing a completely good connection to his guru. Then, in the second segment of the story, Milarepa is able, as Fairbairn would predict, to release his own bad objects. First, he acknowledges their appearance as his responsibility. Initially, he attempts to persuade them to leave with good manners, or, if you will, polite neurotic defenses. Then with somewhat greater urgency he tries to drive them out with techniques he describes as "physical," which can be understood in psychodynamic terms as acting out. The demons only become more irritable in response. He recalls his realization that the demons are projections, illusions arising from his own mind. Instead of seeking to drive them out, he invites them to "play and discourse." The demons collapse and vanish. In some translations (Nalanda, 1980), he steps into the largest demon's mouth, and the demon then vanishes into a rainbow. Milarepa's experience serves to clarify an apparent tension in Fairbairn's advocacy of demonic metaphors for conceiving of bad objects and the metaphor of exorcism for psychotherapy. Exorcism may connote an aggressive procedure of driving out demons. Ironically, Milarepa rids himself of demons by inviting them to stay out of compassion and love. Milarepa furthermore does not rid himself of demons by calling on Marpa to do his exorcising for him. Rather, when he calls on Marpa, Marpa does not take Milarepa's demons away but brusquely reminds him to return to his analytic task, that is, meditation. Marpa's irritated suggestion that his teachings are efficacious and his explicit statement of his own permanence as a good object for Milarepa permit Milarepa to release and free his own demons and recognize them as aspects of his own mind. But in confronting Milarepa, Marpa reminds Milarepa not only of his (Marpa's) goodness, but also of his strength. Recall that Milarepa had been devoted to a despairing, enraged, controlling, and suicidal mother who demanded that he enact her murderous impulses. Thus, in reminding Milarepa of his strength, Marpa may be thought of as deliberately marshaling Milarepa's devotion to his mother for the purpose of furthering Milarepa's psychological liberation. In a commentary by Chogyam Trungpa, a contemporary Tibetan teacher, Marpa's skill in doing this has been noted and understood as a transferential process. Trungpa (1973) notes that Milarepa was still in an "adolescent stage" at Red Rock Jewel Valley and that Marpa was still a "daddy" to him.

Transference itself is an illusory, transitional phenomenon. Transference phenomena must be analyzed as though external while recognized as projective illusions. Milarepa, by his confidence in his meditative practice and his relationship to his teacher, is able to recognize his demons as illusions and to interpret them as manifestations of genuine evil. (He was, after all, a murderer.) In Zen, it is said that there is a mountain, then there is no mountain, then there is. In Milarepa's story, first there are demons, then there are no demons, then there are. Milarepa does not rest in the absolute truth of the illusory nature of demons but recognizes the relative truth of evil aggression. He then returns to help beings in the relative world. In psychoanalytic treatment, as for Milarepa, childhood demons are reduced in size by interpretation. Thus freed and strengthened, we are better able to face the living cruelty of the world. It is said that Buddhist psychology is like an ancient recipe for good bread: The recipe is as old as time but the bread baked today is completely fresh. It is the singular genius of Buddhism to recognize that a radically psychological approach is in no way discontinuous with what is essentially religious: There is no need for shame over our humanity, or for false cynicism in the face of our potential for compassion and wakefulness.

A typically paradoxical phrase in Tibetan Buddhism is "auspicious coincidence." Having been touched and intrigued by Milarepa's story, I recalled Auden's (1939) poem honoring Sigmund Freud, in which Auden concludes that, most of all, Freud would have us be kind to the big-eyed demons of the night. It is an auspicious coincidence that almost 900 years earlier in the mountains of Tibet, the same image was used to invite us further into ourselves and the world.

Chapter 8

Between Religious Psychology and the Psychology of Religion

Benjamin Beit-Hallahmi

The wider context of this chapter is the relationship of psychological theories to beliefs, ideology, and ideals. The human sciences are marked, burdened, or endowed (depending on your value judgment) with value judgments. Here systematic inquiry is never far from human nerve endings, sentiments, and burning passions. Taking a stand is inevitable, as has been shown time and again. "Whose side are you on?" is the question for each of us in psychology, something that is less obvious to our colleagues in engineering or chemistry (Beit-Hallahmi, 1974, 1975, 1976, 1977, 1987, 1989). Arguably, the most serious controversy in the history of psychology has to do with the interpretation of IQ measurements (Beit-Hallahmi, 1981). The issue of interpreting religious beliefs may be less visible, but it is not less controversial. Neither does it lack for partisans. What follows is a case study in the history of modern ideas about religion.

The human sciences are by definition a threat to religion because they take religion as an object of study and not as a representation of a special reality or a special mode of knowledge. They are a threat inasmuch as they study changes in culture over time and space, and show time and again that beliefs and customs, including religious ones, are relative and culturally conditioned. The study of religion is heresy if it means examining religious faith and religious behavior. Psychology, as the discipline that deals directly with the nature of human beliefs, presents the most direct threat.

The argument between atheists and theists is over whether the sources of religion are to be found in "internal impulses or needs" or "external power or presence'' (see Hammann, 1987). Any theory about religion that goes beyond faith itself is inherently reductionist and atheistic. Any psychological explanation of religious faith rules out its reality and validity; otherwise, there is no need for it. Psychological explanations, which show the genesis of religion in frustration and projection, indeed undo faith.

The psychology of religion, as opposed to religious psychology, focuses on the psychological explanation of religious phenomena (e.g., Cavenar and Spaulding, 1977; Spanos and Hewitt, 1979; Ullman, 1982). The difference between a religious psychology and a psychology of religion is that between defending religious beliefs and explaining them. The psychology of religion treats religion as a phenomenon for systematic psychological study, while religious psychology aims at promoting religion through the adaptation and use of psychological concepts.

Religious apologists wish to set clear limits to analysis itself, just like all religions set limits to reason, because of the supposed supreme validity of revelation and ''religious experience.'' Apologists advise one to be rational and analytic at all times, except when encountering religion. Attempts to reconcile psychoanalysis and religion have been numerous (see Beit-Hallahmi, 1978), and psychoanalytic apologetics embrace everything in psychoanalysis, except the psychoanalytic approach to religion (Leavy, 1988; Zilboorg, 1950, 1958). The next step is proving that psychoanalysis actually supports one's religion (see Beit-Hallahmi, 1989).

One strand of apologetics calls on the psychology of religion to follow the rule of the ''exclusion of the transcendent.'' According to this rule, or ''axiom,'' the psychologist, qua psychologist, must neither affirm nor deny the reality of the object of religious faith (Wulff, 1984). Such judgments are sometimes declared to be the domain of ''experts'' on religious questions: ''But as a researcher I will not make pronouncements appropriate for philosophers and theologians'' (Rizzuto, 1979: 4). It is quite clear that not only apologists themselves, but also psychoanalysts, have not followed this rule. And it is quite clear that pronouncements about religious faith are made by believers (and non-believers) with no special credentials. No religion requires its adherents to earn a doctorate in philosophy or in physics before being admitted into the sacred fold. As we all know, most believers are remarkably ignorant, which does not stop them from issuing statements about ''transcendence'' and the creation of the world.

THE CLASSICAL APPROACH

The classical psychoanalytic interpretation of religion does not come to praise religion but to bury it, analyzing it in every sense of the word. Demystification, which is the opposite of the apologetic impulse, it its final goal. It is by definition an analytical, ''reductionist'' approach, which takes religion as a phenomenon to be examined, and only that. Analysis demands taking the stand of the observer, not the partisan, and this is the normal stand in psychology.

The classical psychoanalytic approach to religion can be summed up in two concepts: projection and illusion. A lucid summary of the classical psychoanalytic interpretation of religion has been offered by Muensterberger:

Who are the gods who panic? Who are the monsters and werewolves, ogres and witches? Or the bogeys, vampires, and vultures who appear in dreams and mysteries and threaten one's life? Whence those fears and figments; the notion of fantastic beings and domains no human is able to fathom? We encounter them everywhere. They are an integral part of the vast repertoire of human imagination, nay, the human condition. Their supernatural craft stems from that inspiration which in one way or the other belongs inevitably to everyone's childlike sense of impending doom or disaster and only magic, ritual, or prayer can tame or dispel. (1972, p. ix)

Object relations theory, the most important theoretical development in psychoanalysis since Freud (Guntrip, 1969; Winnicott, 1971), provides the best theoretical basis for understanding the world of the spirits in relation to the internal world of objects. Its starting point is the existence of an inner world of mental representations, reflecting the self and objects to which it is attached (Hartmann, 1964; Klein, 1948; Fairbairn, 1952b).

PSYCHOANALYTIC OBJECT RELATIONS THEORY AND RELIGIOUS BEHAVIORS

Students of the psychoanalytic approach to the study of religion have been yearning for the greater use of the concepts developed by object relations theory. Rubenstein (1963) complained about the research lag in the psychoanalytic studies of religion, which were still using the old instinctual framework although the newer object relations framework was available. If the psychoanalytic study of religion was to make serious advances, it had to take advantage of the great and glorious revolution brought about by what was first known as the British school, whose notions of personality structure and function have become the standard for psychoanalysis everywhere.

These prayers have been answered, and we now have a significant body of literature, best represented in the present volume, which embodies a specific object relations approach to religious phenomena. As we survey this body of literature, we must be struck by a dominant voice—one of not just tolerance, but empathy and sympathy with religious believers and religious beliefs. (The use of terms such as "spirituality" or "mature religion" is typical.)

In many cases, one cannot ignore the faint, sweet aroma of apologetics that hangs over the writings, and in most of those, the authors do not hide their strong commitments to religion. Often the apologetic stance is mild, gentle, or half-hearted, but we can easily detect the undercurrent of theistic commitment.

Is this demarche an advance, or progress, or progression? Is it to be seen as an advance over the classical approach? One interpretation of this New Wave

sees it as a more mature, mellow, born-again psychoanalysis, which has overcome Freud's obsession with rationalism in favor of a new, more moderate,
discourse of rapprochement and dialogue. But is a dialogue between psychoanalysis and religion really possible? Isn't analysis the death of faith?

Another question is whether there is an inevitable connection between the
transition from classical "instinct" theory to the study of object relations and
the new sentiments about religion. Is there something in the theory that compels
this change? Is object relations theory especially tied to or conducive to pro-
religious sentiments or religious apologetics? Is there something inherent in its
theoretical stance? The larger part of this chapter will be devoted to this question.

BACK TO BASICS

Let us go back to some of the original observations and survey what the great
originators of object relations theory had to say about religion.

Pro-religious sympathies were not an integral part of an object relations approach. It is important in this context to quote at length from the writings of
Melanie Klein, the Great Mother of the British school, who demonstrated a
strong atheistic position:

The idea of God, therefore, which equips authority with the most complete omnipotence,
meets the child's omnipotence-feeling half-way by helping to establish the latter and also
by assisting to prevent its decline. . . . For the result of development not to be boundless
utopianism and phantasy but optimism, a timely correction must be administered by
thought. The "powerful religious inhibition of thought," as Freud calls it, hinders the
timely fundamental correction of the omnipotence-feeling by thought. . . . The idea of
God, however, acts as a tremendous ally for this omnipotence-feeling. . . . That the mind
may later at some time perhaps overcome even this hindrance, although many thinkers
and scientists have never surmounted this barrier, and hence their work has ended at it,
nevertheless does not undo the injury inflicted. The idea of God can so shatter the reality-
sense that it dare not reject the incredible, the apparently unreal, and can so affect it that
the recognition of the tangible, the near-at-hand, the so-called "obvious" things in
intellectual matters, is repressed together with the deeper processes of thinking. . . . The
injury done can vary in kind and degree; it may affect the mind as a whole or in one or
other dimension to a greater or lesser extent; it is certainly not obviated by subsequent
enlightened upbringing. Thus even after the primary and fundamental injuries to thought
in earliest childhood, the inhibition set up later by the idea of God is still of importance.
It does not therefore suffice merely to omit dogma and the methods of the confessional
from the child's training. . . . To introduce the idea of God into education and then leave
it to individual development to deal with it is not by any means to give the child its
freedom in this respect. For by this authoritative introduction of the idea, at a time when
the child is intellectually unprepared for, and powerless against, authority, his attitude
in this matter is so much influenced that he can never again, or only at the cost of great
struggles and expense of energy, free himself from it. (Klein, 1948: 36–38)

Marion Milner, in an early paper, expresses this atheistic view of religion, which seems to integrate classical and object relations thinking:

It seems that the elusive inner realities of feeling are continually taking to themselves the form of outer realities. It seems that the discovery of the inner life is made in terms of the outer world. . . . This symbolizing capacity of the mind, its infinite capacity for using metaphor in expressing psychic realities, flows out in a tremendous stream which has many branches: the imaginative play of childhood, art, symbolic rituals, religion. Words become the central mode of expression for most people, after early childhood, and bridge the gulf between the inner and outer realities. But words also become caught up in the original confusion between the two realities and are too often given an absolute value. (Milner, 1987: 14)

Later on, Milner (1969) expressed a more sympathetic view of religion and religious rituals, accepting not only her clients' beliefs, but also institutional rituals as therapeutic.

W.R.D. FAIRBAIRN

Fairbairn's earliest case study (1927) was a fascinating, moving, and poignant story that presents an unusual combination of sexual compulsion and religious fantasies. A young, unmarried woman became obsessed with both masturbation and religious visions, showing a typically psychotic picture. Fairbairn correctly diagnosed this case as representing an extreme rarity among religious believers, but it might be less of a rarity among religious visionaries.

He also stated that ''what is sought by the patient who enlists psychotherapeutic aid, is not so much health as salvation from his past, from bondage to his (internal) bad objects, from the burden of guilt, and from spiritual death. His search thus corresponds in detail to the religious quest'' (Fairbairn, 1952a: 155). And, as we shall see below, Guntrip was to follow Fairbairn's ideas and extend them on this score.

D. W. WINNICOTT

Winnicott's idea of the transitional state has been the major source of theorizing in contemporary writings dealing with religion (Rizzuto, 1979). His original ideas are worth looking at closely: ''I am therefore studying the substance of *illusion*, that which is allowed to the infant, and which in adult life is inherent in art and religion. . . . We can share a respect for *illusory experience*, and if we wish we may collect together and form a group on the basis of the similarity of our illusory experiences'' (Winnicott, 1971: 3; emphasis in the original).

A close reading of Winnicott shows that his idea of transitional phenomena parallels the more traditional psychoanalytic notion of regression in the service of the ego:

It is assumed here that the task of reality-acceptance is never completed, that no human being is free from the strain of relating inner and outer reality, and that relief from this strain is provided by an intermediate area of experience which is not challenged (arts, religion, etc.) This intermediate area is in direct continuity with the play area of the small child who is "lost" in play. (Winnicott, 1971: 13)

Winnicott time and again couples religion and art, as two phenomena belonging to the "intermediate area" (Winnicott, 1965).

According to Winnicott, faith in God is made possible by positive early experience: "To a child who has started life in this way the idea of goodness and of a reliable and personal parent or God can follow naturally" (1965: 97).

And this idea of God is created in the following way: "Man continues to create and re-create God as a place to put that which is good in himself, and which he might spoil if he kept it in himself along with all the hate and destruction which is also to be found there" (1965: 94). Moreover,

Surely Mrs. Knight in the controversy of some years ago was not devaluing God by comparing God with Father Christmas; she was saying or trying to say that you can put some parts of a child into the witch of the fairy story, some of the child's belief and generosity can be handed out to Father Christmas, and all sorts of feelings and ideas of goodness that belong to the child and his or her inner and outer experiences can be put out there and labelled "God." In the same way, nastiness in the child can be called "the devil and all his works." The labelling socializes the otherwise personal phenomenon. (Winnicott, 1965: 95)

HARRY GUNTRIP

Harry Guntrip, whose eloquent writings have done much to make the ideas of the British school accessible to a worldwide audience, has been the most outspoken in his pro-religious stand:

Naturally, religion, dealing as it does with the emotional needs of human beings as persons, will be more liable to adulteration by the importation of infantile dependence into its motivation than will science. Nevertheless, man has shown an age old desire for the emotional security that would result from the knowledge that our life as "persons" arises out of and remains rooted in a fundamentally "personal" element in the structure of the universe. It is the task of philosopher and theologian to show whether that is realistic, but he would be a bold, foolish man who would insist that is in itself a neurotic wish. (Guntrip, 1961: 383)

The origins of religion lie in a basic and universal human need, the need for an object: "Religion, like psycho-analysis, is a search for a psycho-therapy for the emotional and personal ills of human beings even if the method for approach is different" (Guntrip, 1961: 45).

"Religious experience is so very much an expression of human nature as rooted in the primary need for good personal relationships" (1961: 255). "Religion is *about* the human being's innate need to find good object-relationship in which to live his life'' (1961: 257).

Later on, Guntrip stated that "it may well be that integration, maturity, mental health and religious experience are all closely related" (1969: 324).

The need of the human being to retain a fundamental sense of organic unity which is at the same time a latent sense of relationship, and which will develop through a good mother-infant experience into a specific capacity for ego-object relationship, ultimately with the universe itself, the final reality, must have been the core of religious experience all down the ages . . . i.e. Buber's "yearning for the cosmic connexion" as something entirely different from projecting a father-image on to the universe. (Guntrip, 1974: 267)

Non-believers may be schizoid, while religionists are less neurotic:

Science is primarily intellectual investigation of impersonal phenomena, and religion is primarily emotional experience of personal relationships, from which the schizoid person is detached and which he often consciously dislikes and has little capacity to understand. . . . Freud must have had some personal reasons for overvaluing the impersonal scientific method, as also for his hostility to religion." (Guntrip, 1961: 249–50)

While implying a critique of Freud, this approach still incorporates the notions of illusion and projection. There is no defense of a religious reality, but only a yearning, based on human, "temporal" experience, projected onto the universe. Guntrip adopted Winnicott's notions of transitional states and transitional objects as the origins of cultural phenomena, including religion: "It follows that 'culture,' all the arts and religions of mankind, are 'playing.' This is not to trivialize culture, but to reveal the enormous significance of 'playing' at the beginning of life. In fact, it is in his 'playing' that a child is really 'living' " (Guntrip, 1974: 419).

DOES THE THERAPIST'S ROLE FOSTER SYMPATHY FOR RELIGION?

Is the gap between micro and macro levels, between the case study level and the psychology of religion level, created by the nature of therapeutic interaction? Does it explain the appearance of pro-religious sentiments or apologetics in the writings under discussion?

The choice put before us by some of the case presentations is that between empathy and reductionism. Empathy is the sine qua non of psychotherapy, while reductionism is the starting point for science. The psychology of religion perspective seeks to arrive at acceptable generalizations, while the clinical approach must respond to a human cry for immediate help. Morally speaking, helping those in need of solace and support is superior to the schizoid desire for pure knowledge. But isn't this separation between the search for the general in academic science and the respect for uniqueness in clinical work a bit artificial?

After all, when clinicians present their cases, they aim at generalization as well, and they do have much to teach all of us. Moreover, in this context, this separation between micro and macro is superfluous, as much of our theorizing is based on individual cases.

Sympathy and empathy are necessary and commendable in therapy, as the therapeutic stance is guided by human kindness, common sense, and clinical experience. If the goal is treatment only, that is commendable. Sympathy for the believers should be separated from sympathy for faith, if we are to learn from clinical work about the psychology of religion. If the goal is understanding, we need a lot more than mere sympathy.

THE FUNCTIONAL ARGUMENT

Often, the gentle apologists do not dare offer more than the "functional" justification for religion. One of their common observations in clinical discussions is that religion faith seems to help and sustain troubled individuals. There can be little doubt about that, and it does not contradict the classical view. Wasn't it Freud who stated that religion is "born of the need to make tolerable the helplessness of man" (1927: 32)? And indeed that is what we discover time and again. The functional approach to religion, which views it as a form of coping, or as helpful in coping, still does not support or imply any genuinely religious notions about the reality of the religious object.

GENTLE APOLOGETICS

Obviously, pro-religious sentiments are not just the result of over-identification with clients in therapy. There is a prior commitment to religion, and not a "conversion" of the therapist to the client's faith. Just as in the case of the nature–nurture controversy is psychology, it is the basic ideological stance that predicts the specific position taken here (Beit-Hallahmi, 1981; Pastore, 1949).

This mild apologetics does not dare summon us to any real faith, that is, to ontological claims. Meissner (1984) and Rizzuto (1979) follow Guntrip and Winnicott; they seem to claim only that God is a transitional object. "God, psychologically speaking, is an illusory transitional object" (Rizzuto, 1979: 177). If there is a defense here, it is the defense of a non-denominational God, which is supposedly common to all religions, and of nothing more specific. This whole business of sophisticated, gentle apologetics is another chapter in the long, inexorable process of secularization and the psychologizing of religion. Actually, this variety of apologetics is an admission of defeat, because it presents a psychologized religion, devoid of the common faith of common believers who do not need any sophisticated apologetics. Those who need it are intellectuals, for whom defending the faith remains an impossible mission.

The inherent danger in apologetics in this case is the creation of another religious psychology (Beit-Hallahmi, 1989). This renewed attempt will not have any impact beyond the boundaries of a small circle of friends, a limited, closed group of religionists.

PROJECTION THEORY AND THE OBJECT RELATIONS APPROACH

If classical psychoanalytic theory can be summed up in the concepts of projection and illusion, there is nothing in the new material, including, and especially, clinical material, that contradicts Freud. On the contrary, object relations theory lends itself rather well to a continuation of the Freudian tradition, which sees all religious ideas as projections. The concepts of object representations and transitional objects seem like the logical extension of projection theory. We are still dealing with illusions and fictions. There is nothing inherent in object relations theory that would make it more sympathetic to religion. It turns out to be more of a restatement of Freud than an opposition view.

The notion of universal, deep, human yearnings and needs in support of religious faith is no more convincing than other arguments in support of theism. Fairy tales also reflect deep needs and universal dreams, but we consider them untrue and we analyze them just as we analyze religion. A universal yearning for X does not prove that X exists. And we find the same yearnings in individual love and in works of art. All theoreticians in the object relations tradition make clear that the religious yearning is for an imaginary object. The internal need is real, but the external object is imaginary. That is simply a rewording of Freud's classical claim.

The great insights about personality development, articulated by the object relations approach, are not the monopoly of the pro-religious. Lutzky (1991) demonstrates the use of the theory toward the understanding of religion in the most basic way. The proposed connection between the sacred and the internal object, between early experience and the numinous is a major discovery. It aims, and succeeds, at illuminating religion as a basic human experience, without in any way assuming its ontological validity.

CONCLUSIONS

It is clear that some of the great theoreticians who created the British object relations school had strong religious commitments, especially Fairbairn and Guntrip. It is also clear that psychotherapy leads its practitioners to empathy and sympathy with clients' experiences and beliefs, as it should. Nevertheless, there is nothing in the theoretical approach itself that compels us to take a pro-religious, or apologetic, approach. The insights offered by object relations theory demonstrate a continuity with Freud's atheistic approach. The notions of object representations and transitional experience do not lend any comfort or consolation to theists. "God" remains a projection and an illusion. If all you can say is that

"God" is a "transitional object," religious faith is in trouble, because that is not what the believers want and say.

At the conclusion of this brief survey, we have not discovered a return from apostasy to faith or a born-again psychoanalysis. The contributions to the understanding of religion from an object relations perspective turn out to be insightful articulations of projection theory, and not sources of support for faith in the religious objects. Object relations theory can offer little solace for established religion or established religions. What we can observe is a moderate pro-religious spirit animating some psychoanalytically inspired writings. It is a general pro-religious sentiment, not a defense of specific religious positions. What we are gratified to realize is that intellectual honesty has kept theorists away from direct apologetics, despite their sympathy for religion.

ACKNOWLEDGMENTS

The author is especially grateful to Shimshon S. Rubin, who has gone over an earlier draft and suggested several improvements. All remaining difficulties and shortcomings are the author's sole responsibility. The preparation of the chapter has been supported by the Research Authority, University of Haifa.

Chapter 9

Images of God: A Study of Psychoanalyzed Adults

Marilyn S. Saur
William G. Saur

Psychoanalysts and psychoanalytic psychotherapists, influenced by Freud's view of religion as an illusion fostered by neurotic man, have had a limited framework with which to analyze religious material from their patients. Recently, neo-Freudian object relations theory has proposed an alternative conceptualization of illusion for understanding an individual's religious experiences and religious development.[1] Object relations theory is concerned with the nature and origins of interpersonal relations, particularly the effect of early internalized object representations on ego and superego development and on present interpersonal relations.[2]

Perhaps the most comprehensive application of object relations theory to religious issues is Rizzuto's study of the origins, evolution, and significance of the God-representation in psychic life. Her work expands Freudian ideas of religion and God by incorporating Winnicott's notion of the transitional sphere. According to Rizzuto, it is in the transitional sphere that a young child creates a highly personalized mental representation or image of God.[3] This understanding of the creation of a personal God-representation does not confirm or deny the existence of God.

In his seminal paper, "Transitional Objects and Transitional Phenomena," the British psychoanalyst D. W. Winnicott laid the foundation for the conceptualization of religion as a transitional experience.

The third part of the life of a human being, a part that we cannot ignore, is an intermediate area of experiencing, to which inner reality and external life both contribute. It is an area that is not challenged, because no claim is made on its behalf except that it shall exist as a resting-place for the individual engaged in the perpetual human task of keeping inner and outer reality separate yet interrelated.[4]

He calls this intermediate area of experiencing "transitional phenomena." Winnicott elaborates: "I am therefore studying the substance of illusion, that which is allowed to the infant, and which in adult life is inherent in art and religion."[5]

Winnicott defines illusion as a way of gaining access and giving meaning to reality while expressing inner subjective experiences. It is not an obstruction to reality. Illusions, along with play, creativity, and imagination, exist in the transitional space. Here, transitional objects are formed. An object such as a stuffed toy or blanket is chosen and imbued with special meaning that is neither fully subjective nor fully objective and initially serves to soothe and defend against anxiety connected with the loss of the mother. Transitional objects are important in that they are readily available and constant. They are not forgotten or mourned but may be put aside at times.[6]

According to Rizzuto, psychologically speaking, God may be described as a transitional object. One's personal image of God has the characteristics of other transitional objects but differs in that a concrete, tactile object does not exist. Rather, a mental representation is created or found from primary images such as parents, siblings, and others. Unlike other transitional objects, the God-image is not forgotten after childhood but remains available for use throughout life and may be recalled during times of crisis or transition. The God-representation is a complex image, not merely an idea but a dynamic, affective representation with conscious and unconscious aspects, with visual, perceptual, emotional, and conceptual components.[7]

Rizzuto suggests that the precursor of the development of the God-image resides in the mirroring provided by the mother with the infant, leading to the child's capacity to utilize transitional space. The origin of the God-representation occurs around two years, when the child's curiosity about how the world works is expressed in the endless questions of "how, what, and why." According to Rizzuto, the child learns that things are made and manipulated by people. In response to the child's long stream of questions about the nature of causality, the parent eventually suggests chance or fate or God. From this suggestion the child receives some notion of a power beyond and greater than people. The child imagines, finds, creates a God-image, using material from representations of other primary objects. This process occurs within the transitional sphere and continues throughout life as part of a struggle to relate inner experience and the outer world. Hence the God-representation may change according to the processes of adaptation and defense, similar to changes in self and other object representations. If the God-representation remains in the original form from early childhood, an adult may experience God as unimportant, meaningless, or intrusive.[8]

The present study was conceived as a method of examining some of Rizzuto's formulations about the development and later use of the God-representation in an individual's life. Based on Rizzuto's conceptualizations of the nature of the God-representation, seven propositions were extracted for investigation in the present study.[9] These propositions are as follows:

1. The young child creates a highly personalized mental representation or image of God drawn from the child's inner world of representations of parents, self, and significant others.

2. The God-image is both conscious and unconscious during its original formation and in later life.

3. The God-image may change, similar to changes in self and object representations, according to processes of adaptation and defense.

4. The God-image contains visceral, emotional, and conceptual components.

5. The God-image may be used in original form, repressed or transformed.

6. Among individuals whose God-image has not changed along with other development, God may be regarded as irrelevant or threatening.

7. Portions of the God-image that have been repressed may emerge, particularly during times of stress or life transition.

The data for this study were obtained from interviews with ten adults who had within the past four years completed a full course of clinical psychoanalysis. Each person had been analyzed four or five times a week over a period of five to seven years. Each had worked with a different analyst. This group was chosen because it was expected that adults who had completed psychoanalysis would have achieved some understanding of their early object relationships[10] and would freely discuss representations of self, objects, and God. The expectation proved to be correct. Half of the subjects had Christian backgrounds, and half had Jewish backgrounds. By self-description, several were currently atheists or agnostics, several were actively struggling with questions of faith, and several professed deep faith. Five of the subjects were female and five were male. All were between 32 and 42 years old.

From an initial phone call, subjects learned that we were interested in talking about aspects of their religious experience. At the beginning of the interview, they were told that the conversation was being taped. They were encouraged to associate to the question: Has there been a time in your life when you have felt close to God? The question was adapted from the written questionnaire portion of Rizzuto's study. It was chosen because it called attention to the relationship between the subject and their God-representation. When themes began to emerge in response to the initial question, the interviewer asked additional questions that encouraged material of an affective and personal nature. The interviews varied from one to two hours in length. They ended when the subjects had expressed themselves fully about their past and present religious experience. The interview data were examined for illustration of the propositions derived from Rizzuto's work.

THE CHILD'S CREATION OF A GOD-IMAGE

Jane's God-representation, that of a warm, caring figure, contained elements of her grandmother and two rabbis she had known in her childhood. She remembered her mother suggesting that God was "a man in the sky with a long white beard" who was interested in cleanliness and obedience. This image never became real for Jane, even though she could remember conversations with her mother that went back to the age of four. As a child, she held a private, more affective image. She was able to describe memories of thinking of her grandmother as being "almost godlike." The qualities of her grandmother that were most meaningful in this connection were her kindness, warmth, and consistently good and loving nature. These qualities became associated to Judaism by the fact that being Jewish was of utmost importance to her grandmother. The fact that they always were together during the Jewish holidays further strengthened the association. The rabbis she knew in her early years also communicated warmth, caring, and respect.

As an adult, she came to think of these qualities of the rabbis and her grandmother as the best of parenting. The loving parental representation was in contrast to her representation of her own mother, who because of major depressive episodes, was not able to maintain a consistently warm rapport. It is interesting to note that for Jane, an image was created principally from an internal representation of a female. Even when individuals use the conventional masculine pronoun, a male God image can't be assumed.

CONSCIOUS AND UNCONSCIOUS GOD-IMAGES

Trudy felt emotionally moved by the interview. She described a dilemma of yearning for faith while at the same time fearing it. On one side, she saw a spiritual life as a way of gaining support, as a resource for self-understanding, and as a way of developing an aspect of herself. She was attracted to the idea of being able to pass this dimension of life on to her daughter. On the other side, she had competing negative feelings, all of which were on the theme of dependency. She imagined that if she came to rely on a "higher being" for comfort and support, she would soon lose her understanding of her feelings. She feared becoming dishonest and manipulative in order to have her needs met. These fears puzzled Trudy, since in her present life, relationships were characterized by mutuality and interdependence. One result of her psychoanalysis was that she knew she could be feminine without behaving in a dependent or needy manner. The image of being in a markedly dependent relationship was in contrast to her most current sense of self. It was as if she unconsciously expected the higher power to exert a pressure that would undo her therapeutic gains.

Her family history gives some insight into what factors could have contributed to the unconscious aspects of her God-representation. Both parents had been deceptive during her childhood. Both had made a strong point of their involvement in church and had expounded moral values. Much later, her mother had made the startling confession that she had no belief, and her father was discovered in an extramarital affair. Trudy was left wondering what her parents stood for and who they really were. With these changes in object representations, the God-representation could have become imbued with aspects of a powerful but deceitful other with whom she could not expect a straightforward and mature interaction.

CHANGES IN THE GOD-IMAGE

A good example of this kind of change is provided by John. One facet of his self-representation was that of being one of the best-behaved boys in his peer group. Being chosen to become an altar boy created a feeling of being good and led to a sense of union with parents, grandparents, nuns, and priests. They, like God, were loving authority figures whom he enjoyed pleasing. In adolescence, the representation changed as his need for autonomy grew. He no longer had to be good in response to authority. The change was acted out at age fifteen when he gave up attending church. He continued to maintain the self-image of a good person and taught catechism to younger children, but he no longer felt that love followed from obedience.

Adulthood and taking on the role of psychoanalyst caused changes in his self-representation such that his sense of self no longer revolved around pleasing idealized authority figures. A personal God no longer fit. He described religion as being helpful in the lives of children but "a little secondary" in the lives of adults. John expressed his most current God-representation in an emotionally distant manner. It was "a feeling produced by the experience of being raised in a human family." It is possible that this sociological-sounding definition was held as a defense against more personal images that might have contained elements from childhood or adolescence that would have been threatening to his self-representation as an autonomous adult and analyst.

VISCERAL, EMOTIONAL AND CONCEPTUAL
COMPONENTS OF GOD-IMAGES

The proposition that the God-representation contains these components was illustrated by Nora, a practicing Christian. She stated that she believed God was available and ultimately reliable. Her concept of God had a negative side, which she came to understand after her psychoanalysis. She had been puzzled about why she felt constrained to be cautious and overly precise even after she had come to recognize caution and precision as being part of her representation of her father. One day, in the few seconds after making an error, she felt that God was looking over her shoulder, watching and disapproving. From that incident, she understood that a part of her experience of God was that he, like her father, was punitive, careful, and exacting.

Nora described other times in her daily life during which she experienced God on an emotional level. She enjoyed the outdoors and often felt a sense of God as being intriguing and exciting, particularly when she was swimming or hiking. She talked of an expansive quality that came to her at those times, a sense of the mystery of the universe that was felt as excitement. She said that the excitement could easily be turned to soothing. The same aspects of nature that could cause her to feel energized could on other occasions communicate the steady, never-ending quality she felt in her God. The visceral component of the representation was also mediated through nature. For Nora, God was felt as an almost tangible presence in the wind. God was also like the buoyancy of a large body of water.

REPRESSION AND TRANSFORMATION OF THE GOD-IMAGE

A different subject will be used to illustrate these possibilities. Rob stated that as an adult he was not aware of having a God-representation. He could only respond by describing what he assumed other people meant when they spoke of God. He termed God "the child's perspective of the all-powerful father, the giving mother, the feeling of oneness." Although from his viewpoint he was not worshiping that God, he was using the original childhood representation to identify the God in which he could not believe.

Repression can be inferred from the associations of John. As was mentioned in the discussion of changes in the God-image, his contact with the Catholic Church was frequent. For more than ten years of his childhood, he attended a parochial school and participated in mass at least six times a week. Considering the degree of personal involvement plus the abundant exposure to doctrine and ritual, memories from that period of his life came slowly and with obvious gaps. While it was clear from the reminiscences that God was real for him in childhood, memories were sketchy and unelaborate, suggesting repression.

Trudy, mentioned in the discussion of conscious and unconscious God-images, described a transformation experience. Prior to her college years, the image had a positive connotation of comfort and facilitation of growth. She was eager to enrich her "good caring self" through involvement in campus religious activities. The disillusionment with her parents signaled a transformation in the God-representation, and the transformation was to a negative image.

GOD REGARDED AS THREATENING AND IRRELEVANT

As mentioned above, Rob had a God-image that had not undergone transformation. The image he had, that of a projection of childish wishes, threatened his professional viewpoints. As he jokingly stated, "It's something of a narcissistic wound to have a patient say therapy helped her get right with God." Presumably, the point of the joke was that a good therapist would have helped a patient move beyond this childlike stage in her development. The data suggest why his God-representation did not change during childhood. Rob's father had insisted that he be a believer. Adolescent doubts about a supreme being were intolerable to his father. His father applied continuous verbal and emotional pressure and often insisted on statements of belief. The pressure culminated in Rob's feeling that the only alternative open to him was to be an agnostic. The insistence on belief seemed to have functioned to deprive him of the space to play with ideas and feelings about God. Belief was not a personal, emotional process of tentative thoughts and later revisions. It was an unexplored yes-or-no commitment.

In Rob's thirties, the topic might have resurfaced during his analysis. He began by expressing to his analyst some of the warmth he felt about Judaism. This was met with an interpretation that he quoted as: "It's the same with you as everyone else. It's identifications you have, and non-identifications with the external group." He commented that he "felt stung" by this response from his analyst and did not feel free to pursue the subject. Once again, he was denied the encouragement to explore some of his thoughts and feelings and perhaps to have transformations occur.

EMERGING IMAGES AS A RESPONSE TO STRESS AND TRANSITION

David described his family as being "unreligious Jews." They retained portions of the cultural heritage through holidays but divorced them from a religious context. For example, at Passover each year there was a meal with all the right foods, but the biblical story was omitted. As a child, he was invited to attend Hebrew school. He had pleasurable memories of age eight, when Bible stories and services were of interest to him. He felt a "religious sense," which led to play at being a rabbi. There were attempts to use the Hebrew School involvement as a means to belong to the community and to grow intellectually. He stopped attending because of lack of parental support, and his interest in religion diminished.

For the next fifteen years, religion was relegated to the foolish and disdainful. At age twenty-six, when his father died, David was suddenly taken with the thought that the event should be marked in a religious way. He went to the temple in his father's memory but continued over the next two years for himself. His attendance culminated in his bar mitzvah. The feelings that emerged at the time of this life transition were similar to those of the eight-year-old boy. His religious involvement generated a sense of comfort combined with a sense of inner productivity and growth. In both instances, he felt that he received a larger context in which to place the events of his life. This must have been a particularly important need in light of the Passover meal that was devoid of meaning.

The God-representation was not a traditional personified deity, but rather it existed as a feeling of support that was exemplified by stories, ritual, and song.

David's summary of this experience of religion echoes Winnicott's conceptualization. He stated: "There it is. All you have to do is take it."

A more detailed discussion of two interviews follows. The data illustrate the overall utility of an object relations perspective in understanding religious experience, particularly the significance of the God-image in an individual's psychic life.

Sandy's conversation began with the statement, "Once upon a time I felt close to God." Indeed, the theme of the fairy tale, that beautiful time long ago, pervades the story of his religious development. At the time of the study, he was forty-one years old. His memories took him back to being a child and feeling that God was like a person. He remembered saying ritual prayers and talking to God about problems. God was a potential helper as long as Sandy pacified him with good deeds.

Many of Sandy's memories came out as retrospective interpretations, since he had struggled with religious issues both alone and in his analysis. One such interpretation is of being four years old and watching adults pray in church.

You went to church all those times and all the adults were there. They know what they're doing, they're in charge of this world. They're all singing to God and talking to God. As a four-year-old I wouldn't think, "Huh, this is strange stuff." God's there. It was a matter for me of constructing God in such a way that fit my intimate internal world, and I fit it with my mother because she was the most important person to me. . . . God was too hard to relate to simply by what I was taught. There was a lot of hocus-pocus dogma that was hard to grasp as a kid. . . . I think I may have even thrown out the dogma and put at the center of my religion the way I related to my mother. God is basically this incredibly powerful being that will treat you like your mother treats you.

He could clearly remember the turning point in this relationship with God. He was a junior in high school and was sitting in a friend's white Cadillac, having a discussion about religion. It was not an emotional moment, but something like an intellectual "Aha!" when he realized that he no longer believed in the existence of God. He recalls feeling as if a solution to a problem had suddenly fallen into place.

In retrospect, Sandy sees this change in his relationship to God as closely linked to breaking away from his family. Previously, he had perceived God as wanting what his mother wanted. As with his mother, he had enjoyed being a good child for God and had enjoyed the feeling of God's love for him in return. After that point in high school when he ceased to believe, he felt he had relinquished the close tie to his mother and with it, feelings of omnipotence and optimism. He no longer had the confidence that if he were a good person, things would work out in his life.

As an adult looking back, he experienced grief and loss at giving up the notion of a God who was in control of the good things in his life. The quality of loss of the fairy tale was most evident here.

It's a cruel hoax . . . giving up the notion that there is a God who is in control of everything you like. I think it's hocus pocus, I can't believe it. . . . It's a setup for pain to believe it and give it up. It's like believing in Santa Claus.

Sandy's intellect became more dominant as he moved away from belief. He stated, "If religious dogma could be proven, I could believe; otherwise, the stuff is nonsense." His knowledge of human nature had led him to see that people constructed a God that would comfort them and would give them some degree of meaning. he all but paraphrased Winnicott's notion of a transitional object when he observed, "It wasn't that as a young child I was enlightened with truth. I made up a God."

It was uncomfortable for Sandy to consider the transitional nature of his religious experience. He reasoned that if a child came to imagine qualities of the unseen, and in the process met some of his own needs, the process would be dishonest.

In his mid-thirties, he saw his analyst's position as that of a critical other who would "keep you honest." The analyst would help him not pretend there was a God, because the pretense would create the false sense of being taken care of in the world. When he caught himself thinking, "Damn, if there was a God like I used to have, it sure would make things better," he would counter that feeling with the argument to himself that "all I want is comfort."

At one point in his analysis, he thought he might analyze the old God-image to the point of discarding it and starting over, but it didn't happen. Sandy felt that the process could not begin because he was not able to disregard his intellect. Thoughts of comfort always circled around to accusations of having made up the comforter. Sandy would reason: "A personal God is the only thing that has meaning to me, but to link it to truth is impossible for me. Once I've thrown out all the personal meaning, what use is it?"

At another point in his analysis, Sandy wanted to know whether his analyst believed in God. He had wished for the analyst to believe, feeling that the analyst represented Freud. Sandy thought that if someone of intellectual stature believed, then perhaps he could, too. When his analyst did not answer the question, Sandy interpreted the non-response as a statement of non-belief. After that, Sandy found a resolution that he termed atheistic prayer. It entailed positive thinking for no other reason than positive thinking, as opposed to talking to God. Another form of his resolution was the use of the Twenty-Third Psalm as a mantra for meditation, said without religious meaning.

Sandy's story had many facets that were interesting from the perspective of object relations theory. The most obvious is the imaging of God from representations of himself and his mother. This image did in fact change as his self and object representations changed, most notably during adolescence. However, changes in the self representation toward being a more intellectual and psychologically oriented adult caused him to be wary of what he felt to be the childlike portions of the representation. A God who was the embodiment of care and comfort seemed to him a contradiction of independent adult functioning. He seemed to firmly believe that psychological equilibrium should come from within, and that reaching to a God implied an unhealthy lack of self-reliance. As Rizzuto points out, further transformations were curtailed and the God-image posed a threat to his self representation.

From a Winnicottian perspective, fairy tales and personal images of God have in common their origin in the transitional sphere. For Sandy, both had a negative connotation because they involved imagination and human need. If what he imagined spoke to his needs, it signified falsity and self-deception.

Linda's story provides an interesting contrast to Sandy's, particularly in the use of the transitional sphere and in the preference for feelings over rational thought. Her interview began by her cautioning the interviewer that she really didn't know what she believed about God, but that she could talk about what she felt. She went on to describe her religious heritage as non-practicing Jewish on her father's side and atheist on her mother's side. Her father had some wish to introduce religion into his children's lives, and he had the children baptized by an Anglican priest and sent them to Sunday school.

The early memories of Sunday School made a lasting impression on Linda. She remembered with pleasure entire mornings of songs, stories, and crafts. After several years, her parents lost their motivation to send the children to Sunday School. Linda missed the church and asked to be allowed to go without her siblings. Her parents agreed and she attended through eighth grade. Along with these positive associations were familiar fond memories of being at camp and happily singing hymns in an outdoor chapel.

In her adult life she reported feeling close to God more at some times than at others. The times of closeness invariably evoked the sense of comfort of the early warm experiences of Sunday School. She felt the comfort as "the sense of a present parent who was available in the midst of a struggle with something." One of the phases in her life when the closeness of God was most salient was during graduate school when she was lonely and overwhelmed by new roles in life.

I wasn't married, I had no family. So church was a way to keep something very important alive when there weren't any real people to be close to. Keeping love alive is the way I used to think about it. . . . For a lot of my life, church was something of a longing.

These statements clearly expressed the sense of object-relatedness in her church experiences. God was in church, in a feeling created by the music and the chants, and these feelings linked to early positive feelings of being parented and cared for.

It is notable that the sense of a present parent was not based on an actual interaction with her parents, who were not as emotionally available as she had wished. She experienced church as a way to feel close to her father, who was often absorbed in his career. The closeness came more from a feeling of identification with him through religious participation. She was identifying with the representation of him as concerned with spiritual matters, even though he had not participated in religious practices. Her most meaningful association to the spiritual aspect of his personality was his interest in having her baptized.

The object-related nature of her religious experience was apparent when she talked about prayer. She likened prayer to the analytic relationship, where the patient talks to someone he doesn't see. She said:

It's the object relatedness of it. . . . It isn't just talking to yourself. It's maintaining the object in tough times or joyous times or transitions. It's the natural expression of the need to maintain object relatedness built into us. No matter what you think about it, I think it's there.

For Linda, the God-representation was connected to her self representation. She said that during her analyses, she did not question who God was but rather who she was in relation to God. Was she a Christian or a Jew? She felt that God would remain the same in either case. Eventually, she came to see that she could not practice Judaism because it had not been part of her early experience. The decision then related to her object relations. She felt that by defining herself as a Christian, she had moved away from her father's heritage in a way that caused her some sadness.

To summarize, both subjects displayed their awareness of the object-related nature of their God-representations. For Linda, it was reassuring to experience parental representations that were evoked in connection with her God-representation. Sandy disliked the connection between his image of God and his representation of mother. Both of them had a way of describing the transitional space as part of the process. Linda felt that God was in church and was present in songs and chants. Sandy acknowledged that it was the imagination that created a feeling of the presence of God.

For both, their attitudes are consistent with their self representations. Linda did not hesitate to describe herself in terms of feelings, particularly longings and loneliness. Sandy described himself as more intellectual, rational, and skeptical about human needs. A comforting God-representation fit with Linda's self representation but created dissonance for Sandy.

The data from the study confirm Rizzuto's conceptualizations about the nature, origin, and functions of the God-representation. The study concludes that object relations theory provides a psychoanalytic framework for a comprehensive understanding of the image of God in an individual's psychic life. From an object relations perspective, religion is not merely an illusion in the traditional use of the term, but rather is an illusion in the fullest sense of the word, a potentially growthful experience related to creativity and imagination.

NOTES

1. See W. W. Meissner, *Psychoanalysis and Religious Experience* (New Haven, Conn.: Yale University Press, 1984); J. McDargh, *Psychoanalytic Object Relations The-*

ory and the Study of Religion (Lanham, Md.: University Press of America); and A. M. Rizzuto, *The Birth of the Living God* (Chicago: University of Chicago Press, 1979).

2. See O. Kernberg, *Object Relations Theory and Clinical Psychoanalysis* (New York: Aronson, 1976); and J. R. Greenberg and S. A. Mitchell, *Object Relations in Psychoanalytic Theory* (New York: Aronson, 1983).

3. Rizzuto, *Birth of the Living God.*

4. D. W. Winnicott, *Playing and Reality* (New York: Basic Books, 1971), 90.

5. Ibid.

6. Ibid.

7. Rizzuto, *Birth of the Living God.*

8. Ibid.

9. Ibid.

10. P. A. DeWald, *The Psychoanalytic Process* (New York: Basic Books, 1972).

Chapter 10

Religious Behavior in the Psychiatric Institute 500

Michael H. Stone

Despite the burgeoning literature on the topic of borderline conditions and their treatment, the role of religion is rarely mentioned. The literature is instead composed of books and articles devoted to exploratory, supportive, behavioral, group, and other forms of therapy that enjoy a higher academic mortgage within the psychiatric community. The works of Kernberg (1975), Searles (1979), Giovacchini and Boyer (1982), Waldinger and Gunderson (1987), Meissner (1988), Rinsley (1982), Linehan (1987), and Stone and Weissman (1988) are exemplary. The questions of whether religion could or, under certain circumstances, should figure importantly in the treatment of borderline and other severely disturbed patients probably would not have arisen in my mind either, nor would this chapter have been written, had it not been for the long-term follow-up study I conducted, beginning in 1985, of some 550 patients who had been hospitalized at the New York State Psychiatric Institute between 1963 and 1976. My colleagues and I have already published a number of papers on various aspects of this study, which, for reasons of simplicity, and in homage to Tsuang and Winokur's elegant study (1975) of the Iowa–500, I have called the P.I.–500 (Stone, 1987, 1988, 1989a, 1990; Stone, Hurt, and Stone, 1987; Stone, Stone, and Hurt, 1987). Thus far, we have focused on the natural history of this large group of borderline, schizophrenic, schizoaffective and other patients, 95 percent of whom were traced from ten to twenty-five years after they had left the hospital. It became apparent in the course of my follow-up contacts with the patients and their families that a large number of the former patients had found it meaningful at some point during the post-hospital years to join a religious cult, or to become actively involved in a religion toward which they had hitherto been indifferent, or to convert from the religion of their original family to a different religion.

Before we turn our attention to the religious organizations that figure in the lives of the P.I.-500, it will be useful to recount in summary fashion the global outcome results in patients from the major diagnostic groups.

GLOBAL RESULTS

For didactic purposes we may divide the outcomes typical of the various former patients into six categories. "Recovered" signifies clinical recovery, with good function both in social and in occupational life; along with the presence of an adequate intimate life and the absence of symptoms. "Good" refers to those patients whose everyday function is sometimes disturbed with minor symptoms and whose intimate life may be rather meager, but who work well and have a circle of friends. "Fair" designates continuing symptoms of moderate severity, a constricted but adequate social life, and a modest if somewhat spotty work record. Patients were considered "marginal" if they required considerable help from family or outside agencies and if they were largely unable to work or form a sustaining social network. "Incapacitated" meant that extramural life was no longer possible, because of breakdown in all areas of life; the patient was (usually) still in a hospital or other residential facility. The patients who took their own lives are placed in the category of "suicide."

The largest diagnostic group, the borderlines, consisted of 299 patients, of whom 206 met DSM III (1980) criteria for borderline personality disorder and Kernberg (1967) criteria for borderline personality organization. The other 93 patients met Kernberg criteria only. The bulk of the remaining patients were either schizophrenic when first seen (99), schizoaffective (64), manic-depressive (39), or schizophreniform, usually as a result of drug abuse (36).

Whereas borderline patients at two- to five-year follow-up function not much above the level achieved by the schizophrenic patients (Carpenter, Gunderson, and Strauss, 1977), two-thirds of the P.I.–500 borderlines reached the Good or Recovered levels at intervals of ten years or more after hospitalization. In contrast, the schizophrenic patients rarely recovered (8 percent); the majority were either incapacitated (23 percent) or marginal in function (43 percent). The schizoaffective and manic-depressive patients achieved intermediate results: Their most characteristic outcome was fair, although there were sizable groups of patients in all outcome categories. The suicide rate was approximately 10 percent across all diagnostic groups, including the DSM III borderlines (9 percent), except for the schizoaffectives, whose suicide rate thus far has reached 22 percent, and the patients classified as borderline by Kernberg criteria only (2 percent). Because of the large size of the borderline group, I was able to identify several factors whose presence served as predictors of an outcome either better or worse than the average for the whole group. High IQ, artistic/musical talent, high attractiveness in the women, and obsessional personality traits all augured well for the post-hospital life course. The most positive factor was continued membership in Alcoholics Anonymous (for those patients with alcohol-related problems). AA, of course, has many of the characteristics of, and had its origins as, a religious organization. Negative factors included father-daughter incest, antisocial traits, and a history of severe parental brutality.

As for joining a religious cult or converting to a different religion, the impact on outcome is not so easy to assess. AA is a homogeneous organization aimed at treating one particular problem. The patients of the P.I.–500 who turned to religious groups and cults for help started out with a wider spread of functional levels and diagnostic subtypes; of the thirteen who joined AA, all but one were borderline when first evaluated. Furthermore, those who joined religious movements showed considerable diversity in their selection. Some simply moved from one mainstream religion to another (Judaism to Methodist Protestantism), while others made changes of a far more radical sort, moving from mainstream to (as it would be viewed by the family of a child raised in New York state) the exotic— from Catholicism, for example, to Hare Krishna. In the section that follows, I enumerate the various religious groups with which the patients became involved, highlighting those chosen by the borderline as distinct from the schizophrenic and other patients.

THE VARIETY OF RELIGIOUS GROUPS

Of the 550 patients from the original study, I was able to trace 520. A little over 6 percent (thirty-two of the 520) of the patients eventually joined a cult, sect, or other religious group. In this tendency, the major diagnostic categories were evenly distributed. I have outlined these groups in Table 1, indicating the relevant diagnostic partitions and the numbers of patients in each.

Given the relatively small numbers with which we are dealing—thirty-two patients in approximately twenty identifiable groups—it is hard to draw generalizations. One can discern a trend on the part of the borderline patients to gravitate toward both cults and organizations that are less exotic (relative to the patients' origins) and less controlling than the cults adopted by the less well-functioning schizophrenic and other psychotic-level patients. Among the schizophrenics, for example, one each joined Jehovah's Witnesses, the Rosicrucians and Subud (discussed in this chapter). One of the patients who joined Scientology, an extremely defensive and controlling sect, was borderline when first hospitalized but later became schizophrenic (a rare evolution among borderlines) and has been chronically psychotic and dysfunctional over the past nineteen years. Another schizophrenic patient became enmeshed within a satanic cult whose "enemies" were burned in effigy by its members. The borderline patients, in contrast, usually joined religious movements that, however exotic with respect to their families' beliefs, allowed a greater measure of personal freedom than

Table 10.1
Borderline and Other Patients of the P.I.–500 Who Joined Religious Groups and Cults

Religious Group	No. of Borderline Pts. who Joined	No. of Sz & Other Pts.
Born Again Christian	1	1
Buddhism	3	
EkInkar	1	1
Fundamentalist Christian Sects	1	1
Hare Krishna	1	2
Judaism to Protestantism	1	
Maha Baba	1	
Maharishi Mahesh Yogi	1	
Oral Robert's Sect	1	
Scientology	2	
Speaking in Tongues	1	
SIDDHA	1	
Yoga	1	1
(Precise nature unclear)	1	2
(Became a Catholic Monk)	1	
Jehovah's Witness		1
Rosicrucianism		1
Subud		1
(Patient joined an ashram)		2
(Patient joined a Satanic cult)		1

would be permitted a follower of Rev. Moon or L. Ron Hubbard. The woman who lived in the commune of the Maharishi Mahesh Yogi, for example, was able to visit her family whenever she wished and was not asked to turn over all her earnings to the leaders of the commune. Two of the borderline patients joined fairly rigid sects shortly after leaving the hospital, but after a year or two left these groups for more conventional denominations of a still conservative and fundamentalist bent. The transition in one case had been from an evangelical sect practicing glossolalia (speaking in tongues) to a less fervent Baptist group.

Certain groups, such as the Hare Krishna, had appeal over a wide range of personality and diagnostic subtypes, attracting persons of quite contrasting characteristics, each for a highly specific reason. One schizophrenic man, for example, felt alienated from the world of competitively more successful, more socially related people around him. For him, Hare Krishna was appealing because of its Eastern exoticism. Its membership included many other disaffected young people with the same complaints (and the same inability to fit in) as he had. Hare Krishna offered him the profound consolation of belonging, of being like everyone else. But this sect is at the same time vehement in its denunciation of illicit drugs, for which reason one of four former borderline patients was drawn to it: For him, Hare Krishna provided not only camaraderie (a secondary consideration for this man) but, more importantly, a protective circle, hemming him from all sides against what he had come to realize was his self-destructive tendency to abuse drugs. In the era of the P.I.–500, opium, as if to stand Karl Marx on his head, had become the religion of the people. And to complete the irony, the best cure for addiction, to opium or to anything else, was religion, whether in the form of a cult, a major sect, or AA.

In the remarks above I have alluded to a few of the functions religious groups regularly perform. The dynamics underlying religious membership are varied and complex. Some of the former patients immersed themselves in religious groups for one predominant reason; others appeared to require their support for several reasons at once. Certain themes recurred again and again, allowing the motivating forces propelling these thirty-two patients into intense involvement in religion to be analyzed into a number of categories. These include (1) the containment of socially unacceptable impulses; (2) the gratification of impulses (of socially acceptable ones, in the case of excessively repressed persons; of socially unacceptable ones, in the case of poorly socialized persons seeking validation through cults that repudiate conventional society); (3) provision or enhancement of a sense of identity; (4) offering a sense of structure and of purpose; (5) bolstering self-esteem; and (6) the alleviation of despair, the offering of hope, and the reduction of existential malaise (through group support, belief in an afterlife, and so on). Examples of these phenomena are found in the sections that follow.

THE DYNAMICS UNDERLYING CULT AFFILIATION AND CONVERSION

Containment of Unacceptable Impulses; Making a New Life

Many of the patients who joined religious organizations appeared to do so out of a desire to curb impulses that either society in general or their original families considered unacceptable. These patients usually selected highly controlling cults, such as the Hare Krishna or one of the stricter, fundamentalist Christian groups. The borderline patients seemed less likely to affiliate with these groups than did the schizophrenic, though impulsivity was a common problem among the former. The one borderline patient who did join Hare Krishna had lived, after eloping from our hospital unit, as a vagrant, homosexual prostitute and petty thief. After a brief jail sentence, he became a member of the Hare Krishna group. This move helped him gain control over his antisocial impulses. He has not, however, regained self-sufficiency, but rather relies on family support and public assistance.

One of the schizophrenic men joined an unusual and intrusively controlling sect called Subud. This sect practiced a severe asceticism, requiring its initiates to stand naked in a circle, to test whether they could stifle sexual excitement. The patient, ironically, seemed troubled more by an impoverishment of lustful feelings than by an excess, as though he had what Paul spoke of (in Corinthians I) as "the gift of celibacy." Subud allowed him to feel accepted by—even superior to—the other adherents (since he had so little lust to begin with). He no longer had to dwell on the uncomfortable reality that he was in fact a joyless person in whom something regularly present in others was missing.

In some of the patients with antisocial traits, religion not only served to contain impulses hitherto left unchecked but also marked the end of their years-long immersion in delinquency. Provided they lived up to the moral dictates of the cult, they could henceforth consider themselves new persons with a clean slate. One alcoholic borderline man, on the run from the law for years for larceny, speeding violations, and so on, finally joined a Buddhist sect. He also began to attend AA meetings with regularity at the same time. For the past six years he has lived as a "born-again" person, as law-abiding socially and as successful occupationally throughout this time as he had been sociopathic and unsuccessful before. The borderline man who became, literally and figuratively, a born-again Christian had been in less trouble with the law than the preceding patient, but had an equally serious problem with drugs.

The Gratification of Impulses

Religious cults, probably more than the major religions, sometimes function, via their intensely personal approach, as agencies for the sanctioning and reinforcing of impulses that would otherwise be denied gratification. The power of the group, depending on its orientation, will either grant permission to normal impulses that had been kept excessively in check (as from a repressive family), or will grant license for the acting out of antisocial impulses. In both situations, the organization fosters a sense of entitlement—in the one case, of a normal sort, in the other, of a pathological sort. The multiplicity of cults and the fervor of their adherents is in part a testimonial to the need many people feel for this, if one can excuse the oxymoron, externalized superego. But that is the point: Some lack an adequate (internalized) superego, and others have internalized an intolerably harsh set of guidelines, with the common result that both must turn to an extrafamilial group for readjustment.

None of the patients in the P.I.–500 turned to religious organizations for the purpose of rationalizing and justifying antisocial impulses. Even the one woman who briefly joined a satanic cult and who practiced a kind of "witchcraft" did so as a way of expiating her guilt over an incestuous relationship with her father—and not (as is all too common in various parts of the country) for the purpose of harming others.

One of the borderline women had been raised in a severely ascetic environment, her family having preached since she was small the evils of attractiveness and sex. Torn between her loyalty to her parents and her natural yearnings, she broke down and became suicidal after a premarital sexual relationship. Shortly before she left the hospital, she became involved with an ecstatic sect that practiced glossolalia. The sect espoused the notion of joyfulness and rightness in marital sex—a comforting compromise from the position of her family, for whom sex was repugnant under any circumstances. After about two years, she left the sect, married, and joined a more conventional Protestant group, congenial to herself and her husband and not unacceptable to her parents. She has functioned at a high level for the past fifteen years.

Firming up a Sense of Identity

Problems in identity were near universal among the patients of the P.I.–500. Only the seven neurotic patients could be said to have anything approaching a cohesive sense of self. The others, almost all of whom were in their late teens or early twenties, manifested marked confusion in such areas as gender, group allegiance, ethical values, or occupational direction. Many of these problems were only partly resolved when, after a typical stay of twelve or thirteen months on the unit, they re-entered the everyday world. Some of the patients whose parents had been unusually intrusive, imposing their vocational and other desires on their offspring, rejected everything about their background: the good, the bad, and the neutral, repudiating the family's religion in the process. One of the Jewish borderline patients, for example, found solace in the religion of his (Protestant) therapist and is now studying for the ministry. Similarly, one of the beleaguered Protestant borderlines found refuge and a more comfortable and secure sense of identity in a Hindu sect.

Hospitalized patients with fragile identities are often at risk for what Olsson (1983) has called "malevolent surrender" to perverse cults practicing total mind control via brain-washing and other heavy-handed techniques. Only two of the P.I.–500 patients succumbed to the blandishments of the Scientologists; none joined the Moonies. One borderline woman spent several years as a "captive" of a fundamentalist midwestern sect until rescued by her brother. Having been an incest victim, she was burdened with the problems in self-esteem and gender-identity characteristics of this group of women (Stone, 1989b). She felt guilty over her participation in the illicit sexual relations, even though the latter began long before she could have had any choice in the matter. As she grew older, she despised men, but also her own womanhood, as though femaleness condemned her to being taken advantage of over and over again. The fundamentalist sect only confirmed her sense of "badness," although it offered her some hope of expiation. With her brother's help, she later joined a more compassionate denomination, whose membership had a more realistic grasp of who had been the real "sinner" in her family.

Fear of intimacy, while by no means negligible in many of the borderline patients, was intense and pervasive among the schizophrenics. Routinely, the schizophrenic men misread their interpersonal anxieties with women as proof of being homosexual. Others held concretistic notions about masturbation as somehow "weakening" their manhood—ideas we now regard as quaint, but that exercised a malignant dominion over these schizophrenic men even as late as the 1960s. These were the patients who, like the man who joined Subud, gravitated toward the ascetic Eastern cults, where they could exchange the humiliating "couldn't"—vis-à-vis their inadequate sexual prowess—to a pride-engendering "shouldn't." This was true of the two schizophrenic men who became devotees of Hare Krishna. Analogously, the one borderline man who became a monk was homosexual and had never been able to accept his sexual orientation. Instead, he found consolation and a better sense of identity (as a man doing God's work) in a monastery where, in addition, his avoidance of women needed no further explanation. However, this man's consolation was not complete even within the monastery. There, he had still the need to confront the Pauline denunciations of homosexuality, as in Romans 1:24–27 and 1 Corinthians 6:9–10. But the benefits of monastic life far outweighed the drawbacks for this man, who has continued to do well for the past seventeen years.

Providing Structure and a Sense of Purpose

In the same way a religious organization might envelop a once delinquent man within a carapace of moral rectitude, its exterior framework compensating for his inner deficiency, religion could also provide a supporting exoskeleton for other borderline patients whose inner structure, although not lacking as to social mores, was otherwise grossly undeveloped.

Few borderline patients demonstrate adequate self-discipline; one might almost say that a lack of this attribute goes toward defining someone as borderline. One outward manifestation is the tendency to be frantic when alone, a symptom that varies inversely with one's ability to contain this anxiety through hobbies, sports, reading, and other sublimatory activities. Manic-depressive and borderline patients both tend, owing to the abrupt shifts in their mood, to leave various tasks and pursuits short of completion; female patients with these disorders frequently have severe premenstrual tension, which also has the effect of interrupting projects recently undertaken.

Religious groups, especially the tightly knit communities in which everyone knows everyone else, provide structure through programmed activities and strictly observed rituals that are performed each day at the same time. For patients who struggled with feelings of anomie, the pointlessness of existence and the like, the cults and similar religious groups gave a sense of purpose. Often, this sense of purpose arose out of group activities that helped sustain the group itself (through farming, carpentry, and so on) or that performed useful services within some neighboring community. Gratifying activities of this sort were especially rewarding for the many borderline and schizophrenic former patients who did not find a sense of purpose through the more conventional channels of marriage and children. In the P.I.–500, for example, the borderline women married only about half as often as did women in the general population; the men married only a fourth as often. The marriage rate in the schizophrenics was much lower than even these figures. One of the schizophrenic women who had never married suffered a recrudescence of her psychosis shortly after leaving our unit. Afterward, she was given lodging in a church near where she was living. For the past twelve years, she has made the church her life, performing various chores for the sacristan in return for bed and board. The church has given her everything: structure, purpose, identity, self-esteem, hope, and the containment of her once overwhelming anxieties. The two most successful of the 97 traced schizophrenic patients both found structure and purpose in a religious cult. Both are married businessmen with several children. Both spent years "pulling themselves together" in communes, eventually leaving them as they became more capable of independent life.

Enhancement of Self-Esteem

The patients of the P.I.–500 came for the most part from middle- to upper middle-class families. The presence of a severe emotional disorder will often, in and of itself, undermine self-esteem. This will be all the more true when one of the inciting causes of the illness was humiliation or other abusive behavior on the part of the parents. Another powerful detractor from one's self of self-worth, even in the absence of parental cruelty, is the spectacle of unusual success in the remaining members of the family. A schizophrenic patient capable only of intermittent work at a low level of complexity will tend to feel as less painful the gap in work potential between himself and, say, his father, if the latter runs a small shop, whose maintenance tasks are mostly within the abilities of his son. The same schizophrenic man, comparing himself with a father or mother who is a highly respected professional or the leader of some large enterprise, cannot help but feel belittled, even if his parents have been models of sensitivity and circumspection. Men are more burdened with expectations of achieving self-sufficiency in the work sphere than are women in Western culture, and are proportionally more "at risk" if they fail to measure up. A generation of women's liberation has not leveled the balance in this domain. This factor may account for some of the heightened risk for completed suicide in schizophrenic males from affluent families. In the P.I.–500, I noted the "paradox" that the higher the IQ and social status of a schizophrenic male, the higher was his suicide risk, a phenomenon that is not so paradoxical in the light of the foregoing remarks. Completed suicide occurs about three times as often in white males as in females in our culture during the (currently) vulnerable third decade of life (Solomon and Murphy, 1984). Religious organizations appeared to have played a significant role in reducing the suicide risk, and, more importantly, in improving the quality of life and in enhancing self-esteem for many of the patients who joined these organizations. Of the thirty-two patients mentioned in Table 10.1, none of the eighteen borderlines has committed suicide; only one of the psychotic-level patients has died by his own hand (the patient who had once been a member of Subud).

One of the borderline women has spent the last fifteen years in India as a member of SIDDHA-Foundation commune, deriving great satisfaction from her charitable work. I do not know whether she has converted form the Judaism of her original family; she does, however, live within the framework of a Hindu religious organization.

Hope and the Alleviation of Despair and Existential Malaise

One could fairly make the claim that all of the patients of the P.I.–500 who joined cults suffered from chronic feelings of hopelessness. This despair, some-times generalized and "existential," while in other cases, arising out of more specific sources, was often the propelling force behind their decision to seek out these groups.

A schizophrenic man in his late twenties eventually joined a Buddhist sect five or six years after leaving the hospital. He was unable to get a foothold anywhere in life; work, friendship, romantic attachments all seemed to elude him. He felt alone and without purpose. His affiliation to the Buddhist sect alleviated this existential despair, giving him a renewed sense of belonging such as he had not experienced since leaving his original family.

A borderline woman, after leaving the hospital, lived with a man for three years and had a child by him. They then drifted apart. She had both to support herself and care for her daughter. In the immediate aftermath of the breakup, she felt devastated. A friend suggested she become a member of a Hindu sect whose leader ran a nearby commune. For the next two years, she lived with this group and adopted the religion. The latter she has retained, even though in the recent years she has become self-supporting and lives with her child in a different city.

Two of the former patients, one a borderline woman and the other a schizo-phrenic man, each joined a cult that emphasized reincarnation. The woman did so in response to the despair she felt following three suicides in close family members. The male patient joined this cult shortly after his miraculous (and the word is not hyperbolic here) rescue from a suicide attempt in which he was nearly dead from trying to hang himself.

One of the incest victims, who appeared schizoaffective when first on the unit but who probably suffered from a post-traumatic stress disorder in response to the molestation, left the hospital still in a demoralized state. She found renewed hope in a religious cult in which she remained for some years. Currently (fifteen years after she came to our unit) she functions at a high level, having completed a graduate course and having recently become engaged.

A schizophrenic adolescent was still severely handicapped when he left the hospital. For several years, he lost touch with his family and lived as a vagrant, having by this time abandoned hope of finding even menial temporary jobs let alone any form of sustained work or social contacts. A member of the Rosicrucian sect, whom he chanced to meet, invited him to join that organization. Throughout his twenties he found friendship, solace, and hope in this group, became largely asymptomatic (he had been quite delusional earlier), and later reunited with his family. Over the last twelve years he has held an executive position, married, and helped raise three children. Having come to regard the Rosicrucian beliefs as rather eccentric, he now becomes somewhat alarmed whenever his thoughts turn toward this sect. He suspects that these thoughts are a sign that some family matter is troubling him more than he can admit, and he will right away schedule some sessions with his psychiatrist in order to get to the bottom of the problem.

Hopelessness for some of the patients was, as in several of the above-mentioned vignettes, the residue of ruined ambition, as when it became clear that one's dreams of success would never be realized. By "success," one usually meant a prestigious job, a fully realized talent, finding a mate who was stunning or rich, and so on. These patients were dealing, in other words, with "narcissistic" blows that permeated their beings, despite their wide circles of friends. For many others, hopelessness stemmed from finding themselves utterly alone and unable to make friends. Among those who found hope again through religion, it was often to a small cult that they turned—one led by a charismatic leader who knew each of the followers personally. Or, in a related fashion, these patients turned to larger groups whose leaders nevertheless instilled in each new adherent a sense of personal, vivid connection to the deity. Those who turned to Christian sects, for example, came to feel themselves warmly encircled by Jesus. They were not alone. This was demonstrated to me most poignantly by one patient whose real father had abandoned his family, leaving her and her brothers devastated until they reconstituted a sense of belongingness through Jesus. Christ, in other words, although invisible and impalpable, became far more real and, in a way, touchable, more sustaining and comforting than their real father had ever been, even before he deserted them.

AFTERWORD

In the preceding remarks, I have concentrated on the various benefits the religious groups were able to confer on many of the former patients who joined them. The reader must keep in mind that the cults, sects, and other religious groups mentioned here were those sought by this particular population of patients. I was not writing about the entire spectrum of such collectives which, as one would note from Halperin's book (1983), include destructive as well as con-

structive communities. There are, after all, criminal cults that simply drape
themselves in the mantle of religion by way of justifying atrocities. One recalls
the satanic cult headed by Charles Manson (Emmons, 1986). The psychopath
cum healer Jim Jones, for whose followers the kingdom of heaven was ushered
in prematurely by cyanide Kool-Aid, offered an even more grisly example (Reston, 1981). The spectrum also includes brainwashing cults that lure with their
blandishments the unstable and the weak, lock them in a mental vise, and exploit
them as fodder for the grandiosity and enrichment of the leaders. Fortunately,
the patients of the P.I.–500 were, with few exceptions, not drawn into spiritual
black holes of this sort. One of the borderline women, as mentioned, was
extricated form a financially exploitative cult by her brother.

It would not surprise me to learn that some of the cults contain in their
membership more than their share of fragile persons, some of whom we might
diagnose as borderline, schizophrenic, and so on. But only some of these cults
could be said to exert negative influences; the majority might have more in
common with the religious groups alluded to above, which served well in the
sustaining, esteem-enhancing and other functions I have outlined.

Most of the therapeutic effects wrought by the religious groups could, at least
in principle, have been achieved by other means. Much would depend on community resources, cultural and other factors in the patients. If we were to add
the patients who joined AA, Nar-anon, and political (as opposed to religious)
communes to the thirty-two who joined cults, we would be left with some 80
percent of the P.I.–500 who did not use these resources. Yet many recovered,
especially among the borderlines. Almost all of the borderlines were impulsive,
and lacked what Foon (1987) calls an "inner locus of control." For some, the
religious organization compensated by providing an external locus of control.
For the rest, this need was fulfilled by group therapy, shared and supervised
living arrangements, day hospitals, and the like. What I believe is a unique
power of religion—especially in the form of a charismatic cult led by a "benevolent despot"—is the transformation of severely antisocial persons into law-
abiding and community-minded citizens. To be sure, even religion has its limits.
Mengele (to say nothing of Hitler), Ted Bundy, and Ian Brady (the English
child-torturer) are most likely beyond redemption (Stone, 1989c). Two of the
borderline males in my study each murdered three people, in one case with
cruelty and premeditation. One is still in jail (eighteen years after his crime);
the premeditated killer escaped punishment, having been under-age when he set
fire to a neighbor's house. These were the only two (though there were five
other murderers in my study) whom I consider beyond resocialization. But
retreating from these extremes, we encounter people like those in former President Nixon's inner circle who became, after their indictment, born-again Christians, and who appear to have put their arrogance and exploitativeness behind
them. The same evolution could be observed in the life of Malcolm X, who was
in trouble as an adolescent for breaking and entering houses, stealing, and so
on, but who, after his conversion to Islam, became a man of great integrity and

rectitude. God is bigger than the biggest man, so the same pompous or contemptuous man who would "make mincemeat" of any therapist's efforts might still be chastened by a religious experience. In the P.I.–500, the alcoholic petty thief became, literally, a new man after embracing Buddhism. But his was a chance encounter, brought about through a girlfriend. No one could have "prescribed" religious conversion for this man, even though probably nothing else would have worked. And what kind of "therapy," short of religious conversion, could ever convince a nine-year-old boy pocketing $500 a week selling crack that honesty is a better policy or that earning $50 a week helping out in a store is a much better way for a young person to work?

These last comments raise a related issue concerning mental structures: specifically, internalized objects. As with conventional psychotherapies, religion has an easier time replacing overly harsh internalized objects (that is, abusively punitive parents whom their child transforms into a crushingly severe superego) than firming up to appropriate social standards a conscience that was undeveloped to the point of amorality and callousness. Older people who have never had proper role models with whom to identify when they were children are notoriously unenthusiastic about completing this unfinished business as adults. Still, some of the patients of the P.I.–500 were able, belatedly, to negotiate this step through the help of religious sects whose leaders served as powerful father-figures and mother-figures with whom to identify.

The possibility of an inverse relationship between religion and suicide needs further study. In the P.I.–500, as mentioned above, none of the borderlines who joined a cult has committed suicide. But the numbers do not reach statistical significance. To test whether such a trend is real and not just apparent would require an even larger sample in combination with mine. Such samples are not as yet available. Whatever the relationship, it is probably not a simple one. Although the Catholic Church condemns suicide, for example, there is a high suicide rate in some Catholic countries (Hungary) and a low rate in others (Italy). However, in their literature review, Gartner, Larson, and Allen (forthcoming) found a negative relationship between religious commitment and suicide.

Diekstra and Moritz (1987) have suggested that the alarming increase in the suicide rate among young Europeans and Americans (especially males in the fifteen to thirty age group) over the last twenty years may reflect a number of destabilizing factors in society: the heightened incidence of divorce and family dislocation, a shrinking economic frontier, the continuing drug abuse epidemic, and the weakening hold of organized religion. As an antidote to these social ills, religion may become increasingly important in the coming years: It is *there* for everyone, including young persons who have lost family, work, and their accustomed community.

Given the social impoverishment in the lives of many of our schizophrenic patients, the wonder is that the suicide rate in the P.I.–500 (10 percent in this group) was not higher. For them, the existence of an appealing support group— one that was not time-limited, that might be available life-long if necessary—

often made the difference between life and death. In some countries, the psychiatric centers themselves offer excellent rehabilitative and custodial services, almost obviating the need for facilities unconnected with psychiatry. Some examples are: in Pakistan, the Fountain House in Lahore; in Australia, the state-run hospital in Adelaide; and in Switzerland, the centers in Berne and in Zürich run by Drs. Ciompi and Angst, respectively. There is little in our country that equals these facilities. But certain religious organizations, both of the major denominations and the smaller cults, create for the mentally ill an environment of purposefulness and self-respect. We saw this with the schizophrenic woman who for years has lived in dignified symbiosis with her church. Religion succeeds better than many of our other institutions in giving the disabled what Freud summed as life's two essential ingredients: love and work.

Afterword

Ana-Maria Rizzuto

The task of reflecting on the explorations of old lands with new instruments for surveillance and mapping requires the capacity to cast one's view afar to encompass the past, present, and future unveiling of hitherto unknown landscapes. Finn suggests in his Introduction that a new instrument has been found to explore psychoanalytically the territory of religious experience: "The emergence of the importance of early relationships articulated by the family of object relations theories opened a door through which religious life can again center psychoanalytic discussion" (p. vii).

The new instrument has great potential to clarify and refine the understanding of many issues of human relatedness and their implications for the significance of religious experiences, individually and collectively, as a particular instance of the constant human search for meaningful relations with human and symbolic objects, including the universe conceived as a living reality.

Object relation theories have advantages and limitations in carrying out the task of making sense of the religious experiences of humankind. The specific and irreplaceable advantage of psychoanalytic object relations study of religious experiences is its capacity to provide exquisitely detailed descriptions of subjective perceptions and feelings about the divine object of belief. Such descriptions provide cumulative data that may permit the finding of general patterns in very diverse subjective and external religious behaviors. In *The Sociology of Religion*, Max Weber affirmed the significance of understanding subjective experience:

The external courses of religious behavior are so diverse that an understanding of this behavior can only be achieved from the viewpoint of the subjective experiences, ideas, and purposes of the individual concerned—in short, from the viewpoint of the religious behavior's meaning. (p. 1)

Religion, however, as a personal experience or as a social reality of organized beliefs, institutions, and systems of social organization extends far beyond personal involvement with or rejection of a divine being. It calls for intelligent questioning of perceived reality. It demands integration into powerful social structures found at the moment that early object relations are being established. Religious ceremonies at birth mark a new infant as the member of the parental group, sometimes by an indelible bodily imprint as in circumcision. Such collective imprinting and relatedness go far beyond the boundaries of individual object relations. The careful researcher endeavors to keep in mind these broader types of relations to tease them out of the more private components of object relatedness. There is a methodological need to refrain from extending to these broader realities findings that apply only to individual personal relations. For these reasons, the student of object relations must restrain his conclusions to the boundaries of the field, that is, the subjective experiences of individual persons with their objects of belief. Religion, with all its social, anthropological, cultural, mythological, philosophical, theological, artistic, and political implications, extends far beyond the realm of object relations to encompass the entirety of the human mind and experience. In my opinion, the object relations theorist must refrain from using the word "religion" as a noun. The adjective "religious," as applied by a person to qualify as experience of relatedness, best describes the object relations theorist's field of specific competence.

The next issue is philosophical: Is there an apologetic stance in those who have found militant comfort in the insights provided by the study of religious experiences under the light of object relations theories? Do they have the right to be advocates of religion? Finn answers: "It would be disingenuous not to say that there is an underlying apologetic for at least the potentially adaptive role of religion" (p. viii).

Beit-Hallahmi makes a distinction between the psychology of religion and religious psychology. The psychology of religion explains the religious phenomenon. Religious psychology defends religious phenomena and religion itself as legitimate realities, therefore "promoting religion through the adaptation and use of psychological concepts" (p. 120). To Beit-Hallahmi, this is an inexcusable apologetic. He believes that those who have taken refuge in the object relation theories oppose the classical analytic approach of understanding belief in a divinity as nothing but a projection and an illusion and indulge in theoretical and clinical sympathy with the belief in religious realities and with the sentiments of religious believers. He denounces them: "In many cases, one cannot ignore the faint, sweet aroma of apologetics that hangs over the writings, and in most of those, the authors do not hide their strong commitment to religion" (p. 121).

If there is such a "sweet aroma," it can be detected in some of the contributions to this volume, perhaps not so much in the intentions of the writers as in the lapses in the precision of their language. For example: "The generally accepting God can be distorted, in the narcissistic or manic patient, into an omnipotent God with whom the youngster identifies in contempt of his or her parents" (Banschick, p. 76).

One gets the impression that there exists a real God who is, in fact, "accepting" and whose characteristics are "distorted" by the abnormal perception of the patient's pathological mind. Such language has left the realm of psychology to make a reference to a reality beyond it. The author does not intend to say it, but the slipping of his language reveals an implicit acceptance of a God out there.

I agree with Beit-Hallahmi that the psychology and the psychoanalysis of religion are natural disciplines incapable of going beyond their phenomenological level of discourse. All they affirm or negate refers exclusively to psychological realities, be it God, people, or fictive beings. He is right in saying that a universal yearning for a divine being does not prove that it exists. However, based on the same epistemological premises, psychology and psychoanalysis have neither the authority nor the competence to say that it does not exist. The realm of reality in which a divine being may exist rests beyond the scope of their field of competence and their level of discourse. They must abstain from affirmation and negation. Freud's atheistic approach is as unjustified as the "sweet aroma" of religious apologists. Both the psychologist of religion and the psychoanalyst, as psychological experts, must remain agnostics because they do not have the competence to know.

Beit-Hallahmi is close to the dangerous edge of psychological discourse when, in commenting on my conclusion that "God, psychologically speaking, is an illusory transitional object," comments: "If all you can say is that 'God' is a 'transitional object,' religious faith is in trouble, because that is not what the believers want and say' (p. 127).

I think Beit-Hallahmi is in trouble! He has forgotten that we can and must speak nothing but psychological language. It is not our task to say what God is or to declare that God is not at all. He confuses the existence of God as an actual being with the psychological process of affirming that something exists or that something is one way and not another. The psychological function of affirming is related to other psychological ego functions such as reality testing, belief, and conviction. These three aspects of psychic life are the least known of our disciplines. We have not as yet described the psychological conditions for any belief or conviction. Freud never wrote about it. Empirically, however, he believed psychoanalysis to be based on solid ground when, in reaching conclusions about a particular patient, he could count on the patient's sense of conviction. He affirmed in his work *Constructions in Analysis* (1937):

Quite often we do not succeed in bringing the patient to recollect what has been repressed. Instead of that, if the analysis is carried out correctly, we produce in him an assured conviction of the truth of the construction which achieves the same therapeutic result as a recaptured memory. The problem of what the circumstances are in which this occurs and of how it is possible that what appears to be an incomplete substitute should nevertheless produce a complete result—all of this is a matter for later inquiry. (p. 266)

The "later inquiry" should be an imperative *now* for those seriously interested in an empirical psychology of religion. It may well be that similar psychological conditions occur spontaneously to give "an assured conviction of the truth of the construction" to the religious psychic realities of a person. I have given some suggestions along these lines in my book (1979). The findings of the inquiry would reveal the psychodynamic and object-related conditions for religious conviction about the existence of a divinity; it would say nothing about the divinity itself. And believers would not be in trouble. True believers do not care what psychologists and psychoanalysts think about their beliefs for the very simple reason that belief and conviction are not free psychological actions. They are overdetermined by myriad psychodynamic processes far beyond our conscious control.

I agree with Beit-Hallahmi that projection and illusion are essential components of any religious object. They are, however, not sufficient. Projection is a psychic mechanism and can only project the representations it finds. The question is how the projected representation, or the transitional object, or the illusion have been formed. Only gravely psychotic people have God-representations that resemble with certain closeness people in their lives. Most God-representations are very complex constructions, the constructions of a living mind, as the transitional object is. To fully understand religious beliefs, projections, illusions, transitional objects concepts are not enough. What is needed is a detailed and well-documented theory of the process of transformation of representations at the service of the psychic life of the individual. To my knowledge, this is the most significant theoretical task psychologists and psychoanalysts must undertake if they intend to advance their knowledge of the fascinating process of human belief.

Beit-Hallahmi is right in reminding us of Freud's comments about the restriction of freedom of thought implicit in religious beliefs, and of Melanie Klein's stern warnings about the damage that the idea of God inflicts on the reality sense, and on the need to tame the feeling of omnipotence. These are real dangers present in any religious belief that postulates an omniscient and omnipotent God. Psychic freedom in this respect requires that the therapist help the patient examine all beliefs with equal honesty. Religion and God should not be an exception. I agree with Beit-Hallahmi that "sympathy for the believer should be separated from sympathy for [faith of the believer]" (p. 126). There are two reasons to abstain from "sympathy for the faith." The first and most important is that, like the rest of psychic life, faith is always ambivalent and the God-representation partakes its share of ambivalence. To sympathize with what is conscious at a particular moment means to foreclose the possibility of exploring other components. The second is that the therapeutic relation requires absolute abstinence and any sympathy for particular contents creates unmanageable collusions and may even qualify as a seduction (Hoffer, 1985). Religion has no privileges in the therapeutic situation. It only requires the full respect bestowed on any other disclosures from the patient and the commitment to a careful exploration of all issues involved.

Finally, I want to say a word about religious psychology. If by religious psychology is meant a discipline at the service of "defending religious beliefs," I have no use for it. Religious beliefs need no defense. They exist whether we like it or not. We have no power to bring them to existence or to make them disappear. If by religious psychology we mean a discipline that documents and correlates the connections between religious phenomena and other aspects of psychic life, it seems to me to be a perfectly legitimate enterprise, as long as it does not become a means for "scientific" apologetics, or, even worse, an advertisement for the "goodness" of religion. Such a consumer-society approach to belief is one more trivialization of the human experience typical of our market mentality.

Melanie Klein has provided two interesting topics for such studies. Is it true that believers in an omnipresent God have less freedom of thought than non-believers? The question is valid and it is answerable. We need people to study it and decide whether Klein was objectively correct or simply prejudiced against God. Her assertion about the narcissistic enhancement of pathological grandiosity provided by the belief in an omnipotent God is another excellent subject for a research project. Are believers more grandiose and narcissistically fixated than non-believers? Or if we select Freud, are believers more childish, clinging, and dependent than "mature" non-believers? The questions are waiting for laborers who care to answer them.

Having discussed the philosophical and methodological issues involved with the volume, I proceed now to discuss the individual chapters. They seem to fall naturally into four categories: four chapters focus on representations; two chapters describe the Buddhist's experience; one chapter explores the psychodynamics of the particular psychic act of forgiveness; and two chapters attend to the function of religion in specific pathological situations.

In his chapter, "The Deep Structure of Religious Representations" McDargh introduces the notion of "deep structure":

Where we hope to build upon Rizzuto's contribution is in suggesting a more nuanced account of what we might term "deep structure" of a religious representation, specifically, its roots in aspects of self-experience that are prelinguistic—what Eugene Gendin was pointing to with his language of feeling or "felt sense" and what Christopher Bollas implies with his phrase, "unthought known." (p. 2)

McDargh does not give a definition of what he means by "deep structure," a phrase that has Chomskian echoes. He connects it with the Jamesian "dimension of feeling,'' the ''experience of aliveness,'' and with Gendlin's '' 'felt sense' of how it is with us at any given time'' that we live our lives in the context of our bodily ways. He concludes after discussing Milner's treatment of Susan with a quotation from Christopher Bollas about the function of the ''transformational object'' as: ''an identification that emerges from symbiotic relating, where the first object is 'known' not so much by putting it into object representation, but as a recurrent experience of being—a more existential as opposed to a representational knowing'' (p. 12).

I agree with McDargh's emphasis on the great significance of our bodies, the centrally organizing function of affect and the undeniable connection between our capacity to ''know'' existentially, in the flesh of the other and of our own, and our capacity to feel alive in a context of meaning, religious or otherwise.

I object, however, to the lack of parsimony encountered in the introduction of new terms to say what has already been said in the psychoanalytic literature. If we truly mean to establish a meaningful discourse between psychoanalysis and the study of religion, we must respect any terminology that is capable of saying what we want to say. Let me ask a few questions to make the point. Is a ''deep structure,'' the unconscious, a part of the unconscious body ego, a complex organization of early life experiences memorial processes? Or is it none of the above? And if not, what is it? It seems to me that there is no need to create new words that add what psychoanalysts call a ''mystical'' flavor to our discourse. McDargh could have remained consistent with psychoanalytic theory by conveying the same concept with known words.

In my book, *The Birth of the Living God*, I went to great pains to provide a comprehensive psychoanalytic theory of object representations, in which I describe explicitly what I think McDargh calls ''deep structure'':

Memories of objects are of critical importance in human life because the child has all his needs and wishes in the hands of the mothering person. Those multiple exchanges leave memories that are visceral, . . . propioceptive, sensorimotor, eidetic, iconic, and (later on) conceptual. . . . Accordingly, the memories of a given object follow a developmental line from visceral to conceptual. It may be impossible to evoke some of these memories by conscious recall, although they may persist in bodily attitudes, postures, habits, and patterns of behavior that unconsciously perpetuate the experiences with the object. (p. 76)

To separate feeling, sense of one's self, and subjective experience from this representational matrix is an impossible task. They come together, and they are but complementary aspects of each other. Only scientific dissection may tease them apart, while it is never possible in the concrete psychic experience. I say in the book:

The consequence of this process [representational memory] is that any single corner of our bodies, any of our organs, any of our most hidden wishes or fantasies, any of our impulses, any of our encounters with any aspect of reality is object-related. . . . We have never experienced life out of the context of objects. (76–77)

To be oneself, therefore, is to be the history of our encounters with our objects. If we cannot retrieve consciously from the experience any other memory than a sense of being that is colored with a particular affective quality, it does not mean that we are not dealing with representational processes. It means that the processes are unconsciously registered and presently not accessible to conscious recall.

It seems to me that the difficulty rests in the persistence of a psychology of representation within the framework of psychoanalysis that belongs to cognitive schools incapable of conceiving the notion of affect-laden unconscious representations. In *The Shadow of the Object* Bollas seems to fall into this difficulty when he says: "The first object is 'known' not so much by putting it into an object representation, but as a recurrent experience of being—a more existential as opposed to representational knowing" (p. 14).

I agree with Bollas that the mode of remembering the first object is an existential mode of being, but I disagree that such a mode is not representational. The representations are visceral, propioceptive, sensorimotor, and it is their physiological, affective, self-experiential characteristics that provide the subjective existential quality for the individual. This is the bedrock of human experience. To say otherwise is to deny the representational significance of the body, which Freud called the body ego.

Such subjective representational reality seems best illustrated in the example presented by McDargh.

These new body sensations begin to open up for Susan a sense of interiority and the beginning of a sense that she might have a valuable inner experience that is in some relationship with an outside world. . . . Susan [feels she is] inhabiting her body for the first time as well. (p. 13)

I claim that such experiences could not have been possible if her body representations had not registered in early infancy a modicum of maternal care that could now be used for subjective conscious self-discovery, when reawakened by actual maternal figures.

These preverbal experiences are, as McDargh states, the foundation of our mode of being, our search for transformational objects, that is, objects that change us for the better. He is right, I think, in considering them as the foundation of the inclination to search for a divine object. However, their counterpart must be stated. Distressing experiences at this early time may prompt a person to avoid people and themselves (as happened with Milner's patient Susan). For some people, the only transformation an object seems to promise is further suffering, destructiveness, humiliation. The search for the transformational object requires the complementary concept of the avoidance of the dangerous object. To believe that religious faith deals only with the search for the transformational object is to underestimate the complexities of the human search and perhaps to do a little bit of apologetical work for the "goodness" of religion.

The comments presented above apply to Shafranske's chapter, "God-Representation as the Transformational Object." he says that his chapter

presents an understanding of God-representations as the expression of an individual's
desire for or acknowledgment of psychological, spiritual, or physical transformation. . . .
It is proposed that contained within religious faith and within the background of all God-
representations lies the transformational object. (p. 57)

I must concede that in a large number of religious experiences, the people who are going through them are in search of a process of transformation. When that is the case, I agree with Shafranske that the ultimate source of search must be indelible moments of transformation in early infancy, when the early mother was the transformational object.

Some clarifications are, however, in order. I cannot agree with the understanding of the God-representation "as the expression of an individual's desire." I have shown in my book that representational processes and concrete representations are immensely complex processes of an essential unconscious nature. Our conscious awareness of some of them follows regular psychic laws that we do not control. The representation, by definition, cannot be an expression of anything. Rather, the opposite is true. A religious desire reveals the search for an object whose representation promises transformations that are deemed necessary. This clarification is essential because many God-representations harbor in their traits promises of great psychic danger: annihilation, invasion, overpowering, humiliation, punishment, rejection, hatred. They are not usable as objects of self-syntonic transformation.

Shafranske's central thesis is that the "God-representational process is rooted in the earliest period of an individual's ontogenesis is and is based not only on its function as a transitional object but is also related to the infant's experience of what Bollas has termed the transformational object" (p. 62).

My response is yes and no. Yes, this conceptualization is apt for those whose transitional object period and later elaborations and transformations of the God-representation permitted them to form and use unconsciously the representation of a God capable of transforming their inner states. An individual who has such representation reveals, without knowing it, the history of his earliest experiences, during moments of helpful transformation. But no, for so many people who, due either to very bad early experiences or derailments at any other level of human relatedness, have come to form unconsciously a representation of God that is not suitable to bring about any desirable transformation and might or must be avoided. This second individual keeps us in the dark. We cannot tell whether or not he had the experience of a helpful transformational object. All we can say is that he has no desire now to be involved with God. The research task ahead is to determine what conditions in the past history of the individual and what circumstances in his present situation create the opportunity for the search of a transformational experience with God, as opposed, let us say, to the avoidance of God.

Shafranske proves himself an example of what Beit-Hallahmi calls "subtle apologetics." It is, in my opinion, incorrect to apply the notion of the transformational object to religion in general. It is correct and useful to conceptualize the connection between religious (notice my use of the adjective) search for a God that can effect inner change and the notion of the transformational object. It has heuristic value for the understanding of some religious experiences. Theoretically, it seems impossible to say that it applies to all religious experiences. Only detailed empirical studies may help us discover to what cases it applies and to what situations it does not.

I do not see why we have to restrict the notion of the transformational object to its earliest source. It seems to me that, like any other object, it must change the type of function it performs according to the progressive transformation of the subject itself. Once the function of the transformational object has been accomplished, it leaves an open road for many other types of transformational objects at any time in life. It would be interesting to explore whether we can describe types of transformational objects for each developmental age.

The case presented illustrates not so much the function of the transformational object as its failure. Such failure seems to be the source of all addictive behaviors, even if the addiction is to God. The failure is shown in the absence of results: The transformational object of the young man failed to transform him, to help him move to the next stage in search of the next transformation. I believe that many religious behaviors reveal a similar failure, an addictive use of God without inner change. I would like to suggest that we undertake empirical studies to ascertain the conditions of the object (the God-representation) and the subject in the religious experience that permit a true moment of transformation. In infancy we see it dramatically: The baby changes in front of our eyes and moves to the next stage, the transitional space signaling oncoming self-awareness. What could have been the limitations of this young man's God-representation or, for that matter, of the objects of his early past, that he could not use his God except as an addiction?

Banschick discusses in his chapter, "God-Representations in Adolescence," what he calls the functional quality of the adolescent representation of God. He suggests that the "experience of God can provide a sense of order and consistency in a world that appears hopelessly arbitrary and futile." Furthermore, he affirms that "in healthier young people, the God experience may actually serve as a creative facilitation of the developmental process."

I do not know what Banschick means by God experience. I wish he had given some definition or description of the connotations of the words. On page 75 he says that it "represents the experience a person has of either himself or herself or of the world at large." On page 76 he considers the God experience a transitional phenomenon, which can be "extremely functional in the developing person" (p. 76). He concludes on page 83: "Thus God is never really experienced and never really lost, which gives Him a unique status among internalized objects.''

These words seem contradictory to me. It is not that I disagree that the adolescent's complex dealings with whatever God he or she has are very significant at that moment of development. It is that we need conceptual clarity. What is a God experience? A type of religious experience according to William James? A subjective experiencing of oneself that needs not be religious? A transitional phenomenon without a concrete object representation? The clarification is essential because religious people, adolescents among others, have a religious way of experiencing something they frequently call God, and what they feel at the time, they call religious. If we want to talk about experiencing God, we must declare what we mean and be specific about distinguishing ''experiencing'' God from thinking about him, philosophically or religiously. We must also separate ''experiencing'' from the complex defensive maneuvers of avoiding, suppressing, repressing, or splitting an ego-dystonic representation of God.

I agree that the ''experience'' of God, when it happens, is a significant event in adolescence. It is age-appropriate, as we know from observing normal developing young people. They enter adolescence with a period of normal doubts about whatever they have learned about religion, and by the close of the period, a good number have decided whether to believe in God or not. This is a necessary psychological task indicating that, as Blos (1979) has shown, the adolescent is completing the oedipal resolution by separating from the internal representation of the object. God, as a representation, partakes of the time-specific transformations of the internal objects.

Banschick's observations about prayer in adolescence are very interesting. His data indicate that ''more than half the hospitalized adolescents with whom I had contact pray quietly at night in order to self-soothe'' (p. 77). The figures are interesting and suggest another excellent area for formal, systematic research, because I am inclined to doubt that soothing oneself is the only motive for the adolescent's prayer. Prayers have always been used not only for self-consolation but also to placate, to propitiate, to magically influence the divinity or to extract from it what one deems indispensable for oneself. The type of prayer reveals the type of psychic function and the type of object relatedness of the supplicant. We need to know the content of prayer in the context of the life circumstances of a person before we can conclude what psychic function it provides.

Banschick presents the painful history of an adolescent who had been subjected to massive psychic and physical trauma in the name of God. The case illustrates that such weighty and persistent injury inflicted by the parents leaves no psychic room for a transformation of the God and the self-representations. God is an existing sadist like his parents. John is a satanist, and, at heart, believes himself to be a devil of sorts. This case illustrates that when pathology is so massive, the object representations are not available for psychic transformation. God and the sense of self are undisguised and enlarged transpositions of malevolent, sadomasochistic characters and relationships to the larger realm of belief. The encomiastic use of his satanic poetry to make sense of himself was a respectful and most valuable way of meeting him where he found himself to be, where he had always been.

I question if it is true that his God-representation changed. The evidence is not there. I would not be surprised if the gains of the treatment were mostly the result of his concrete relationship with the therapist and the staff and his separation from his parents. The effort needed to transform the object representations stemming from such sadistic relationships goes far beyond what can be accomplished in a year of treatment. The psychic defenses cannot and should not permit it because the risk of annihilation is too great.

The Saures, in Chapter 9, have carried out an ingenious research project by taking advantage of the insights of analyzed individuals to examine ''some of Rizzuto's formulations about the developmental and later use of the God-representation in an individual's life'' (p. 130). They selected seven propositions from my book, *The Birth of the Living God*, and set out to prove or disprove them.

Their description of the methodology employed is not clear. I am not sure whether they interviewed the subjects in person or they just taped the phone interviews. The interpretation of the data seems to follow the clinical method, but the Saures do not tell us what criteria they use to organize and classify the large amount of information gathered in a two-hour interview. This information is useful for the reader to be able to study critically the conclusions and for future researchers who would like to compare their results with the present one.

Their conclusions should make me happy and, in fact, they give me great satisfaction:

The data from the study confirm Rizzuto's conceptualizations about the nature, origin, and functions of the God-representation. The study concludes that object relations theory provides a psychoanalytic framework for a comprehensive understanding of the image of God in individual's psychic life. (p. 139)

With such friends I need now an enemy, that is, someone willing to prove all that is wrong with my theorizing. I am not searching for defeat but for the learning that ensues from intelligent exploration of the progressive subtlety of conceptualizations. What I appreciate about the Saures study is the systematic exploration of issues with a well-defined group and a clear hypothesis. It is from studies of this kind—empirical, concrete, and theoretically well-thought through—that we learn the most. The greatest risk in this field is generalization without concrete and repeated evidence.

We owe gratitude to Mark Finn and Jeffrey Rubin for studying the Buddhist's experience. My own studies, and most psychoanalytic studies, focus exclusively in the Western Judeo-Christian tradition. This tradition is particularly suited for the study of religion under the light of psychoanalytic object relations theory. The Judeo-Christian tradition begins with a living and active God, who speaks the language of Abraham, establishes himself as his Lord, his guide, his protector, and the master of his future (Genesis 12:1–3). Such a God is psychologically so close to parental representations that it makes the theory of object relations and representations specifically suitable for the study of the psychic processes involved in religious belief.

Buddhism is a drastically different tradition. As Huston Smith (1958) describes it, the religion of Buddha was "without authority, without ritual, without theology, without tradition, without grace, and without the supernatural" (p. 108). The question of God in Buddhism is a difficult one. Buddhism does not have a personal God as the Judeo-Christian tradition has. Smith, following Edward Conze's careful study of the concept of nirvana and the terms used to describe it, compares it with traditional Western descriptions of God as Godhead. He concludes: "Nirvana is not God defined as a personal creator but stands sufficiently close to the concept of God as Godhead to warrant the name in this sense" (p. 127).

Whether a particular practitioner of Buddhism intends a search for nirvana or to attain insight, wisdom, compassion, and the eradication of suffering, the object of his attention is his inner world of mental reality as the only realm in which they and reality can be found. The person must find liberation from suffering in the meditative exploration of his or her inner world. Whether this self is conceived as an individual self (the Theravada tradition) or as a self bound to the manifold manifestations of life (the Mahayana tradition), the experience of meditation itself is a solitary exercise, a private encounter with oneself. The encounter may be presented to a revered teacher, but the experience itself occurs in solitude. This aspect of Buddhism contrasts sharply with the emotion-laden communal rituals addressing the Godhead of the Judeo-Christian tradition.

Whatever Buddhists search for in their meditation—nirvana or insight—they are certainly not searching for an encounter with a personal God. Such a situation provides the opportunity to ask several questions about the functions and transformations of object representations in those who have been born in a Buddhist community, and even, more interestingly, in those who, having being born in a Western theistic tradition, have later become Buddhist. The careful and detailed study of this subject could provide the psychologist of religion with new and fascinating insights.

I must say a few words in relation to what we know today about the process of formation of the human mind. We know that we become a self because we are born and raised in a matrix of caring people. Among them, the maternal object is the first and most significant facilitator of the immediate and lasting subjective organization of experience. The interactions with the maternal and other objects are organized in extremely complex object representations that are capable of transformation and updating following the progressive transformation of self-representations. The object and self-representations are the essential constitutive elements of all human mentation. Inanimate objects exist as representations in an internal environment of private object- and self-related meanings that bestow affective significance on them. No human being is able to carry out any mental activity outside its matrix of self- and object representations. Meditation, therefore, must partake in this general process. What happens in the Buddhist's meditation experience to the representations of the parental objects and of oneself as a child or an adolescent? Do they undergo creative, somehow religious transformations in a mode or shape different from the Western formation of a God-representation? Is the self-representation, as Rubin suggests, most affected by the meditative process? And if so, how? What are the consequences in the intrapsychic representational reality for the object representations and the interpersonal world for the relationships to significant objects?

Rubin concludes about Steven, the Western Buddhist meditator: "We gradually came to understand that Buddhism had taken on constructive, defensive, reparative, and restitutive functions for Steven, simultaneously enriching and limiting his life" (p. 102).

This conclusion, I suggest, obtains not only in Steven's Buddhist experiences but in all religious experiences. We are not able to construct a better side of ourselves without defending against a less acceptable aspect of it, and to repair what we felt was damaged or missing without closing other doors of possibility. This is as true of religious experience as it is of love, career, advocation, and even dreams. We are creatures limited by time and space, including intrapsychic time and space. The great tensions of human life stem from our capacity to conceive and wish for more possibilities than we can carry out in a limited lifetime, with a limited psyche that is able to afford only some of them.

The psychology of religion gains from studies of cases such as Steven's. They may clarify for us the functions and limitations of a given religious experience to organize the intrapsychic reality of the person. Rubin elegantly illustrates that Steven's strenuous efforts to solve and avoid the repetition of his conflicts brought him to replay them in a new key:

Buddhist emphasis on self-purification and transformation had a dual unconscious function: It provided a means of attempting to win his perfectionist father's approval and to atone for his unconscious guilt over his imagined crime of not saving, and wishing to destroy, his damaged brother. . . . But it also became an agent of self-condemnation and self-inhibition. The quest for purity of action, like his father's demand for perfection, became one more ideal that he could never attain and thus one more occasion for self-condemnation. (p. 104)

Rubin concludes that Buddhism's emphasis on "cool" emotions reinforced his defensive passivity and prompted Steven to focus on "detaching from negative affects rather than experiencing them. . . . The possibility of Steven being appropriately assertive or angry was thus unfortunately stifled" (p. 105).

I have some questions about Steven. His parents' atheistic upbringing deprived him of their permission to use whatever God-representation he must have formed as a member of an American culture that explicitly believes in God. What were the consequences of not being allowed to have a usable God like other children for his capacity to sublimate and transform his parental representations? What was his unconscious, or perhaps conscious, representation of the Godhead before he became a Buddhist? Did he have a personal relation to a Buddhist master? Did he use the analyst not only as an analyst but also as a guiding master? Did he have fantasies about his relation to Buddha? The purpose of my questioning is to find what happened affectively and representationally to the representations of his primary objects in the religious experience. I am unable to comprehend changes in the sense of self and the mediatory self-representations without changes in the object representations. Could it be that the intrapsychically objectless Buddhist religion was partly responsible for the limitations of Steven's capacity to change? Was his Buddhism a search for the Buddha's experience, that is, a religious search or a socially sanctioned *method* and an analytic resistance to avoid a painful encounter with his internal and actual parental objects? These questions and many others must wait for exquisitely particularized analytic case studies that may provide answers to such subtle but essential questions.

In Chapter 7, "Transitional Space and Tibetan Buddhism: The Object Relations of Meditation," Finn addresses some aspects of the questions I have asked. He reflects:

Separating the technique from the tradition creates the impression that meditation is a completely solitary activity. While in a sense this is true, it is also true that in the Buddhist tradition, meditation practice is learned within a committed relationship to a teacher. (p. 110)

Finn selects a case study, the famous Tibetan saint, Milarepa, from early Tibetan Buddhist literature. The relation between teacher and student is described with emotional details as a way of exemplifying "the interpenetration of the spiritual and the psychodynamic" (p. 111). In the Buddhist understanding of the universe, this affirmation makes eminent sense: "One cannot take absolute truth without relative truth, yet absolute truth is in fact absolute. Thus, the relative psychological world and the absolute spiritual world are inseparable" (p. 112).

Aquinas would agree, saying that grace presupposes nature (psychology) and can only exert its divine effect by acting on the natural psychological disposition and the free consent of the person. I am bringing in Thomas Aquinas as a way of saying that two very different traditions have arrived through different roads to the conclusion that spiritual life cannot be separated from its psychic foundations. Psychoanalysis concurs with this conclusion and affirms that it applies to all religious experiences.

Milarepa's story presents a young child and man who is caught in the inescapable wave of his elders' crimes and hatred. He is driven to commit murder by the power of religion's step-sister, black magic. He is capable of remorse and searches for a guru, a good parental object, to guide him in his spiritual journey.

The story of the man's journey can be described in object-related psychodynamic terms without losing its spiritual meaning. First, he discovers loneliness, 'the futility of the world''; second, he desires closeness with his guru, experiencing ''a great, unbearable longing'' that moves him creatively to evoke his image in a song about him. Third, the guru, Marpa, appears to him and makes a remarkable promise: ''You may be certain that we will never part.'' One may think of object constancy and of this ''always being there'' as the essential attribute of the accepted God that I found in my research. Fourth, fear of objects (the result of psychic ambivalence toward them their transformation into universal childhood fantasies about monsters) brings Milarepa face to face with horrifying demons. Fifth, through his use of Marpa's teaching, Milarepa realizes that he is dealing with internal monsters and, by a remarkable act of reality testing, invites them to play with him. Of course, they vanish. As a result of this experience at the Red Rock Jewel Valley, ''Milarepa gained great spiritual progress and . . . became a great teacher'' (p. 116).

This moving and beautiful story has a profound teaching in it. It shows that all psychically usable religion is based on the permanence of the object who ''is always there.'' It also illustrates that a move to a more mature form of religion requires some transformation of the ambivalently held object, mediated by the psychic courage of the individual to face the horrifying and frightful components of all objects—human, demonic, and devine. Peter Blos described this separation from the internal representation of the object as the essential intrapsychic task of adolescence (1979). The story of Milarepa seems to illustrate that confronting the demonic side of all objects frees the person and permits the experience of a more solid sense of self. This is another example of the dialectical relations between self- and object representations.

I agree with Finn that the space for this transformation is the transitional space. We witness, as he says, in Milarepa's struggle, his use of music, song, the clouds of the landscape, and explicit language in playful enactment of his paradoxical invitations to the demons to play with him. What we see is the richness of human fantasy, displayed with emotional courage, under the indispensable guiding light of solid intellectual discovery (''I have already fully realized that all being and all phenomena are of one's mind'') participating in a process of self-transformation in the world that can only occur in the transitional space. What differentiates the more normal experience from pathology is the simultaneous presence of all the components: a protective and mentally present object (Marpa, God), childhood derivatives of frightening objects (demons), emotional involvement, intellectual clarity, and the freedom to play. I am inclined to say that perhaps these are the conditions for transformational moments in religious experience.

Finally, I would like to comment on a significant observation made by both Finn and Rubin. They notice the similarities between the method of Buddhist meditation and the psychoanalytic method of free association, including not only the intrapsychic events but the setting itself. These observations are of great interest. They pay attention to the consequences of conditions that alter our habitual mode of consciousness. their comments are to be taken seriously. I would like researchers to go beyond the descriptive level and undertake a systematic examination of the type of changes that occur in psychoanalysis and meditation to determine their obvious similarities and their differences. This area of research could throw unsuspected light on some aspects of religious experience.

John Gartner focuses on a particular psychic action in his chapter on "The Capacity to Forgive: An Object Relations Perspective." He defines mature forgiveness as "an integrated realistic view that contains both good and bad aspects of self and others. Forgiveness allows us to absorb the full impact of the evil that men do while not losing sight of their humanity" (p. 23).

Gartner understands the dynamics of the inability to forgive in Kleinian and Kernbergian terms. It results from the splitting of self- and object representations and the inability to integrate in one person good and bad object representations. For Gartner,

the failure to forgive is a manifestation of splitting, for it [says]: "Someone has behaved destructively toward me (bad object representation) stimulating feelings of hate (connecting negative affect) in me (bad self-representation." Thus the view of the other is a caricatured "all bad" one. (p. 23)

The level described above involves representational and reality testing processes organized under the power of the splitting mechanism of defense. Following Hunter, Gartner links this defensiveness to "the fear of retaliation and paranoid anxiety" (p. 24).

In discussing these theoretical approaches and a clinical case, he describes the conditions for emergence of the psychological capacity to forgive. He lists among the interpersonal events between two people the experience of having been forgiven, not having been rejected in spite of overt injurious behavior, the subjective experience of feeling liked by the other person, and the persistent behavior of not giving up on the misbehaving person. This last condition should be called hope (the patient said: "That gave me hope") for the other, an essential component of all treatments and human relations. Among the intrapsychic changes, Gartner lists the undoing of the splitting of self- and object representations, which is mediated by the capacity the patient has to test the reality of the absence of rejection in the therapeutic situation. Next is the capacity to develop positive, affectionate feelings for the therapist, and finally, the actual capacity to remember some positive affect and empathy for a parent. I conclude that the mediatory representation of a respectful therapist permitted the transformation of formerly intolerable self- and early object representations into more integrated and acceptable ones. Such transformations are clearly shown in Gartner's case and lead to his conclusion about his patient's change in her capacity to tolerate contradictory affects without splitting: "the patient's act of forgiveness . . . allowed her to feel both grateful and furious at the same person at the same time."

Gartner has presented a much-needed description of the psychodynamics of forgiveness. It is elegant, and it makes sense. I believe, however, that it is incomplete. Forgiveness cannot be fully understood without looking at the narcissistic component of all human suffering. Perhaps the shortest way of making my point is to go back to the case and observe that all of the reported moments in which the patient rejects Dr. Gartner involve a humiliation of him as a person or as a professional and are aimed at "getting" him. To all the aspects so well described by Gartner, one must add the undoing of the narcissistic injury suffered by the patient. In the past, she seemed to have experienced the parting of her therapist not only as abandonment but also as a narcissistic injury. The situation had changed with Dr. Gartner because the patient felt that he did not give up on her. I interpreted this as her feeling that she is valuable in his eyes, and not deserving the death her mother wished on her. It is the "me" of "you didn't give up on me" that feels narcissistically respected even at the moment of abandonment.

I would like to see comparable studies detailing the conditions for the acceptance of forgiveness, a situation that may have some other psychodynamic components.

David G. Benner presents a comprehensive examination of a case in his chapter, "The Functions of Faith: Religious Psychodynamics in Multiple Personality Disorder." The patient is a 39-year-old woman, the child of two Holocaust survivors. She has a history so full of massive trauma that one wonders how she is still able to feel or talk. An orphan at age five, she was tortured by her stepmother since the second year of life and repeatedly raped by her stepfather, who also aborted her two pregnancies by him. Her stepparents forced her to participate in a satanic cult and in human sacrifices. She had to abandon her child to save herself. What else can be expected from her but an endless bewilderment about her self, others, the world, and God?

Benner carefully documents his patient's manifold relations with a God she believed in with most aspects of herself (personalities). It is a valuable documentation of the complexities of the representational processes and affective states involved in belief and also of the psychic conditions for belief. God cannot be used as an object for belief in three of her "personalities." Alter 5 relates to the six-year-old girl and is "associated with abusive experiences in the orphanage. . . . She felt herself to be a misfit in the world of the other personalities." She felt alien to herself, to her body, to her family, and to her language (p. 42).

Her subjective experience was of being lost in the world and with herself. In this condition, she felt the most anti-religious because she feared religion would tempt her to change her perception of a harsh reality. Unbelief seemed a necessary condition to protect her sense of reality, her reality testing, by insisting that life is harsh. She did not want to be "softened" by religion.

Alter 8 "was associated with the rage experienced at the abortions performed by her stepfather." She "rejected the God she had been raised to believe and trust" (p. 43). Unbelief seemed to protect her affective sense that no one should be trusted, not even God. Finally, alter 10, which she linked to age seventeen, indicated that she was not interested in religion. She discovered how to escape from pain by retreating into academic accomplishment (p. 43). Seventeen is the age at which one must confront the internal objects (Blos, 1979) to separate from them and consolidate a personal sense of self. Alter 10 preferred to avoid them, to escape from the internal pressure of overwhelming objects, God included. These commentaries of mine about the dynamics of her unbelief bring to focus some postulated psychic conditions for her to be able to believe in a God whose representation she obviously had in mind. Benner comments that this case "does illustrate the multiple and complex ways in which religious faith can function within the individual" (p. 54).

It seems to me that it also illustrates the relation between the sense of self and the sense of the object, as conceived at a particular moment of psychic experience. Belief as a conscious process requires that a certain type of subjective experience be established between the object of belief, the God-representation of a particular moment, and the contemporary sense of self. The type of experience of relatedness to God at that moment of belief must allow the person "to maintain a sense of self which provides at least a minimum of relatedness and hope" (Rizzuto, 1979: 202).

It seems to me that the three alternate personalities that are unable to believe appear in desperate situations of intense alienation between the patient and her external and internal worlds. It makes her unable to believe in a God that cannot offer her a minimum of relatedness and hope, without forcing her to renounce either her reality testing or her internal safety. In the first instance, she is so disoriented that she does not even recognize her body or her language; in the second her rage (and despair, I think) overwhelm all other experiences; in the third, unable to confront the internal objects, she has to avoid them at all costs, and God together with them. In none of these cases could she afford to believe without losing her sense of herself or her reality testing. Not believing was her best defense. It allowed her to keep a minimum of relatedness to herself, while she was sustained by the conviction that she was perceiving correctly and that she had to watch out to protect herself. The common element to the three instances of unbelief seems related to her need to keep faith in herself and nobody else. Perhaps it was her capacity to use reality testing at the service of her sense of self at the time that protected her from psychosis, even if the price she had to pay to be able to tolerate her suffering was the splitting of her experiences into morsel personalities.

What the case illustrates best is the contradictory, complementary, many-layered components of representation, affect, and experience that condition a moment of belief in God. A natural experiment in pathology, a personality divided in some of its component parts, is like an enlarged photograph. It permits the observation of components present in all of us that remain invisible without the great magnification provided by a pathological development.

We should be grateful for Benner's description of a complex and interesting case and hope that it encourages others to report their cases and the data necessary to discover the conditions for and patterns of belief in God.

Michael H. Stone discusses in his chapter, "Religious Behavior in the Psychiatric Institute 500," the significance of a benign cult experience for the 6 percent of borderline and psychotic patients who joined a religious group or cult after discharge from the hospital. The study is a statistical and descriptive follow-up of patients ten to twenty-five years after their discharge from the hospital. Stone draws two main conclusions from his study. The first is the power religion has, "in the form of a charismatic cult led by a 'benevolent despot,' " to transform "severely antisocial persons into law-abiding and community-minded citizens" (p. 152). The second is that religion "has an easier time replacing overly harsh internalized objects . . . than firming up to appropriate social standards a conscience that was undeveloped to the point of amorality and callousness" (p. 153). For people as impaired as severe borderlines and schizophrenics, the religious group acts as an "externalized superego," an exoskeleton, to support their efforts to achieve internal and external self-control.

Stone describes what religious groups offer to these patients' marginal existence: the easing of their existential malaise by providing hope, membership, and a sense of identity. To these functions, he adds the significance of the structure and purposefulness of the group to help contain impulses at one level while facilitating their satisfaction at another. Belonging, affiliation, and participation are significant experiences that contribute to increase the patient's always limited self-esteem.

Stone is well aware that these benefits could have been achieved by other means, such as intense political involvement, or by any other involvement that provides an opportunity to belong to a solidly structured group. We are talking about religion as a social institution, as an organization of people defining themselves clearly and firmly in their manner of partaking of the complex act of living. We are talking about the social, cultural, psychological, and pragmatic functions of religious organizations in their efforts to make sense of the human experience at one level, the level of meaning, and to provide structures capable of harnessing human forces that appear overwhelming, at the pragmatic level. In this sense, one could say that social groups are always re-creating old and new religions and cults to accommodate the manifold needs of a constantly evolving human experience. In our fragmented and isolating society, the experience of anomie threatens all of us. Marginal people find pockets of safety in the many cults available, if the leader and the group are benevolent. There they can function and feel the desperately needed sense of belonging, of counting to others, of having purpose and meaning. This is in essence the group psychology component of all religious experiences, including the common belief in a God-head for all. It is interesting to reflect about the connections between group psychology and the private experience of religious relatedness.

In the case of the patients described by Stone, the actual objects of the religious group, the people there, carry a tremendous significance for humans in need of protective leaders. The people in these cults are for them probably more important than the beliefs themselves. I would, however, add immediately that even the most exalted and mature of private religious experiences never occurs without a background context of human relatedness that supports it. Here, human relations complete a circle with religious experience. Religion, defined in the strictest terms as a relation to a postulated Godhead, cannot exist outside the context of the human group relatedness and the institutions created for both. However, to follow this subject would take me too far afield.

Stone has made us aware of the functions cults may have for people who need "externalized superegos." I hope that his findings encourage all mental health field workers to take a careful religious history and to fully learn about and respect the religious circumstances of even the most impaired and hopeless of patients. As he well demonstrates, nobody knows what reserves of strength remain available within a person until such a person has found a meaningful and esteem-enhancing group that welcomes him or her.

There is much to be learned about human religion. This book is a valuable beginning. The field is broad and requires a careful separation of the levels of investigation as well as the ways of finding the connections between them. We need a great amount of discipline and dedication, discipline of an intellectual nature in our use of the vocabulary at our disposal, and of the focus we select each time we attend to a particular phenomenon. If we are talking about God as a mental representation, we should not talk about religion without noticing that we have made a conceptual leap. If we use the word "religion," we should define at the outset how we mean it, whether as a system of concrete beliefs, as a social phenomenon, as an anthropological phenomenon.

Religion is intrapsychic and an existing societal reality. It is also, in most cases, a postulation of the existence of a transcendent reality (even if it is imminent, as in Buddhism). This postulation is absolutely essential to any re-ligious phenomenon understood in the light of psychoanalytic object relations theory. However, we should listen to Beit-Hallahmi. As scholars of the psy-chology of religion, we have nothing to say about that transcendent reality. Our method is phenomenological and must remain there, where the phenomenon is. It is a fact that many among us do believe in that transcendent reality. It is here, then, that we are required to keep the most austere of disciplines. We must not make assumptions, sentimentalize belief, sell the goodness of religion, or its "healthy" effects. If there is a God, it does not need us and our discipline to do well. He/She has lived well for centuries without us. We can, nonetheless, contribute a detailed and progressively subtle exploration of all the psychic components of the experiences of belief and unbelief, and their intrapsychic, personal, and group psychology consequences. This would be an indisputable contribution, not only for the psychological disciplines but also for all practitioners of religion. The work is there, waiting to be done. This book represents a first step in this work. As I have tried to show in my commentary, it opens more questions than it answers, which is perhaps as it should be. A question well asked is always the beginning of its own answer.

REFERENCES

Blos, P. (1979). *The Adolescent Passage*. New York: International University Press.

Bollas, C. (1987). *The Shadow of the Object*. New York: Columbia University Press.

Hoffer, A. (1985). "Toward a Definition of Psychoanalytic Neutrality." *Journal of the American Psychoanalytic Association*, 33: 771–96.

Smith, H. (1958). *The Religions of Man*. London: Harper & Row.

Rizzuto, A-M. (1979). *The Birth of the Living God: A Psychoanalytic Study*. Chicago: University of Chicago Press.

Weber, M. (1963). *The Sociology of Religion*. Boston: Beacon Press.

Bibliography

Alexander, F. (1931). Buddhist training as an artificial catatonia. *Psychoanalytic Review*, *18*, 129–45.

Aronson, H. B. (1985). *Guru Yoga-A Buddhist meditative visualization: Observations based upon psychoanalytic object relations theory and self-psychology*. Paper presented at the American Academy of Religion in Anaheim, Calif.

Ashbrook, J. (1972). Paul Tillich converses with psychotherapists. *Journal of Religion and Health*, *11*(1), 40–72.

Auden, W. H. (1939). In memory of Sigmund Freud. In W. H. Auden, *Collected shorter poems 1927–1957*. New York: Vintage Books.

Ausburger, D. (1973). *The freedom of forgiveness*. Chicago: Moody Press.

———. (1981). *Caring enough to forgive. Caring enough not to forgive*. Pelham, N.Y.: Herald Books.

Baker, H., and M. Baker. (1987). Heinz Kohut's self psychology: An overview. *American Journal of Psychiatry*, *144*(1), 1–9.

Barbour, I. (1974). *Myths, models, and paradigms*. New York: Harper and Row.

Bateson, G., and M. C. Bateson. (1987). *Angel's fear*. New York: Macmillan.

Beit-Hallahmi, B. (1974). Salvation and its vicissitudes: Clinical psychology and political values. *American Psychologist*, *29*, 124–29.

———. (1975). Encountering orthodox religion in psychotherapy. *Psychology: Theory, research and practice*, *12*, 357–59.

———. (1976). On the "religious" functions of the helping professions. *Archive fur Religionpsychologie*, *12*, 48–52.

———. (1977). Humanistic psychology—Progressive or reactionary? *Self and Society*, *12*, 97–103.

———. (1978). *Psychoanalysis and religion: A bibliography*. Norwood, Pa.: Norwood Editions.

———. (1981). Psychology and the explanation of inequality. In R. Solo and C. H. Anderson (eds.), *Value judgment and income distribution*. New York: Praeger.

———. (1987). The psychotherapy subculture: Practice and ideology. *Social Science Information, 26*, 475–92.

———. (1989). *Prolegomena to the psychological study of religion*. Lewisburg, Pa.: Bucknell University Press.

Benner, D. G., and C. S. Evans. (1984). Unity and multiplicity in hypnosis, commissurotomy, and multiple personality disorder. *Journal of Mind and Behavior, 5*, 423–32.

Benner, D. G., and B. Joscelyne. (1984). Multiple personality as a borderline disorder. *Journal of Nervous and Mental Disorders, 172*, 98–104.

Blos, P. (1967). The second individuation process of adolescence. *The psychoanalytic study of the child, 22*, 162–86.

Bollas, C. (1979). The transformational object. *International Journal of Psychoanalysis, 60*, 97–107.

———. (1986). The transformational object. In G. Kohon (ed.), *The British school of psychoanalysis*. New Haven, Conn.: Yale University Press.

———. (1987). *The shadow of the object*. New York: Columbia University Press.

Boor, M. F. (1982). The multiple personality epidemic. *Journal of Nervous and Mental Disease, 170*, 302–304.

Boor, M. F., and P. M. Coons. (1983). A comprehensive bibliography of literature pertaining to multiple personality. *Psychological Reports, 53*, 295–310.

Boucher, S. (1988). *Turning the wheel: American women creating the new Buddhism*. San Francisco: Harper and Row.

Bowman, E. S., P. M. Coons, E. S. Jones, and M. Oldstrom. (1987). Religious psychodynamics in multiple personalities. *American Journal of Psychotherapy, 41*, 542–54.

Brandsma, J. (1982). Forgiveness: A dynamic theological and therapeutic analysis. *Pastoral Psychology, 31*, 40–50.

Braun, B. G. (ed.) (1986). *Treatment of multiple personality disorder*. Washington, D.C.: American Psychiatric Press.

Brink. T. (1985). The role of religion in later life: A case of consolation and forgiveness. *Journal of Psychology and Christianity, 4*, 22–25.

Buddhaghosa. (1976). *The path of purification*. Translated by B. Nyanamoli. Berkeley: Shambhala Press.

Buie, D., and G. Adler. (1982). The definitive treatment of the borderline personality. *International Journal of Psychoanalytic Psychotherapy, 9*, 51–87.

Campbell, P., and E. McMahon. (1985). *Bispirituality: Focusing as a way to grow*. Chicago: Loyola University Press.

Carpenter, W. T. Jr., J. G. Gunderson, and J. S. Strauss. (1977). Considerations of the borderline syndrome: Longitudinal and comparative study of borderline and schizophrenic patients. In P. Hartocollis (ed.), *Borderline personality disorders*. New York: International University Press.

Cavenar, J. C. Jr., and J. G. Spaulding. (1977). Depressive disorders and religious conversions. *Journal of Nervous and Mental Disease, 165*, 209–12.

Chang, G.C.C. (1977). *The hundred thousand songs of Milarepa*. Boulder, Colo.: Shambhala Press.

Close, H. (1970). Forgiveness and responsibility: A case study. *Pastoral Psychology*, *21*, 19–25.

Coltart, N. (1986). 'Slouching towards Bethlehem . . . ' or thinking the unthinkable in psychoanalysis. In G. Kohon (ed.), *The British school of psychoanalysis*. New Haven, Conn.: Yale University Press.

Coons, P. M. (1980). Multiple personality: Diagnostic considerations. *Journal of Clinical Psychiatry*, *41*, 330–36.

Dalbiez, R. (1936). *La Methode psychanalytique et la doctrine Freudienne*, 2 vols. Paris: Desclee de Bouwer.

Damgaard, J., S. Van Benschoten, and J. Fagen. (1985). An updated bibliography of literature pertaining to multiple personality. *Psychological Reports*, *57*, 131–37.

Davis, M., and D. Wallbridge. (1981). *Boundary and space*. New York: Brunner Mazel.

Deikman, A. (1976). Bimodal consciousness and the mystic experience. In P. Lee, R. Ornstein, D. Galin, A. Deikman, and C. Tart (eds.), *A symposium on consciousness*. New York: Viking Press.

———. (1982). *The observing self: Mysticism and psychotherapy*. Boston: Beacon Press.

DeWald, P. A. (1972). *The psychoanalytic process*. New York: Basic Books.

Diekstra, R.F.W., and J. M. Moritz. (1987). Suicidal behavior among adolescents. In R.F.W. Diekstra and K. Hawton (eds.), *Suicide in adolescence*. Dordrecht, Holland: M. Nijhoff.

Donnelly, D. (1982a). *Learning to forgive*. Nashville, Tenn.: Abingdon.

———. (1982b). *Putting forgiveness into practice*. Allen, Texas: Argus.

———. (1984). Forgiveness and recidivism. *Pastoral Psychology*, *33*, 15–24.

Draper, E. (1965). On the diagnostic value of religious ideation. *Archives of General Psychiatry*, *13*, 202–207.

DSM-III. (1980). *Diagnostic and statistical manual of mental disorders*, 3rd edition. Washington, D.C.: American Psychiatric Association.

Emmons, N. (1986). *Manson in his own words*. New York: Grune Press.

Engler, J. H. (1983). Vicissitudes of the self according to psychoanalysis and Buddhism: A spectrum of model of object relations development. *Psychoanalysis and Contemporary Thought*, *6*(1), 29–72.

———. (1986). Therapeutic aims in psychotherapy and meditation. In K. Wilber, J. Engler, and D. Brown (eds.), *Transformations of consciousness: Conventional and contemplative perspectives on development*. Boston: Shambhala Press.

Epstein, M. D. (1988). The deconstruction of the self: Ego and "egolessness" in Buddhist insight meditation. *Journal of Transpersonal Psychology*, *20*(1), 61–69.

Erikson, E. H. (1959). *Identity and the life cycle*. New York: International University Press.

Eskalona, S. (1968). *The roots of individuality*. Chicago: Aldine.

Fairbairn, W.R.D. (1924). The repression and return of bad objects. In P. Buckley (ed.), *Essential papers on object relations*. New York: New York University Press.

———. (1927). Notes on the religious phantasies of a female patient. In W.R.D. Fairbairn, *Psychoanalytic studies of the personality*. London: Routledge & Kegan Paul (1952).

———. (1952a). *Psycho-analytic studies of the personality*. London: Tavistock.

———. (1952b). *An object relations theory of personality*. New York: Basic Books.

Fitzgibbons, R. P. (1986). The cognitive and emotive uses of forgiveness in the treatment of anger. *Psychotherapy*, *23*, 629–33.

Foon, A. F. (1987). Locus of control as a predictor of outcome of psychotherapy. *British Journal of Medical Psychology*, *60*, 99–107.

Fowler, J. (1974). *To see the kingdom: The theological vision of H. Richard Niebuhr*. Nashville, Tenn.: Abingdon Press.

——. (1981). *Stages of faith: The psychology of human development and the quest for meaning*. New York: Harper and Row.

——. (1989). Strength for the journey: Early childhood development in selfhood and faith. In D. Blazer (ed.), *Faith development in early childhood*. Kansas City, Mo.: Sheed and Ward.

Freud, S. (1900). *The interpretation of dreams*. Standard edition, *4* and *5*. London: Hogarth Press.

——. (1909). *Family romances*. Standard Edition, *9*, London: Hogarth Press (1959).

——. (1926). *Inhibitions, symptoms and anxiety*. Standard Edition, *20*. London: Hogarth Press.

——. (1927). *The future of an illusion*. Standard Edition, *21*. London: Hogarth Press (1964).

——. (1930). *Civilization and its discontents*. Standard Edition, *21*. London: Hogarth Press.

——. (1933). *New introductory lectures on Psycho-Analysis*. Standard Edition, *22*. London: Hogarth Press.

Fromm, E., D. T. Suzuki, and R. DeMartino. (1960). *Zen Buddhism and psychoanalysis*. New York: Harper and Row.

Galanter, M. (1989). *Cults*. New York: Oxford University Press.

Gampopa, S. (1981). *The jewel ornament of liberation*. Translated by H. Guenther. Boulder, Colo.: Prajna Press.

Gartner, J., D. Larson, and G. Allen. (1991). Religion and psychopathology: A review of the empirical literature. *Journal of Psychology and Theology*, *19*, 6–25.

Gay, P. (1987). *A godless Jew*. New Haven, Conn.: Yale University Press.

Gendlin, E. (1962). *Experiencing and the creation of meaning*. Toronto: Free Press of Glencoe.

——. (1965). Existential explication and truth. *Journal of Existentialism*, *16*, 135.

——. (1966). Existentialism and experiental psychotherapy. In C. Moustakas (ed.), *Existential child therapy: The child's discovery of himself*. New York: Basic Books.

——. (1981). *Focusing*, revised edition. New York: Bantam Press.

Gilkey, L. (1973). The problem of God: A programmatic essay. In G. F. McLean (ed.), *Traces of God in a contemporary culture*. New York: Alba House.

Giovacchini, P. L., and L. Bryce Boyer. (1982). *Technical factors in the treatment of the severely disturbed patient*. New York: Jason Aronson.

Goldstein, J. (1976). *The experience of insight: A natural unfolding*. Santa Cruz: Unity Press.

Goleman, D. (1977). *The varieties of the meditative experience*. New York: Dutton.

Greaves, G. B. (1980). Multiple personality: 165 years after Mary Reynolds. *Journal of Nervous and Mental Disease*, *168*, 577–96.

Greenberg, J. R., and S. A. Mitchell. (1983). *Object relations in psychoanalytic theory*. New York: Aronson.

Grotstein, J. (1980). A proposed revision of the psychoanalytic concept of primitive mental states. *Contemporary Psychoanalysis*, *16*, 479–546.

―――. (1984). A proposed revision of the psychoanalytic concept of primitive mental states: Part 2. *Contemporary Psychoanalysis*, *20*, 266–343.

Group for Advancement of Psychiatry, (1968). *The psychic function of religion in mental illness and health*. GAP Report No. 67.

Gruenwald, D. (1977). Multiple personality and splitting phenomena: A reconceptualization. *Journal of Nervous and Mental Disorders*, *164*, 385–93.

Guntrip, H. (1961). *Personality structure and human interaction*. New York: International Universities Press.

―――. (1968). Religion in relation to personal integration. *British Journal of Medical Psychology*, *42*, 323–33.

―――. (1969). *Schizoid phenomena object relations and the self*. New York: International Universities Press.

―――. (1974). *Schizoid phenomena object relations and the self*. London: Hogarth Press.

Habermas, J. (1973). *Theory and practice*. Boston: Beacon Press.

Halperin, D. S. (1983). *Psychodynamic perspectives on religion sect and cult*. Boston: John Wright/PSG Inc.

Hammann, L. J. (1987). *Exploring the labyrinth: Four approaches to understanding religious traditions*. Lanham, Md.: University Press of America.

Hartmann, H. (1964). *Essays on ego psychology*. New York: International Universities Press.

Heinrichs, D. (1982). Our Father which art in Heaven: Parataxic distortions in the image of God. *Journal of Psychology and Theology*, *10*(2), 120–29.

Higdon, J. F. (1986). Association of fundamentalism with multiple personality disorder. In *Proceedings of the Third International Conference on Multiple Personality/ Dissociative States*, Rush-Presbyterian-St. Luke, Chicago.

Horney, K. (1945). *Our inner conflicts*. New York: Norton.

―――. (1987). *Final lectures*. New York: Norton.

Hunter, R. (1978). Forgiveness, retaliation and paranoid reactions. *Journal of the Canadian Psychiatric Association*, *23*, 167–73.

James, W. (1904). *The varieties of religious experience*. New York: New American Library (1958).

―――. (1985). *The varieties of religious experience*. Cambridge, Mass.: Harvard University Press.

The Jerusalem Bible. (1984). Israel: Koren Publishers.

Jones, E. (1975). *The life and work of Sigmund Freud*, vol. 3. London: Hogarth Press.

Jung, C. (1936). Yoga and the west. In his *Psychology and religion: West and east*. Princeton: Princeton University Press.

―――. (1938). *Psychology and religion*. New Haven, Conn.: Yale University Press.

Kaufman, M. (1984). The courage to forgive. *Israel Journal of Psychiatry and Related Sciences*, *21*, 177–87.

Kelman, H. (1960). Psychoanalytic thought and Eastern wisdom. In J. Ehrenwald (ed.), *The history of psychotherapy*. New York: Jason Aronson (1976).

Kernberg, O. (1967). Borderline personality organization. *Journal of the American Psychoanalytic Association*, *15*, 641–85.

―――. (1975). *Borderline conditions and pathological narcissism*. New York: Aronson.

————. (1976). *Object relations theory and clinical psychoanalysis*. New York: Aronson.

————. (1980). *International world and external reality*. New York: Aronson.

————. (1982). The psychotherapeutic treatment of borderline personalities. In L. Grinspoon (ed.), *Psychiatry*, vol. 1. Washington, D.C.: American Psychiatric Press.

————. (1984). *Severe personality disorders*. New Haven, Conn.: Yale University Press.

Klein, M. (1937). *Love, guilt and reparation*. London: Hogarth Press (1975).

————. (1946). Notes of some schizoid mechanisms. *International Journal of Psychoanalysis*, *27*, 99–110.

————. (1948). *Contributions to psychoanalysis 1921–1945*. London: Hogarth Press.

————. (1955). On identification. In her *New Directions in Psychoanalysis*. London: Hogarth.

Kluft, R. P. (1984). An introduction to multiple personality disorder. *Psychiatric Annals*, *14*, 19–24.

————. (ed). (1985). *Childhood antecedents of multiple personality*. Washington, D.C.: American Psychiatric Press.

————. (1987). An update on multiple personality disorder. *Hospital and Community Psychiatry*, *38*, 363–73.

Kohon, G. (1986). *The British school of psychoanalysis: The independent tradition*. London: Free Association Books.

Kohut, H. (1971). *The analysis of the self*. New York: International Universities Press.

————. (1984). *How does analysis cure*? Chicago: University of Chicago Press.

————. (1985). *Self psychology and the humanities*. New York: W. W. Norton.

Kornfield, J. (1977). *Living Buddhist masters*. Santa Cruz: Unity Press.

Kramer, J., and D. Alstad. (1989). Personal communication.

Kutz, I., J. Z. Borysenko, and H. Benson. (1985). Meditation and psychotherapy: A rationale for the integration of dynamic psychotherapy, the relaxation response and mindfulness meditation. *American Journal of Psychiatry*, *142*(1), 1–8.

Lasky, R. (1978). Psychoanalytic treatment of a case of multiple personality. *Psychoanalytic Review*, *65*, 355–80.

Leavy, S. A. (1988). *In the image of God: A psychoanalyst's view*. New Haven, Conn.: Yale University Press.

Lhallungpa, L. P. (1982). *The life of Milarepa*. Boulder, Colo.: Prajna Press.

Linehan, M. (1987). Dialectical behavior therapy for borderline personality disorder. *Bulletin of the Menninger Clinic*, *51*, 261–76.

Loewald, H. (1976). Perspectives on memory in psychology vs. metapsychology: Psychological issues. *Monograph*, *36*(9, no. 4). New York: International University Press.

————. (1978). *Psychoanalysis and the history of the individual*. New Haven, Conn.: Yale University Press.

Lovinger, R. (1989). *Religion in the stabilization and regulation of the self*. Unpublished.

Lutzky, H. (1991). The sacred and the maternal object: An application of Fairbairn's theory to religion. In H. Siegel, J. Lasky, and S. Warshaw (eds.), *Psychoanalytic reflections*. New York: New York University Press.

Marmer, S. (1980). Psychoanalysis of multiple personality. *International Journal of Psychoanalysis*, *61*, 439–59.

Masson, J. (1980). *The oceanic feeling: The origins of religious sentiment in ancient India*. Dordrecht, Holland: D. Reidel.

Masterson, J. (1985). *The real self: A developmental, self and object relations approach.* New York: Brunner Mazel.

McDargh, J. (1983). *Psychoanalytic object relations theory and the study of religion: On faith and the imaging of God.* Lanham, Md.: University Press of America.

———. (1984). The life of the self in Christian spirituality and contemporary psychoanalysis. *Horizons, 11*(2), 344–60.

———. (1989). Personal communication.

Meissner, W. W. (1969). Notes on a psychology of faith. *Journal of Religion and Health, 8*, 47–75.

———. (1984). *Psychoanalysis and religious experience.* New Haven, Conn.: Yale University Press.

———. (1987). *Life and faith: Psychological perspectives on religious experience.* Washington, D.C.: Georgetown University Press.

———. (1988). *The borderline spectrum.* New York: Aronson.

Meng, H., and E. Freud. (eds.) (1963). *Psychoanalysis and faith: The letters of Sigmund Freud and Oskar Pfister.* New York: Basic Books.

Menninger, K. (1942). *Love against hate.* New York: Harcourt, Brace and Jovanovich.

Merkur, D. (1990). Freud's atheism: Object relations and the theory of religion. *Religious Studies Review, 16*, 11–18.

Miller, A. (1981). *The drama of the gifted child: How narcissistic parents form and deform the emotional lives of their gifted children.* New York: Basic Books.

Milner, M. (1950). *On not being able to paint.* London: Heinemann.

———. (1969). *In the hands of the living God: An account of a psychoanalytic treatment.* New York: International Universities Press.

———. (1973). *The suppressed madness of sane men.* London: Tavistock (1987).

———. (1981). *A life of one's own.* Los Angeles: J. P. Tarcher.

———. (1987). *The suppressed madness of sane men: Forty-four years of exploring psychoanalysis.* London: Routledge.

Mitchell, S. A. (1984). Object relations theories and the developmental tilt. *Contemporary Psychoanalysis, 20*(4), 473–99.

Moore, S. (1980). *The fire and the rose are one.* New York: Seabury-Crossroads Press.

Munensterberger, W. (1972). Introduction. In G. Roheim, *The panic of the gods.* New York: Harper.

Nalanda Translation Committee. (1980). *The rain of wisdom.* Boulder, Colo.: Shambhala.

Nyanaponika. (1962). *The heart of Buddhist meditation.* New York: Samuel Weiser.

———. (1972). *The power of mindfulness.* San Francisco: Unity Press.

Ogden, T. (1983). The concept of internal object relations. *International Journal of Psychoanalysis, 64*, 224–27.

———. (1984). Instinct, phantasy, and psychological deep structure. *Contemporary Psychoanalysis, 20*, 500–25.

———. (1989). *The primitive edge of experience.* Northvale, N.J.: Aronson.

Olsson, P. A. (1983). Adolescent involvement with the supernatural and cults. In D. A. Halperin (ed.), *Religion, sect and cult.* Boston: John Wright.

Pastore, N. (1949). *The nature-nurture controversy.* New York: King's Crown Press.

Pattison, E. M. (1965). On the failure to forgive or be forgiven. *American Journal of Psychotherapy, 19*, 106–15.

Peterfreund, E. (1978). Some critical comments on psychoanalytic conceptualizations of infancy. *International Journal of Psychoanalysis, 59*, 427–41.

Pfister, O. (1948). *Christianity and fear*. Translated by W. H. Johnston. London: George.

Phillips, A. (1988). *Winnicott*. Cambridge, Mass.: Harvard University Press.

Piaget, J. (1969). The intellectual development of the adolescent. In G. Kaplan and S. Lebovici (eds.), *The intellectual development of the adolescent: Psychological perspectives*. New York: Basic Books.

Pruyser, P. (1971). Assessment of the psychiatric patient's religious attitudes in the psychiatric case study. *Bulletin of the Menninger Clinic*, *35*, 272–91.

———. (1973). Sigmund Freud and his legacy: Psychoanalytic psychology of religion. In C. Y. Glock and P. E. Hammond (eds.), *Beyond the classics*. New York: Harper and Row.

———. (1974). *Between belief and unbelief*. New York: Harper and Row.

———. (1975). What splits in 'splitting'? *Bulletin of the Menninger Clinic*, *39*, 1–46.

———. (1977). The seamy side of current religious beliefs. *Bulletin of the Menninger Clinic*, *41*, 329–41.

———. (1983). *The play of the imagination: Toward a psychoanalysis of culture*. New York: International Universities Press.

Quinn, S. (1987). *A mind of her own: The life of Karen Horney*. New York: Summit Books.

Reston, J., Jr. (1981). *Our father who art in hell*. New York: Times Books.

Ricoeur, P. (1970). *Freud and philosophy: An essay on interpretation*. New Haven, Conn.: Yale University Press.

Rinpoche, K. (1986). *The dharma*. Albany, N.Y.: State University of New York Press.

Rinsley, R. (1982). *Borderline and other self disorders*. New York: Aronson.

Rizzuto, A.-M. (1974). Object relation and the formation of God. *British Journal of Medical Psychology*, *47*, 83–89.

———. (1976). Freud, God, the devil and the theory of object representation. *International Review of Psycho-analysis*, *31*, 83–89.

———. (1979). *The birth of the living God: A psychoanalytic study*. Chicago: University of Chicago Press.

Roland, A. (1988). *In search of self in India and Japan: Toward a cross-cultural psychology*. Princeton, N.J.: Princeton University Press.

Rubenstein, R. L. (1963). A note on the research lag in psychoanalytic studies of religion. *Jewish Social Studies*, *25*, 133–44.

Rubin, J. B. (1985). Meditation and psychoanalytic listening. *Psychoanalytic Review*, *72*(4), 599–613.

Saffady, W. (1976). New developments in the psychoanalytic study of religion: A bibliographic review of the literature since 1960. *Psychoanalytic Review*, *63*(2), 291–99.

Sandler, J. (1960). The background of safety. *International Journal of Psychoanalysis*, *41*, 352–56.

Sandler, J., and B. Rosenblatt. (1962). The concept of the representational world. *Psychoanalytic Study of the Child*, *17*, 132.

Sandler, J., and A. M. Sandler. (1978). Object relations and affects. *International Journal of Psychoanalysis*, *59*, 291.

Schafer, R. (1968). *Aspects of internalization*. New York: International Universities Press.

———. (1976). *A new language for psychoanalysis*. New Haven, Conn.: Yale University Press.

———. (1983). *The analytic attitude*. New York: Basic Books.

Scharfenberg, J. (1988). *Sigmund Freud and his critique of religion*. Translated by O. Dean, Jr. Philadelphia: Fortress Press.

Schwartz, K. M. (1986). The meaning of cults in the treatment of late adolescent issues. In S. C. Feinstein et al. (eds.), *Adolescent Psychiatry*, vol. 13. Chicago: University of Chicago Press.

Searles, H. F. (1979). *Countertransference*. New York: International University Press.

Sexton, R., and R. Maddock. (1978). The Adam and Eve syndrome. *Journal of Religion and Health, 17*, 163–68.

Shafranske, E. (1989). *The clinical case study method in the psychoanalytic study of religion: A review and critique*. Paper presented at the annual meeting of the American Psychological Association in New Orleans.

Shea, J. (1987). *Religious experiencing: William James and Eugene Gendlin*. Lanham, Md.: University Press of America.

Silberer, H., (1917). *Problems of mysticism and its symbolism*. New York: Moffat.

Smedes, L. (1984). *Forgive and forget: Healing the hurts we don't deserve*. New York: Harper and Row.

Smith, B. L. (1989). Of many minds: A contribution on the dynamics of multiple personality. In M. Fromm and B. Smith (eds.), *The facilitating environment*. Madison, Wisc.: International Universities Press, pp. 424–58.

Smith, M., J. Bruner, and R. White. (1956). *Opinions and personality*. New York: John Wiley.

Smith, W. C. (1979). *Faith and belief*. Princeton, N.J.: Princeton University Press.

Solomon, M. I., and G. E. Murphy. (1984). Cohort studies of suicide. In H. S. Sudak, A. B. Ford, and N. B. Rushforth (eds.), *Suicide in the young*. Boston: John Wright/PSG.

Spanos, N. P., and E. C. Hewitt, (1979). Glossolalia: A test of the "trance" and psychopathology hypotheses. *Journal of Abnormal Psychology, 88*, 427–34.

Spence, D. (1982). *Narrative truth and historical truth*. New York: Norton.

Spero, M. H. (1981). Countertransference in religious therapists of religious patients. *American Journal of Psychoanalysis, 35*, 565–76.

———. (1985a). Psychotherapy of the religious patient. Springfield, Ill.: Charles Thomas Publisher.

———. (1985b). The reality of the image of God in psychotherapy. *American Journal of Psychotherapy, 39*(1), 75–85.

Spidell, S., and D. Liberman. (1981). Moral development and the forgiveness of sin. *Journal of Psychology and Theology, 9*, 159–63.

Stern, C. R. (1984). The etiology of multiple personalities. *Psychiatric Clinics of North America, 7*, 149–59.

Stern, D. (1985). *The interpersonal world of the infant*. New York: Basic Books.

Stolorow, R. D., and G. E. Atwood. (1979). *Faces in a cloud: Subjectivity in personality theory*. New York: Aronson.

Stolorow, R., B. Brandchaft, and G. Atwood. (1987). *Psychoanalytic treatment: An intersubjective approach*, Hillsdale, N.J.: The Analytic Press.

Stone, M. H. (1987). Psychotherapy of borderline patients in light of long-term follow-up. *Bulletin of the Menninger Clinic, 51*, 231–47.

———. (1988). Exploratory psychotherapy in schizophrenia spectrum patients: A reevaluation in the light of long-term follow-up of schizophrenic and borderline patients. *Bulletin of the Menninger Clinic, 50*, 287–306.

————. (1989a). The course of borderline personality disorder. *Annual Periodical of Psychiatry*. Annual Review 8. Washington, D.C.: American Psychiatric Press.

————. (1989b). Psychotherapy of incest victims. *Psychiatric Clinics of North America*. Forthcoming.

————. (1989c). Murder. *Psychiatric Clinics of North America*.

————. (1990). *The fate of borderline patients*. Guilford Press.

Stone, M. H., S. W. Hurt, and D. K. Stone. (1987). The P.I.–500: Long-term follow-up of borderline inpatients meeting DSM-III criteria. I. Global outcome. *Journal of Personality Disorders*, *1*, 291–98.

Stone, M. H., D. K. Stone, and S. W. Hurt. (1987). Natural history of borderline patients treated by intensive hospitalization. *Psychiatric Clinics of North America*, *10*, 185–206.

Stone, M. H., and R. Weissman. (1988). Expressive group therapy with borderline patients. In N. Slayinska-Holy (ed.), *Borderline and narcissistic patients in therapy*. Madison, Conn.: International University Press.

Suzuki, S. (1970). *Zen, mind, beginner's mind*. New York: Wetherhill.

Tendzin, O. (1982). *Buddha in the palm of your hand*. Boulder, Colo.: Shambhala Press.

Thera, S. (1941). *The way of mindfulness: The Satipatthana Sutta and commentary*. Kandy, Sri Lanka: Buddhist Publication Society.

Todd, E. (1985). The value of confession and forgiveness according to Jung. *Journal of Religion and Health*, *24*(1), 39–48.

Trungpa, C. (1973). *Cutting through spiritual materialism*. Boulder, Colo.: Shambhala Press.

Tsuang, M. T., and G. Winokur. (1975). The Iowa 500. *Canada Psychological Association Journal*, *20*, 359–65.

Ullman, C. (1982). Cognitive and emotional antecedents of religious conversion. *Journal of Personality and Social Psychology*, *43*, 183–92.

Vergote, A. (1988). *Guilt and desire*. New Haven, Conn.: Yale University Press.

Vitz, P. (1988). *Sigmund Freud's Christian unconscious*. New York: Guilford Press.

Waelder, R. (1930). The principle of multiple function. *Psychoanalytic Quarterly*, *15*, 45–62 (1936).

Waldinger, R. J., and J. G. Gunderson. (1987). *Effective psychotherapy with borderline patients*. New York: Macmillan.

Walsh, R. (1980). The consciousness of disciplines and the behavioral sciences: Questions of comparison and assessment. *American Journal of Psychiatry*, *137*(6), 663–73.

Walters, O. (1985). Psychodynamics in Tillich's theology. *Journal of Religion and Health*, *24*(1), 39–48.

Wapnich, K. (1985). Forgiveness: A spiritual psychotherapy. *Psychotherapy and the Religiously Committed Patient*. Special issue of *Psychotherapy Patient*, *1*, 47–53.

Wilber, K. (1984). The developmental spectrum and psychopathology. Part I: Stages and types of pathology. *Journal of Transpersonal Psychology*, *6*, 75–118.

Wilber, K., J. Engler, and D. Brown. (1986). *Transformations of consciousness: Conventional and contemplative perspectives on development*. Boston: New Science Library, Shambhala Publications.

Wilson, W. (1974). The utilization of Christian beliefs in therapy. *Journal of Psychology and Theology*, *2*, 125–31.

Winnicott, D. W. (1951). Transitional objects and transitional phenomena. In P. Buckley (ed.), *Essential papers on object relations*. New York: New York University Press.

——. (1953). Transitional objects and transitional phenomena. *International Journal of Psychoanalysis, 34*, 2.

——. (1958). Transitional objects and transitional phenomena. In his *Collected papers: Through pediatrics to psychoanalysis*. London: Tavistock.

——. (1965). *The maturational process and the facilitating environment*. London: Hogarth Press.

——. (1971). *Playing and reality*. New York: Basic Books.

——. (1986). *Home is where we start from*. New York: Norton.

Wulff, D. M. (1984). Psychological approaches. In F. Whaling (ed.), *Contemporary approaches to the study of religion*, vol. 2. The Hague: Mouton.

Zilboorg, G. (1950). *Psychoanalysis and religion*. New York: Barnes & Noble.

——. (1958). *Freud and religion: A restatement of an old controversy*. Westminster, Md.: Newman Press.

Zimmer, H. (1951). *Philosophies of India*. Princeton: Bollingen Series 26, Princeton University Press.

Index

adolescent development: biological, 74; clinical cases on, 78–82, 83–84; experience of God and, 73–74; God representation and, 74–77, 84; identitiy search and, 75; inquiry and, 73, 74; object representation and, 169; oedipal drama and, 74–75; operational thinking and, 74; prayer and, 77; religious faith and, 164; tasks of, 73

affect regulation, 103

Alcoholics Anonymous, 143

American Academy of Psychoanalysis, 91

American Journal of Psychoanalysis, 91

Aquinas, Thomas, 168

atheism *v.* theism, 119–20

Atwood, G., 103

Auden, W. H., 118

Australia, 154

Banschick, Mark R., 163

Baptist group, 144

Beit-Hallahmi, Benjamin, 156, 157, 158

Benner case: alter egos and, 41–44, 171–72; God representations and, 40, 41–42, 47–48, 49, 50, 51–53; host personality and, 39–41; integration and, 53; patient background and, 38–39, 171; patient guilt and, 40, 47–48; religion's function in, 48–50, 51–54; satanism and, 50–51; sexual relationships and, 39, 48–49

Benson, H., 110

Bible, 25, 78, 135

Birth of the Living God, The, 62, 92, 160, 165

Blos, Peter, 74, 164, 169

Bollas, Christopher, 2, 12, 15, 64, 65–66, 67, 160, 161

Borysenko, J. Z., 110

Bowman, E. S., 37, 47, 49

Brady, Ian, 152

Brandchaft, B., 103

Buddha, Gautama, 96, 111

Buddhism: central tenets of, 97; clinical case and, 96, 97–98, 101–2, 104–5; despair alleviation from, 150; duality and, 112–13; ethics and, 97; goal of,

111; God and, 166; inner focus of, 166; Judeo-Christian tradition and, 166; meditation practices and, 97, 111–12; Milarepa and, 115–18, 168–69; object representations and, 166–67; paradoxical logic of, 112–14; psychoanalysis and, 91, 92, 93, 109–10; psychoanalytic listening and, 93, 102, 110; as psychology, 110–11; psychology of religion and, 109; Smith quoted on, 166; Theravadin, 96–97; Tibetan, 97, 111, 113, 118; time and, 113; transformation and, 167–68; Western psychology compared with, 97, 98; Western students of, 109; Winnicott and, 114; Zen, 91, 92, 97, 111, 118
Bundy, Ted, 152

China, 89
Christianity, 25, 89, 165–66
Civilization and Its Discontents, 89
Coltart, Nina, 61
Comprehensive Textbook of Psychiatry, 21
Constructions in Analysis, 157–58
Conze, Edward, 166
Coons, P. M., 37
Corinthians, 148

Dalbiez, R., 101
deep structure, 2, 159–60
Deikman, A., 105
DeMartino, Richard, 92
demystification, 120
depressive position, 22
Diekstra, R. F. W., 153
dream interpretation, 106
drive theory, 7, 35, 36
drug abuse, 77, 142, 145, 146
dual-instinct theory, 22

ego fragments, 38
ego psychology, 35, 36
Egypt, 40
electroconvulsive therapy (ECT), 7–8, 12, 14
Engler, J. H., 15, 109, 110

Epstein, M. D., 110
Erikson, E. H., 5, 75, 77
exorcism, 117

Fairbairn, D.R.D., 35–36, 48, 50, 51, 114–15, 117, 123, 127
Final Lectures, 91
Finn, Mark G., 156, 165, 168–69
Foon, A. F., 152
forgiveness: conditions for, 171; effects of, 27; by Gartner's patient, 31–32; by God, 27; Holocaust and, 24; Hunter and, 24; immature, 24–25; integration and, 26, 31–32, 170–71; Kernberg and, 23; literature on, 21; object relations theory and, 22; operational definition of, 23; patient-therapist relationship and, 27; psychological importance of, 21–22, 25; psychotherapy and, 26; self-, 25–26; splitting and, 24–25, 27
Fountain House, 154
Fowler, James, 4
fragmentation (splitting), 24–25, 26, 27, 45, 47, 53, 90, 170–71
Freud, Sigmund: acceptance of, 89; analyst's mental state and, 93, 102; atheistic approach by, 157; Auden and, 118; dream interpretation and, 106; dual-instinct theory of, 22; "family romance" and, 82; God-representation theory by, 2; Guntrip quoted on, 125; illusion and, 88; life's essence and, 154; Meissner and, 93; object relations theory and, 35–36, 121–22, 127; over-valuation of science by, 125; psyhotheraputic results and, 157–58; religion and, 35, 54, 61, 83, 88–89, 90, 92, 126; Rizzuto and, 92; science and, 105
Fromm, Erich, 92
Future of an Illusion, 89

Gallup Poll, 87
Gartner, John, 170–71
Gartner case: forgiveness and, 31–32; hatred by patient and, 29, 30; patient background and, 27–28; patient

progress and relapse and, 30, 31; patient-therapist relationship and, 29–30, 31; therapy sessions and, 28–31

Gendlin, Eugene, 2, 5–6

glossolalia, 147

God: addictive use of, 163; Buddhism and, 166; forgiveness by, 27; ineffable nature of, 83; as transitional object, 76, 126, 127–28, 130, 137, 157

God experience, 73–74, 163–64

God representation(s): adolescent development and, 74–77, 84; adolescent clinical cases and, 78–79, 80, 82, 83, 84; atheistic parents and, 167–68; Benner case and, 40, 41–42, 47–48, 49, 50, 51–53; change of, 130, 131, 133, 134; child's creation of, 132; clinical case on transformation and, 68–70; complexity of, 158, 162; concept and images of God and, 3; conscious and unconscious, 131, 132–33; emotion and, 3, 5–6, 134; Freud and, 2; human development and, 76; individuality and, 58; infancy and, 67; interpersonal experience and, 3–4; Milner case and, 11–12; multiple personality disorders and, 37; negativity from, 58; object relations theory and, 61–62, 75; origin of, 130; parental representations and, 37, 138–39, 166; power of, 58; prayer and, 67; psychic danger and, 162; psychoanalytic conceptions of, 59; repression of, 131, 134; Rizzuto and, 2–3, 62, 130, 131; self representation and, 67, 137–38, 139; source of, 92; stress and emergence of, 135; threatening, 134–35; transformation and, 57–58, 62, 66, 68–70; transformational object and, 66–68, 70–71; trust and, 77; visceral, 133, 134

Greaves, G. B., 45

Grotstein, J., 47

Group for the Advancement of Psychiatry, 87

Gruenewald, D., 45

guilt absorption, 47

Gunderson, J. G., 27

Guntrip, Harry, 5, 58, 75, 124–25, 127

Hare Krishna group, 143, 144–45, 148

Hartmann, Heinz, 35

Hinduism, 150

Holocaust, 24, 171

Home Is Where We Start From, 93

homosexuality, 148

Horney, Karen, 91

Hubbard, L. Ron, 143–44

human sciences, 119

Hungary, 153

Hunter, R., 21, 24

Huxley, Aldous, 91

ignorance, 1

In the Hands of the Living God, 7

India, 89, 111, 115, 150

infancy: affect regulation and, 103; articulation of experience in, 66; experience and, 62–64; God representations and, 67; mother representation and, 65, 66; object representations and, 63; self-discovery by, 63; sensory experience in, 65; transformation in, 163; transformational object and, 64–66

Inquisition, 105

integration: Benner case and, 53; forgiveness and, 26, 31–32, 170–71; multiple personality disorders and, 47; of psychoanalysis and Buddhism, 93; of religion and social structures, 156; patient-therapist relationship and, 27

IQ measurements, 119

Islam, 152

Israel, 26

Italy, 153

James, William, 3–4, 59, 61, 91

Jehovah's Witnesses, 143

Jesus, 26, 40, 49, 58

Jewel Ornament of Liberation, The, 114

Jikei-Kai Medical School, 91

John the Baptist, 58

Jones, Ernest, 37, 89

Jones, Jim, 152

Joscelyne, B., 47
Judaism, 89, 132, 135
Judeo-Christian tradition, 25, 165–66
Jung, Carl, 27, 61, 90

Kelman, Harold, 91–92
Kernberg, O., 22, 23–24, 26–27, 142
Khas, Masud, 7
Klein, Melanie, 7, 22, 23, 24, 104, 122, 159
Kohut, Heinz, 93, 95
Kutz, I., 110

Lasky, R., 45
Lawrence, D. H., 11–12
Loewald, H., 36, 113, 114
Lucretius, 88
Lutzky, H., 127

Mahamudra meditation, 113, 115
Maharishi Mahesh Yogi, 144
Mahler, Margaret, 103
Malcolm X, 152
Manson, Charles, 152
Marmer, S., 45
Marpa, 115–16, 117–18, 169
Marx, Karl, 145
McDargh, John, 36, 75, 159–60, 161
Meissner, William W., 36, 54, 67, 75, 87–88, 93, 126
Menninger, Karl, 90–91
metapsychology, 61
Meunsterberger, W., 121
Middle Ages, 90;
Milarepa, 115–18, 168–69
Milner, Marion, 7, 92, 123
Milner case: capacity for illusion and, 10–11; client background and, 7–9; God representation and, 11–12; interpretation and conclusions on, 14–16; Milner's growth and, 7; mystical experience and, 13; patient background and, 12–14; patient complaints and, 7, 12; religious experience and, 14, 15; sexual abuse and, 9; symbolic play and, 11
Moon, Sun Myung, 143–44

Moonies (Unification Church), 39, 43–44, 147
Morita, Shomo, 91
Moritz, J. M., 153
Moses, 40
multiple personality disorders, 36–37, 45, 47, 53. See also Benner case

Naropa, 115
Narrative Truth and Historical Truth, 95
New Introductory Lectures on Psycho-Analysis, 105
New York State Psychiatric Institute, 141

object relations theory: apologetics and, 156; classical psychoanalysis compared with, 94; deep structure and, 160; definition lacked by, 94; focus of, 36, 129; forgiveness and, 22; Freud and, 35–36, 121–22, 127; God representation and, 61–62, 75, 139; guilt and, 48; human possibility and, 116; infant perception and, 64; Judeo-Christian tradition and, 165–66; multiple personality disorders and, 45, 47; original concepts of, 122; personal relations and, 156; personality development and, 127; premise of, 94–95; projection theory and, 127; psychoanalytic approach to religion and, 121; psychology of religion and, 109; religion and, 36, 122, 123, 124, 127–28, 155, 156, 174; self-psychology compared with, 95; self-representations and, 25, 137; transformational object and, 71
Ogden, T., 65, 69
Oldstorm, M., 37
100,000 Songs of Milarepa, The, 115
Our Inner Conflicts, 91

Pakistan, 154
paranoid-schizoid position, 22
pathological reductionism, 110
Perennial Philosophy, The, 91
Peterfreund, E., 61
Pfister, Oskar, 89–90
Pharisees, 26

Piaget, Jean, 73
prayer, 67, 77, 139, 164
projection theory, 127
Pruyser, Paul, 3, 10, 45, 84–85, 87
Psalms, 77, 83
Psychiatric Institute 500: despair and, 150–51; global results from, 142–43; identity problems and, 147–48; impulse containment and, 145–46; impulse gratification and, 146–47; murderers and, 152; patient status in, 142; religious group and, benefits from, 151–52; role models and, 153; self-esteem and, 149–50; sense of purpose and, 148–49; structural provisions and, 148–49; variety of religious groups and, 143–45
psychoanalysis: analyst's mental state and, 93, 102; believers' status and, 159; Buddhism and, 91, 92, 93; Eastern thought and, 91–92; generalization and, 165; God representation and, 59; God's existence and, 157; meditation and, 92, 170; object relations theory and, 94, 121; religion and, 59–62, 87–88, 89, 93, 120–21, 174–75; science and, 105; terminology and, 160
Psychoanalysis and Religious Experience, 93
psychoanalytic investigation, 60–61
psychoanalytic reductionism, 105–6
psychology: Buddhism and, 97, 98, 110–11; ego, 35, 36; God's existence and, 157; religion threatened by, 119–20; religious, 120, 126–27, 156; self-, 95
psychology of religion, 120, 125–26, 156
psychopathology, 22
psychotherapy: empathy and, 125, 126, 127; forgiveness and, 26; Jung and, 27; patient-therapist relationship and, 26–27, 114; religious issues and, 84–85, 87; topics of inquiry and, 84–85

Ramakrishna, 88
Red Rock Jewel Valley, 115, 118, 169
religion: apologetics and, 156; Asian, 89, 94; childhood needs and, 88; classical

psychoanalytic approach to, 120–21; as constructive and pathological, 36; divisive function of, 53, 55; drug addiction and, 145; Eastern, 90, 91–92; Freud and, 35, 54, 61, 83, 88–89, 90, 92, 126; Fromm and, 92; functional justification for, 126; guilt and, 48; Guntrip and, 124–25; health and, 93; Horney and, 91; human nature and, 87, 124–25; individuality and meaning of, 106–7; integrative function of, 53, 54; Jung and, 90; Kelman and, 91–92; Kohut and, 93; meditation and, 110; Menninger and, 90–91; Milner and, 92; multiple personality disorders and, 37, 47, 48–50, 51–54; object relations theory and, 36, 122, 123, 124, 127–28, 155, 156, 174; origin of, 124, 126; Pfister and, 89–90; potential effects from, 94; power of, 152–53, 173; psychic foundation of, 168; psychoanalysis and, 89, 174–75; psychoanalysts' conception of, 35, 36, 87–88, 93; psychoanalytic approach to, recommendations for, 106–7; psychoanalytic literature and, 89, 94; psychoanalytic study of, 59–62, 121, 174; psychology's threat to, 119–20; Roland and, 93; science and, 105, 119; self-psychology and, 95; sex exploitation in, 104, 105; Silberer and, 90; suicide and, 153; theraputic benefits from, 91, 92, 93; transformational object and, 161–62, 163; as transitional experience, 129–30; Winicott and, 36, 93. *See also names of specific religions*
religious apologists, 120
religious behavior, 155–56
religious faith: adolescent development and, 164; analysis and, 122; Benner's patient and, 49, 50; conditions for, 172–73; dangers of, 158; Gallup Poll on, 87; meaning of, 4–5; Meissner's definition of, 54; multiple personality disorders and, 36–37; psychological maturity and, 107; therapists' attitude

toward, 158–59; theraputic function of, 126; Winnicott and, 124
religious groups. *See* Psychiatric Institute 500; *names of specific groups*
religious imagery, 1, 106
religious language, 24–25
religious psychology, 120, 126–27, 156
Rinpoche, Kalu, 111
Rizzuto, Ana-Maria: development potential and, 116; Freud's views and, 92; God representation and, 2–3, 62, 70, 92, 130, 131; God's existence and, 126; object and self representations and, 66; object relations theory and, 36, 75, 129; self-representation and, 138; transformation and, 57–58; transitional sphere and, 129
Roland, A., 93
Rolland, Romaine, 88
Roman Catholicism, 39, 134, 143, 153
Romans, 148
Rosenblatt, B., 64
Roshi, Suzuki, 113
Rosicrucians, 143, 151
Rubenstein, R. L., 121
Rubin, Jeffery B., 165, 167
Rubin case: Buddhism and, 96, 97–98, 101–2, 104–5; deautomization and, 105; patient background and, 96, 97–100; patient progress and, 102–3; patient-therapist relationship and, 100–101; self-demarcation and, 103; self-punishment and, 104–5

sadomasochism, 30
Sandler, A. M., 63
Sandler, J., 63, 64
satanism, 39, 50–51, 78, 79, 146, 152, 171
Saur, Marylin S., 165
Saur, William, G., 165
Schafer R., 35, 95–96
Schaffer, Peter, 2
science, 105, 119, 125
Scientology, 143, 147
Scripture, 67
self-demarcation, 103

self-psychology, 95
sexual abuse, 9, 28, 39, 45, 147, 150
Shadow of the Object, The, 161
Shafranske, Edward P., 162–63
SIDDHA Foundation, 150
Silberer, H., 90
Smith, B. L., 47
Smith, Huston, 166
Smith, Wilfred Cantwell, 4
Sociology of Religion, The, 155–56
Socrates, 1
sorcery, 115
Spence, D., 95, 60
Spero, M. H., 75
Stern, C. R., 61, 63–64, 65, 103
Stone, Michael H., 173–74
Storolow, R., 103
Subud, 143, 146
suicide, 28, 43, 142, 149–50, 153–54
Sullivan, Hary Stack, 97
Suzuki, D. T., 91, 92
Switzerland, 154

Tendzin, Osel, 112, 114
time, 113
transference phenomena, 118
transformation: God representations and, 57–58, 62, 66; in infancy, 163; religious cults and, 173; religious experiences and, 162; Rizzuto and, 57–58; transformational object and experience of, 64–66
transformational object: clinical case on God representation and, 68–70; dangerous object and, 161; experience of transformation and, 64–66, 70–71; God representations and, 66–68, 70–71; infant development and, 64–66; mother and, 64, 65, 162; object relations and, 68, 71; prayer and, 67; religion and, 161–62, 163; transformation of subject and, 163
Trungpa, Chogyam, 117–18

violence, 78, 79

Waldinger, R. J., 27
Weber, Max, 155–56
Wesley, John, 26
Wilber, K., 109, 110
Winnicott, D. W.: Buddhist psychology
    and, 114; classical psychoanalysis and,
    35–36; development potential and, 116;
    "false self" structure and, 9; illusion
    and, 36, 114, 123, 130; multiple

personality disorders and, 47; religion
    and, 36, 93, 124; solitude and, 10;
    transitional experience and, 112
women's liberation, 149

yoga, 90

Zen Buddhism and Psychoanalysis, 92
Zimmer, H., 110–11

About the Editors and Contributors

MARK R. BANSCHICK is Medical Director at Four Winds Hospital, Katonah, New York.

BENJAMIN BEIT-HALLAHMI is Associate Professor of Psychology at the University of Haifa, Haifa, Israel.

DAVID G. BENNER is Associate Professor of Psychology at Redemer College, Ancaster, Ontario, Canada.

MARK FINN is Chief Psychologist at North Central Bronx Hospital, Bronx, New York.

JOHN GARTNER is Clinical Assistant Professor of Psychology at Johns Hopkins University, Baltimore, Maryland.

JOHN McDARGH is Associate Professor of Theology at Boston College, Boston, Massachusetts.

ANA-MARIA RIZZUTO is Training and Supervisory Analyst at the Psychoanalytic Institute of New England, Boston, Massachusetts.

JEFFREY RUBIN is in private practice of psychotherapy and psychoanalysis in Westchester and New York, New York.

MARILYN S. SAUR is Clinical Assistant Professor of Psychiatry at the University of North Carolina School of Medicine, Chapel Hill, North Carolina.

WILLIAM G. SAUR is Consulting Associate in Psychiatry at Duke University Medical Center, Durham, North Carolina.

EDWARD P. SHAFRANSKE is Associate Professor of Psychology at the Graduate School of Education and Psychology, Pepperdine University, Los Angeles, California.

MICHAEL H. STONE is Professor of Clinical Psychiatry at Columbia College of Physicians and Surgeons, New York, New York.